Aeneas

Lee T. Pearcy

UNIVERSITY OF MICHIGAN PRESS

ANN ARBOR

Published in the United States of America by the
University of Michigan Press
Manufactured in the United States of America
Printed on acid-free paper
First published July 2021

A CIP catalog record for this book is available from the British Library.

Library of Congress Cataloging-in-Publication data has been applied for.

ISBN: 978-0-472-07490-7 (hardcover : alk. paper)
ISBN: 978-0-472-05490-9 (paper)
ISBN: 978-0-472-12903-4 (e-book)

Aeneas

For my students at
the Episcopal Academy,
1985–2013

Contents

Preface

This book grew from two sets of questions, and its writing spanned two different times. I began writing in the autumn of 2014, midway through the second term of President Barack Obama, and finished in the spring of 2020, as America struggled with pandemic disease, civil unrest, economic recession, and ineffective presidential leadership. At first I wondered about two questions: Why do my students not like Aeneas, and why has the nature of their dislike changed? As 2014 gave way to the election of 2016 and the calamities of 2020, a second set of questions began to surface: What happens when a society looks at its own collapse, contemplates its history, and sees an ingrained, perhaps ineradicable flaw; and how do individuals respond to revolution that is not only political but cultural and to a transmutation of values that sweeps away the worlds in which they have grounded their identities? Readers will find traces of both sets of questions in this book.

I first tried to help students read the *Aeneid* in the 1969–1970 academic year, and since then, I have taught the poem perhaps two dozen times, most recently in the spring of 2014. Most of my students have been young people in their second, third, or fourth year of high school, but some have been college undergraduates or postgraduate students. I soon grew used to the idea that my students would not like Aeneas or find him in any way sympathetic, especially after reading book 4. Still, they responded to him as a person, as a literary representation of a human being, about whom they could form the same kind of judgments that they might form about someone they knew. The last few times I taught the *Aeneid*, however, my students seemed not to know how to respond to Aeneas at all. To them, he seemed unreal—not a human being, but an impersonal center of narrative gravity. They could talk about him but not to him. What, I wondered, had happened?

It may be possible to view the change under the rubric of "liquid modernity." That phrase, coined by prolific Polish sociologist Zygmunt Bauman, has become a convenient label for phenomena attending the deconstruction of the self into a collection of intersecting identities. My latest students may have been creating an Aeneas for their age. Looking not for a person but for an identity, they found a hero who seems to have no easily defined matrix of personality. Aeneas is many things at once: Bronze Age warrior, Trojan, proto-Roman, precursor of Augustus, Roman Hercules, Trojan Achilles, and more. He mirrors the complexity of the *Aeneid* itself. Somehow, though, those roles and personae fail to cohere into the kind of intersection of identities in which my students could recognize a fellow human being. They may, also, have recoiled from something else in Vergil's big, dangerous poem. For Rome to come into being, Troy and Aeneas must cease to exist. In an age of liquid modernity, when our unitary sense of self often fractures under the technology that creates it, the chief task of being human sometimes seems reduced to constructing an identity from external, social cues, from likes and followers. In this world, the ultimate terror may be the kind of loss that Aeneas suffers when the external cues of his identity fall silent. To respond to my students and to my first set of questions, this book sketches an Aeneas for an age of liquid modernity, a hero who vanishes into the multiple roles that he fails, in the end, to negotiate.

The *Aeneid* is also a profoundly political poem, and at its center lies a core of political clarity: the fated progress of Roman history from Aeneas through Romulus to Augustus, from Troy and Italy through the city of seven hills to a world empire. That vision is qualified by endless suffering, by the ingrained curse of civil war, and by Vergil's own sense of inevitable recurrence, but it never vanishes entirely. Part of the greatness of the *Aeneid* comes from its exploration of the way that individual human beings—Aeneas primarily, but also Dido, Turnus, and countless others—become both agents of progress and suffering victims of it. Thus my second set of questions touches not on the individual's quest for defined identity but on the relationships among person, society, and history; for Aeneas, such relationship finds expression in the complexities of his central quality, *pietas*.

Perhaps in response to the liquidity of its central character, the structure of this book is not linear but recursive. In that attribute, it is like the *Aeneid* itself, which, as I note in chapter 6, "ends by taking us full circle back to its beginning—to Juno's anger, savage grief, and the act of founding Rome." Chapter 1 functions as an introduction and concentrates on the Carthaginian episode in books 1 and 4 of the *Aeneid* and on the Helen episode in book 2. Throughout the book, I return to these passages, expanding and recontextualizing my reading of them. Chapter 2 gives background to help readers appreciate the importance of the civil wars and triumviral period in shaping the despair, pessimism, and anxiety from which Vergil created Aeneas. Chapter 3 centers on the departure from Troy in book 2. Chapter 4 is a midpoint about midpoints: the middle of a journey in Vergil's *Bucolics* and the middle of Aeneas' journey in *Aeneid* 6. Chapter 5 returns to the Carthaginian episodes before focusing on the later books—on the tears of Hercules in book 10 and of Aeneas in book 11. Chapter 6 ends with the *Aeneid*'s ending, book 12, but before doing so, it circles back one final time to the poem's beginning. The epilogue serves as a conclusion and sums up my argument.

Every writer imagines an ideal reader. Mine is one of my former students, someone who has read the *Aeneid*, perhaps in school and in Latin, perhaps a long time ago. Perhaps that reader remembers the title character, recalls disliking him or finding him boring—and if the hero is boring, must not the book be also? My hope is to make Aeneas and the *Aeneid* interesting for that reader.

I have not written this book for classical scholars. They will not find in it much that is new or the kind of step-by-step argumentation that they expect; indeed, after twenty-one hundred years of reading the *Aeneid*, saying anything about it that is both new and true is almost impossible. Both my intended readers and classical scholars may, then, be deceived by appearances, since this book comes equipped with the conventional apparatus of academic writing: footnotes, a bibliography, and so on. I have included these for two reasons. First, I want to acknowledge my debts. Every reader of the *Aeneid* stands on the shoulders of his predecessors, some of them giants, and I am grateful to the scholars who appear in my notes and deeply conscious that I have neglected others. Some giants, such as Heinze, Pöschl, Otis, and W. R. Johnson, have become part of the environment in which I read Vergil, and like David Foster Wallace's fish who have to ask what water is, I have often swum unaware in the river of their insights. Second, I hope that at least some of my intended readers may become curious about something I have said and want to know more.

To that second end, I have cited mostly works in English and have biased my references toward recent and easily accessible work. I have also tried to refer to Greek and Latin works by English titles in common use (a few works, like

Cicero's *De officiis*, either have no agreed English title or have none that I can endorse), and I have avoided the arcane abbreviations that professional classical scholars use to signal membership in their club (for example, I refer to Pliny the Elder's *Natural History*, not to *Historia naturalis* or *HN*). I have not been able to avoid quoting Latin and sometimes Greek, because talking about Vergil means talking about how he deploys words or uses the language of his predecessors, especially Homer. I have given translations or close paraphrases for every passage quoted, and I hope that even a reader who does not know or has forgotten Latin or Greek will find it worthwhile to puzzle out the relation between the words and what I say about them. All translations are my own except where noted.

No one writes alone. I am grateful to the Episcopal Academy for giving me three decades of intelligent, eager Latin students and scores of stimulating colleagues. They are too many to mention, both in classics and in other disciplines and practices, but I must single out Tim Kent and Molly Konopka, with whom I shared the teaching of Advanced Placement Latin 4, the "Vergil course." I gratefully remember two teachers, both now dead, who taught me much about the *Aeneid*: Loreen Lee at Little Rock Central High School and Gilbert Highet at Columbia University. Bryn Mawr College, its Department of Greek, Latin, and Classical Studies, and its librarians and libraries—especially Camilla Mackay and the Carpenter Library for Classics, Archaeology, and Art History—provided scholarly support. Julia Hejduk, Sarah Nathan, Kathryn Pearcy, and Alex Pearson read portions of this book in draft, and it is better because of their comments. I am also indebted to a cadre of anonymous readers and to Ellen Bauerle at the University of Michigan Press for numerous suggestions and improvements. By example and by email, Michael Putnam inspired my project and Matthew Santirocco encouraged it more than they may know. All this book's imperfections are mine, not theirs.

Lately, I have been in the habit of asking my students to approach an ancient text with four questions: What kind of thing is it? How does it work? What does it want? Finally, so what—what does it have to say in our time? How is it, as Pound said, news that stays news? Here is my attempt to answer that question for the *Aeneid*.

Stoddartsville
June 2020

CHAPTER 1

On Not Liking Aeneas

Anyone who has tried to teach the *Aeneid* knows the moment at which students will lose sympathy for its hero, the Trojan prince Aeneas. His journey from the ruins of Troy has brought him to Carthage and its queen, Dido. The monarch and the refugee fall in love. They have lived together for nearly a year, warm in each other's arms through the cold winter nights of North Africa. Suddenly, because fate (another word for the logic of history) demands it, Aeneas receives a command from Jupiter to leave. The supreme god sends Mercury to deliver an unambiguous order: leave Carthage and Dido. Aeneas hesitates and ponders ways to tell her, but he sets plans in motion all the same. She discovers his intention and accosts him. Her speech is fiery, passionate, and moving.

> Is it me you're running from? By these tears, by your right hand
> (in my misery I have nothing else left),
> by our marriage, by the wedding we entered upon,
> if I have done anything to deserve a favor, if there was anything
> sweet about me in your eyes, I beg you,
> have pity on Dido, on her house collapsing about her.
> If there still is room for pleading, change your mind.
>
> *Aen.* 4.314–319

Here is how Aeneas begins his reply:

> Never, your majesty, will I deny that you have deserved
> those very many things which you have enumerated so well

in your speech, nor will I regret remembering Dido
while I am mindful of myself, while breath guides these limbs.
Let me say a few words on the matter.

Aen. 4.333–337

This cold, lawyerly opening is not improved when he goes on to deny that he has intended to slip away from Carthage in secret.[1]

Students are quick to observe that Aeneas is lying. Just a few lines before (*Aen.* 4.288–291), he has given clear orders to three of his most trusted captains: let them fit out the fleet on the quiet and get the men to the harbor; let them prepare weapons and tackle and conceal the reason for these new arrangements. His first four sentences to Dido begin with *ego*, *nec me*, *neque ego*, and *me si*—"I," "nor will I," "nor did I," and "as for myself, if."[2] It is easy to see him as a cold, egotistical seducer, a "cad to the last," as Robert Graves said (1962, 27).

Because much of this chapter may seem to confirm that view, I need to affirm that to dislike the *Aeneid*'s hero is to oversimplify and misunderstand him. His heroism is not like that of one of his Homeric models, Achilles—blazing, godlike, effortless. It is the result of dogged persistence through toil (*labor*), and qualities that make Aeneas admirable are sometimes hard to tease from the text. Good teachers point out that many features of *Aeneid* 4.331–361 tug against the perception created by the first half of Aeneas' speech. Vergil introduces the speech with two and a half lines that focus on the contrast between Aeneas' outer and inner states as he listens to Dido's reproaches.

He kept holding his gaze
unmoving on Jupiter's commands and with a struggle
pressed his feelings deep within. At last he replies, briefly.

Aen. 4.331–333

While Dido pours out her feelings, Aeneas stands with his gaze fixed, looking perhaps at her but seeing the commands of Jupiter, not only the epiphany of Mercury that prompted his decision to leave Carthage and Dido, but also the repeated premonitions that he now remembers and includes in the second half of his speech: dreams in which his father, Anchises, warned him (4.351–353) and thoughts of the wrong that he does his son, Ascanius, by depriving him of his destined inheritance in Italy (4.354–355). Aeneas has suppressed or ignored these concerns, we may infer; certainly Dido knows nothing of the mysterious appearance of Apollo and the Lycian lots that he cites at 345–346, as her scornful reply shows (4.376–379).

To respond to Dido, Aeneas has to crush his feelings for her deep under his heart (*obnixus curam sub corde premebat*, 4.332). From the beginning of the poem, Vergil alerts us to the fact that what Aeneas says to those for whom he cares will not reveal how Aeneas feels. The action of book 1 begins with the storm that drives Aeneas and his Trojans to Carthage. Their fleet is separated, and one part, with their leader Aeneas, is cast up—caked with salt, weary to the bone, and hungry—on the shore of an unknown land that turns out to be North Africa. They manage to salvage some grain soaked with seawater and make hoecakes. Aeneas goes hunting and kills enough deer to feed his men. When they have revived a little, he gives them a talk, his second speech in the poem. It is a good speech.[3] He reminds his men that they have come through worse crises, encourages them, and reminds them of their ultimate goal, to reach Italy and revive the glories of their lost Troy. Someday, he says, they will look back on this day with pleasure. All of this talk is deliberate deception, as Vergil says in his summation of the speech.

> Such things he uttered with his voice, and sick with vast cares
> feigns hope on his countenance, in his heart presses hurt deep.
>
> *Aen.* 1.208–209

Vergil echoes this characterization at the beginning of Aeneas' speech to Dido in book 4.[4] The commander who will not give his men the truth of their situation is the same man who cannot tell the woman he loves how he feels about her.

In the second half of Aeneas' speech at the center of book 4, however, Vergil shows us the facade cracking and Aeneas' resolution just managing to hold firm. The long, pompous constructions of Aeneas' exordium, the "never, your majesty, will I deny" and "nor will I regret," give way to shorter sentences passionate with anaphora and punctuated by inadequately concealed emotion.

> But now Italy—Apollo has ordered me to make for it;
> Italy—the Lycian lots have ordered it.
> It is my love. It is my country. If you, a Phoenician,
> are held by the towers of Carthage and the sight of a Libyan city,
> what envy is there that Trojans settle in Italy's land?

> We too may seek our kingdom in another country.
>
> *Aen.* 4.345–350

After rehearsing the dreams and omens and the final, decisive epiphany, he ends the speech with a desperate cry of agony in a line that Vergil left unfinished.[5]

> Stop tormenting me—and yourself—with your complaints.
> Italy—I go against my will!
>
> *Aen.* 4.360–361

Neither Vergil's explanation of his character's habit of concealing his true feelings nor the barely repressed passion of the second half of Aeneas' speech at the center of book 4 is enough to undo the damage of his leaden, rhetorical, possibly mendacious first few sentences or of Dido's two magnificent arias that bracket Aeneas' speech. Many readers, not just students, find Aeneas unlikable beyond the middle of book 4.

Not liking Aeneas begins with the *Aeneid*, if not before. The jealous Libyan chieftain Iarbas, who hoped to marry Dido, lays out the charges: Aeneas is a perfumed, effeminate, Oriental woman-stealer in a silly foreign hat, no better than his cousin Paris (4.215–217).[6] In the battle for Italy after the Trojans have landed there, Numanus Remulus taunts the Trojans with a similar charge: with their flowing Asian dress and love of luxury, they are Phrygian girls, not Phrygian men (9.614–620). Turnus, the Italian hero who opposes Aeneas when he lands in Italy and competes with him for the hand of the Latin princess Lavinia, adds to the dossier: Aeneas abandoned his Asian home (12.15) and hides behind the skirts of his divine mother, Venus (12.52–53). All these rivals dislike Aeneas for what he does: he competes with them for the love of a woman, wears foreign dress, fights on the losing side, and abandons his homeland. Only Dido, who has a claim to know him more intimately than any other character in the poem, blames him for what he fails to do: he does not show feeling or respond to her entreaties as he prepares to leave Carthage. He is no child of Venus or glorious Trojans, she says; his parents are stony mountains, and tigers were his nursemaids (4.365–367). Dido then distances herself from him with the third person: "Did he groan when I wept? Did he look at me? / Did he shed tears or take pity on his lover?" (4.369–370).

Even before the *Aeneid*, people found uncomplimentary things to say about

Aeneas. The *Iliad* portrays Aeneas as a mighty warrior, second only to Hector among the Trojans; in Homer's epic, *pietas*, dutiful loyalty (or loyal dutifulness), is a hallmark of Aeneas' character almost from the beginning.[7] Long before Vergil, Greek art and literature depict the archetypal example of this quality: the scene when Aeneas, after resisting to the last, leaves Troy carrying his crippled father, Anchises, on his shoulders (*Aen.* 2.705–725). Sophocles in the fifth century BC portrayed this episode in a tragedy that is now lost, and he may have been drawing on an even earlier tradition, in the so-called *Little Iliad*; in the fourth century, Xenophon singled out Aeneas' action in saving his family's gods and his father from Troy (*On Hunting* 1.15).[8] As Vergil wrote the *Aeneid*, though, he found other traditions that showed his main character in a less favorable light. The Greek Dionysius of Halicarnassus, Vergil's contemporary, records several of those stories. In one, which Dionysius attributes to the historian Hellanicus of Lesbos (fifth century BC), Aeneas did not fight to the last and flee Troy only when given a divine command to do so, as Vergil has him tell in *Aeneid* 2; instead, he organized an orderly retreat from Troy to the Ida range and then negotiated with the victorious Greeks to allow the surviving Trojans safe passage from the Troad (*Roman Antiquities* 1.47). The fourth-century historian Menecrates of Xanthus was less flattering: he claimed that Aeneas had betrayed Troy to the Greeks because he resented the way that he had been treated by Paris; in return for his treachery, Aeneas was allowed to save his household and became a Greek (*Roman Antiquities* 1.48). Bits and scraps of evidence suggest that Latin authors before Vergil knew that story as well as the one made canonical by the *Aeneid*.[9] Even after the *Aeneid*, Romans found ways not to like Aeneas; the ancient biography of Vergil deriving from Suetonius mentions that a man named Carvilius Pictor wrote a work called *Aeneomastix*, "The Scourge of Aeneas" (*VSD* 44).[10]

Thinking about Aeneas

Anyone who wants to dislike Aeneas can find plenty of reasons to do so, not only in the *Aeneid* but also in the ancient stories about him. Modern times, too, offer plenty of company to those who dislike the Aeneid's hero.[11] But what does it mean to like or dislike a fictional character? At one level, the answer seems simple: when we like or dislike fictional people, we are forming an opinion about them based on a description of their behavior, just as we form opinions about politicians, celebrities, and other people we know only through hearsay. But characters in literature are not exactly like people we have never met.

Characters exist only as part of narrative and within a literary work. Modernist critics and their successors have been quick to point out that a literary character like Aeneas is, in the end, only a pattern in Vergil's words. Despite such strictures, most readers persist in looking beyond the words and projecting these patterns into their own worlds as three-dimensional persons. Words, however, have their limitations. An artist who uses language to create people must show them in action. Character, as Aristotle saw, depends on plot. His dictum that plot is "the first principle and, as it were, soul of tragedy," while "character is secondary" (*Poetics* 1450a), casts a long shadow on the problem of character in literature. In 1978, one critic could write, "It is remarkable how little has been said about the theory of character in literary history and criticism" (Chatman 1978, 19). More than twenty years later, the most recent edition of a standard handbook of literary theory declared that a systematic theory of character "remains one of the challenges poetics has not yet met" (Rimmon-Kenan 2002, 29). If, as the novelist William H. Gass has opined, "a character, first of all, is the noise of his name," then a flood of nameless characters in fiction may suggest that those who are responsible for creating literary character are profoundly discontented with it.[12] Even creating a character may pose challenges that authors prefer to avoid; writers like Karl Ove Knausgaard, Rachel Cusk, and Siri Hustvedt have developed a genre of "autofiction" that rejects creation of an entirely fictional character in favor of merging the author's life with a novelistic narrative.

There are exceptions to this general neglect of character among people who think about or use literature. The philosophical question of how we can know another mind has led to a spate of recent work on literary characterization.[13] The simplest and one of the oldest ways to think about literary characters, though, is to employ them as examples. Such exempla or *paradeigmata* are a stock feature of ancient and modern moral and historical writing.[14] When ethicist and moral theorist Carol Gilligan wants to explore the complex interactions of love and loyalty in modern human relationships, she focuses on the final meeting of Dido and Aeneas. As Aeneas sailed away from Carthage, Dido killed herself with her lover's sword. On his journey to the underworld in *Aeneid* 6, Aeneas meets Dido in the Lugentes Campi (Fields of Mourning), among those who have died because of love (*Aen.* 6.440–476). For Gilligan, their meeting shows Aeneas "caught between two images of himself—as implicated and as innocent, as responsible and as tossed about by fate" (1989, 50). In her article, Gilligan uses Aeneas' speech to Dido in the same way as she uses words of twentieth-century adolescent girls: to show by example how human beings in all ages have mapped the territory of love and loyalty and how we negotiate the collisions between our sense of ourselves and our sense of others.[15]

Aeneas among the Psychologists

Gilligan is an ethicist and educational theorist, but she is also a psychologist, and her reading of the *Aeneid* branches into a second way that readers may think about character. Psychoanalytic criticism sometimes acquires a bad name for its reductive excesses—Peter Brooks has called it "something of an embarrassment" (1987, 334)—and classics, one critic asserts, "has never tried hard to repress its aggression toward the discourse that appropriated Oedipus."[16] But since, as Lionel Trilling noted more than half a century ago (1951), both psychoanalysis and literature seem to offer a descriptive account of the workings of human nature, it is not surprising that many critics have turned to psychoanalytic concepts to understand literature. Both classics and psychoanalysis seek to recover a lost past and interpret it for the present, and some have traced the affinity between the two hermeneutics back to Freud (R. Armstrong 2005). Paul Allen Miller, Micaela Janan, and other critics have used Freudian and Lacanian theory to open up innovative readings of Latin literature, especially Catullus, Ovid, and the elegiac poets.[17]

Vergil has been more resistant to psychoanalytic readings, but examples can be found.[18] One in particular sheds light on Aeneas' character at the beginning of the *Aeneid* and may illuminate his relationship with Dido. It can serve as an example of Freudian approaches. Ellen Oliensis is not the first to see the erotic electricity in Aeneas' first encounter with his mother, the goddess Venus (*Aen.* 1.314–410). After his shipwreck in North Africa and speech to his men, Aeneas decides to explore the unknown land. He grabs a couple of hunting spears and sets out with a companion called Achates.[19] Along their way, they meet Venus, disguised as a huntress—we readers know her identity, but Aeneas does not. Vergil's description makes her seem like another goddess, Diana,

> with a maiden's face and gait, and a maiden's gear,
> a Spartan girl's, or like that Thracian girl

who tires out horses or outruns rivers in her flight.
From her shoulders she had hung a handy bow,
and the huntress had let her hair pour out on the wind;
her knees were bare, and her flowing garments knotted up.

Aen. 1.315–320

Aeneas senses something uncanny, and as Anchises' son should know, it is never good to encounter a strange, scantily clad woman in the forest at midday. A similar encounter between Venus and the young Anchises in the woods of Mount Ida led to Aeneas' conception, and Aeneas, in Carthage, may seem perilously close to reenacting his father's part in that scene. As the Homeric *Hymn to Aphrodite* tells the story, Venus told Anchises not to boast that he had slept with a goddess; when he did, he was struck by lightning and crippled.

In the woods of Carthage, though, all is piety and politeness. In a speech modeled on Odysseus' to Nausicaa (*Odyssey* 6.148–155), Aeneas asks the stranger how he should address her—as one of the nymphs, perhaps even as Diana—and begs her to favor him and tell him where he is. She obliges and provides him (and Vergil's readers) with the backstory of Dido. Aeneas then introduces himself and tells the mysterious huntress something of his story—which, of course, she already knows. Still keeping up her disguise, Venus claims that her parents taught her the craft of augury, and she offers Aeneas an interpretation of a conveniently happening bird omen: just as a flight of twelve swans that he can see have escaped an eagle and are coming to land, some already on the ground and others still in flight, so his ships, having escaped the storm, will be safely reunited.

The scene is laden with irony and not a little humor: "Oh yes, these purple boots," Venus says, "all the girls from Carthage wear them" (*virginibus Tyriis mos est gestare pharetram / purpureoque alte suras vincire coturno*, *Aen.* 1.335–336). At the end, however, narrative and language take a different turn, as Venus drops her disguise.

The goddess spoke, and as she turned aside light shone
from her rosy neck, her hair exhaled the smell of godhood,
down to her feet poured her garment, and by her walk
the true goddess was revealed.

Aen. 1.402–405

This description brings out the sexual tension that has been lurking under the surface of the episode, as Aeneas found himself almost reenacting the role played by his own father at his conception. The natural interpretation of line 404 (literally, "her garment flowed down to the bottom of her feet") is that Venus' knee-high hunting dress is transformed into the dignified, ankle-length robe of a goddess. Kenneth Reckford (1996) points out that the words will bear another interpretation: that as Venus turns away, she drops her clothing and stands revealed in the goddess of love's traditional costume, nudity.

Vergil's language prompts this possibility by echoing another famous literary striptease from a poem that Vergil certainly knew. As Ariadne, abandoned by Theseus, stands on the shore of Naxos in Catullus 64, she drops her clothing into the surf.

> And all of it, slipping from her whole body everywhere,
> before her feet became the plaything of the salt wave.
>
> *Omnia quae toto delapsa e corpore passim*
> *ipsius ante **pedes fluctus** salis alludebant.*
>
> Catullus 64.66–67

Vergil's description of Venus, *spiravere* ***pedes*** *vestis* ***defluxit*** *ad imos*, has "feet" (*pedes*) in the same metrical position and recalls *fluctus* with *defluxit*. Vergil demands learned readers, and his poems are densely packed with allusions like this; even so, it may seem hard to believe that such a subtle play of sound and sense could be enough to make a reader reject the conventional interpretation that leaves Venus fully robed, as Venus Genetrix, the mother of Rome rather than the voluptuous goddess of the *Hymn to Aphrodite*. The more likely interpretation remains dominant. But the hint, the bare suggestion (or the suggestion of bareness) stays there beneath the surface of the poem. It forms part of the poem's unconscious, and it give us a window into Aeneas; as Oliensis says, "Behind the matronly image of Venus Genetrix shimmers the naked Aphrodite—and this is just Aeneas' problem" (2009, 62).

Vergil's intertextual hint introduces an idea of quasi-maternal incest that reappears, as Oliensis argues, at critical points in the poem's unconscious. When Venus sends her son Cupid (Aeneas' half brother) to inflame Dido with love for Aeneas, she disguises him as Ascanius, Aeneas' son. The goddess tranquilizes the actual Ascanius and spirits him away to Cyprus.

> But along Ascanius' limbs Venus pours restful sleep,
> and the goddess lifts him, cherished in her lap,
> to the groves high on Idalia, where soft marjoram,
> sighing in sweet shadow, embraces him with its blooms.
>
> *Aen.* 1.691–694

With Ascanius out of the way, Cupid is free to join Dido and her guests at the banquet welcoming Aeneas and his men to Carthage. There the disguised god mingles with the crowd and greets his father—so they think.

> When he had embraced Aeneas and hugged him
> and satisfied the love of his pretended father,
> he makes for the queen. With her eyes Dido clings to him,
> clings with her heart, and in her lap cherishes him
> unaware how mighty a god now undermines her.
>
> *Aen.* 1.715–719

Dido embraces the son but loves or will soon love the father, and Venus embraces her grandson, whom her son was replacing. Vergil's language brings out the erotic undertones in Dido's fondling of the boy she thinks is her guest's son; *haec pectore toto / haeret*, "she clings to him with her whole heart," will echo at the beginning of book 4, when the banquet is over and Aeneas' words and facial expressions "cling, planted in her heart" (*haerent infixi pectore vultus / verbaque*, *Aen.* 4.4–5). The phrase *fotum gremio*, describing the real Ascanius "cherished in (Venus') lap," reappears in *fovet gremio*, when Dido holds the false Ascanius. More than reinforcing the identity of the tranquilized youth and the disguised god, the echo helps create an atmosphere of charged, intergenerational eroticism that surrounds and colors not only Aeneas' encounter with his goddess mother but also the coming love between him and Dido.[20]

Freud can easily be carried to extremes, and as Oliensis reminds us, "It is not the case that Virgil is discreetly (allusively) depicting a relation of repressed incestuous desire" (2009, 63). But without the insight into unconscious desires that Freud gave to the twentieth century, it might not have been possible to develop the reading that makes Venus' clothing follow the same trajectory as Ariadne's or the suggestion that in embracing a disguised Cupid, Dido is in a sense becoming Venus, the mother of the man with whom she is falling in love. Here and elsewhere, psychoanalytic criticism provides a way to talk about the unconscious life of the text.

Not every critic who approaches Vergil through psychoanalytic theory comes by way of Freud. The French philosopher and psychiatrist Jacques Lacan (1901–1981) developed ideas on the formation of personal identity that have come to rival Freud's in their influence on literary criticism. Lacan deconstructs the self into a house of mirrors. Rather than being, as in Freud, an overlay of conscious thought and speech that can be stripped away to reveal its foundations in unconscious desires and drives, the human subject becomes a grouping of lacks or vacancies, failed reflections in Lacan's house of mirrors. Lacan's self is defined only in relation to something else; it lacks any anchoring point, any firm, stable "I" from which the world can be seen or against which the world can react. This Lacanian self is formed through the acquisition of language, and so language precedes the formation of personal identity. Language alienates human beings from themselves, complicates and frustrates their desires, and imposes an inescapable barrier between human beings and the world in which they live. Lacan sees the human condition as always and necessarily alienated from both itself and the world by the failures of the language through which it is constructed.[21] As a Lacanian self moves through a world it can never fully apprehend, it can easily seem that neither the self nor the world has any firm reality.

Both Lacan and Freud have fallen out of fashion among clinical psychologists (Lacan, who has been characterized as "the analyst from Hell," may never have been in), but their ideas can provide theoretical frameworks for literary understanding. Literary theories—Freudian, Lacanian, Marxist, feminist, and others—are not, in the ordinary sense of the word, true, but they are useful. They are best seen as a kind of rhetoric; theories gather and systematize figures of thought and speech that help to create a convincing account of a literary work. In particular, Lacan's ideas about language and personality seem to offer a language in which to describe important aspects of Aeneas in the *Aeneid*: the way the hero seems to fade from view as the poem advances, as well as the way in which his destiny as Rome's progenitor cuts him off from his future and makes it impossible for him to live a full, self-realized life.

Aeneas the Unreal

When James I. Porter reads the *Aeneid* through a Lacanian lens, he discovers a poem in which "agents, bodies, and places are made to seem unreal" (2004, 137). This unreality can be clearly seen, Porter suggests, in a strange story that Aeneas tells to Dido after the banquet welcoming him to Carthage. The story is made even stranger for us by the circumstance that we cannot be absolutely sure that Vergil wrote every word of it. In response to a request from Dido, Aeneas tells her of the fall of Troy and his travels from there to Carthage. Despite his protestation that the grief in telling it is "unspeakable" (*Aen.* 2.3), his narrative takes up all but a few lines of books 2 and 3.

Troy is burning. Aeneas has just seen King Priam and his wife, Hecuba, butchered by Achilles' son Neoptolemus, as they take refuge at an altar in the courtyard of the palace. Up to this point, Aeneas has been leading a small company of Trojans in valiant resistance. Now he looks around and sees that he is alone. The slain old king reminds Aeneas of his father and family, and he begins to make his way home (*Aen.* 2.559–566).

Then he sees Helen, the woman who caused the war that has meant a decade of fighting, who has made the coast of Troy drip with blood, who has left his friends and kinsmen dead and his city in flames. She, like Priam and Hecuba a few lines earlier, has taken refuge on an altar, knowing that Trojans and Greeks alike have reason to hate her, none more than Menelaus, the husband that she deserted to run away with her Trojan lover, Paris. Anger consumes Aeneas; there may not be much glory in killing a woman, he thinks to himself, but he will kill this one and exact the punishment that she deserves (*Aen.* 2.567–588).

At this point, his mother, Venus, appears to him. She is not in disguise this time but appears exactly as she does to the other gods in heaven (*confessa deam qualisque videri / caelicolis et quanta solet*, *Aen.* 2.591–592). She takes his hand, as Athena takes Achilles' hand when she checks his anger against Agamemnon at the beginning of the *Iliad*. (Aeneas and his mother will touch one other time in the poem, at *Aen.* 8.615.) Venus asks Aeneas why he is raging with anger. The destruction of Troy, she declares, is not the fault of Helen, or of Paris. The goddess strips away the cognitive mist that normally veils mortal vision and shows Aeneas what is.

> "Here, where you see structures torn asunder, stone
> ripped from stone, smoke and dust clouds billowing,
> Neptune is shaking walls and foundations removed
> by his huge trident; he digs the city up from its roots.
> Over here savage Juno takes the lead, holding
> the Scaean Gate; raging, belted with iron, she summons
> the Greek line from the ships.
> Look behind you: Pallas Athena now sits atop the citadel,

gleaming from her cloud-veil, savage with Gorgon shield.
The Father himself supplies courage and strength to the Greeks,
the Father himself rouses the gods against Trojan arms.
Take flight, my son, put an end to your toil;
I will never desert you, and I will set you safe on your threshold."
She finished speaking and buried herself in thick night.
There they were: implacable shapes of the gods,
great presences hostile to Troy.

Aen. 2.608–623

For just a moment, Aeneas has glimpsed the existence of what a Lacanian might call "the Real." The *numina magna deum*, "great presences of the gods," do not exist elsewhere or on another plane of reality; rather, they are here, a category of existence that is always present but beyond our human ability to imagine or describe. Aeneas sees dust and smoke billowing from the collapsing buildings of Troy, but his mother shows him Neptune. Telling the story to Dido, he has no choice but to employ language and the conventional symbols of these *numina*: Neptune's trident, the Gorgon on Athena's aegis, or Jupiter's symbolic role as father of gods and men. A *numen*, however, is (again, in Lacanian terms) the Real manifest in the sublime or the uncanny. It is beyond the limit of our ability to imagine or speak, but it emerges, as Cicero says (*On the Nature of the Gods* 2.4.1), when we gaze at a starry sky and sense something like an intelligence beyond the human. Yet we can only express it as Aeneas tries to, through language, or, as a Lacanian might say, through the Symbolic. Aeneas' glimpse of the Real, as Porter argues, "works to render *unreal* the wars being waged and the achievements of human agency" (2004, 138)—in fact, everything in Aeneas' life, including, as we shall see later in this book, Aeneas himself.

Aeneas' whole description of the epiphany at the destruction of Troy is shot through by doubts about what is real and what is not, and those doubts function on several levels of reading. Commenting on the poem in the late fourth or early fifth century AD, Maurus Servius Honoratus noted that Helen's behavior as she lurks in the shadows of collapsing Troy contradicts the account that Deiphobus gives later in the poem, when Aeneas meets him in the underworld (*Aen.* 6.509–527). Servius suggests that the contradiction is one reason to suspect that the lines describing Aeneas' encounter with Helen (*Aen.* 2.567–588) ought not to be in the poem at all. If we leave out the "Helen episode," as do most ancient and medieval manuscripts of Vergil, the narrative still coheres.

Aeneas sees Priam butchered by Neoptolemus. He realizes that he is alone. Then his mother Venus appears to him and guides him home. Ever since Servius, scholars, students, and well-informed readers have had to reckon with this problem and form an opinion about it. There are three basic options: Vergil did not write the Helen episode; Vergil did write it, and it belongs in the poem; or Vergil wrote it but left it on the cutting-room floor, and so it belongs with the poem but not in the poem.[22] (I incline toward the last view, though not very confidently.)

A reader looking for Aeneas in the *Aeneid* enters a house of mirrors, both textual and interpretive. Early in the poem Aeneas is literally mirrored as he views an image of himself while exploring Carthage. He and Achates, protected by the cloud of invisibility in which Venus has disguised them, come upon a temple of Juno. In it they find pictures of the Trojan War that, Vergil says, ease Aeneas' fears and give him hope for the first time (*Aen.* 1.450–452). Yet his immediate reaction and first words once again do not sound like a man who feels hope after long despair.

> He stopped and wept. "Achates," he said, "what place,
> what region of earth is not full of our toil?
> Look—Priam. Here too are rewards for glory,
> tears for things, and mortal matters touch the mind.
> Let go your fear; this fame will bring you safety."[23]
>
> *Aen.* 1.459–463

He then "feeds his mind on the empty picture" (*animum pictura pascit inani*, 1.464). Yet this "empty picture" of Trojan defeat includes an image of Aeneas: "He recognizes himself, too, mingled with the Greek chiefs" (*se quoque principibus permixtum agnovit Achivis*, 1.487). *Permixtum* denotes "mixed in combat," as commentators are careful to observe, but it hints at the other Aeneas recorded in Dionysius of Halicarnassus, the one who "mingled with the Greeks" when he negotiated his own passage from Troy or even betrayed the city. Porter asks whether what Aeneas recognizes is that the picture shows who he is or that he is the person the picture shows (2004, 143). That question may be oversubtle except in the context of a Lacanian, decentered self, but the confrontation of two Aeneases, one an empty picture and the other a "real" but literally invisible character, reinforces a reader's growing impression that the *Aeneid*'s central character moves through a world in which his own reality is in doubt.

At the very center of the *Aeneid*, Vergil places the most enigmatic of Aeneas' separations from reality. Book 6 ends as Aeneas and his guide, the Cumaean Sibyl, leave the underworld.

> There are twin gates of Sleep, one (the story is)
> of horn, and through it easy exit is granted true shades,
> the other shining, finished with the gleam of ivory,
> but through these, spirits below send false dreams to the sky.
> With these words then Anchises follows his son
> and the Sibyl and sends them out through the ivory gate.
>
> *Aen.* 6.893–898

This short passage seems designed to throw a reader off balance. The twin gates derive from *Odyssey* 19.560–567, where Penelope tells her disguised husband that "there are two gates of shadowy dreams, one made of horn and one of ivory," and that true dreams come from the gate of horn, false from the gate of ivory. Homer's gates are balanced and antithetical: horn and ivory, true and false. Vergil's gates are gates of Sleep (*somnus*), or perhaps of Dream (*somnium*); the genitive form *somni* is ambiguous. Through them go not one kind of dream and another but true shades—*umbrae*, shadows or ghosts—and false dreams, *insomnia*. Instead of dreams balancing dreams, as in Homer, we have *umbrae* at one gate, dreams at the other. Aeneas and the Sibyl are neither, so it is unclear which gate suits them better. The conjunction "but" (*sed*) joins the two gates at a slight angle; a reader expects another relative, "by which," (*qua*) to balance the same relative two lines earlier and to reflect the strict poise of Homer's paired demonstratives.[24]

All these imperfect parallels reinforce the central riddle of Vergil's gates. Anchises has just shown his son a parade of souls who are waiting to be incarnated. The parade begins with the legendary kings of Alba Longa and includes Romulus, Pompey, Caesar, and Augustus; it ends with Marcellus, Augustus' nephew and presumed heir, who died in 23 BC, as the *Aeneid* was being written. Readers of Vergil, whether in the first century or the twenty-first, know those figures as persons not from the distant future, as they are from Aeneas' point of view within the narrative, but from the historical past. Because we know that the figures Aeneas sees are actors in our world, we believe that Aeneas' underworld vision shares in the truth of history. Why, then, does Aeneas leave by the ivory gates, through which the Manes, or spirits of the dead, send false dreams to the world above? What is false about his exit?

Servius has an answer in his comment on line 893: "The meaning is revealed in poetic terms; he wishes it to be understood, in fact, that everything he has said is false."[25] That is, the passage directs readers to interpret Aeneas' underworld journey as an allegory; if so, no reader has ever been able to propose an entirely satisfactory allegorical interpretation. Others have suggested that the gates of horn and ivory label Aeneas' underworld journey as a dream; that because he is a living human, not a "true shade," he cannot exit by the gates of horn; or that since true dreams were believed to appear only after midnight, Vergil is hinting that Aeneas' journey ends before then.[26] Most readers are at least content, if not satisfied, to acknowledge a mystery at the heart of the *Aeneid*.

Homesick for the Future

But it is Aeneas, the central character of the *Aeneid*, who steps through the gates of horn in book 6. The choice is not entirely his; Anchises, his father, sends him out (*emittit*, *Aen.* 6.898). That lack of agency at the center of the *Aeneid* may hold a clue to what kind of person Aeneas is. Although I do not want to undertake or argue for a full-blown Freudian or Lacanian reading of the *Aeneid*, certain psychoanalytic concepts, especially "belatedness" and "rememoration" (or recollection), may offer a way to probe a little deeper into what the end of book 6 tells us about the hero of the *Aeneid*.

Like Odysseus' summoning of the ghosts in book 11 of the *Odyssey*, Aeneas' visit to the underworld is a journey into his past and a quest for knowledge of his future. At a critical moment in book 5, after most of his fleet has been burned in a conflagration inspired by Juno, Aeneas contemplates giving up his quest for Italy and settling in Sicily (*Aen.* 5.700–703). His father appears to him in a vision and confirms the counsel of Aeneas' advisor Nautes, that the hero should continue on to Italy. Then Anchises gives his son a hint of what is to come: a tough people must be subdued, but Aeneas must first go down to the underworld, where he will be reunited with Anchises and learn "all his descent and what city walls are granted" (5.737). "Descent" (*genus*) can refer to one's ancestry or one's progeny, and it is reasonable for a reader of line 737 to imagine that in the underworld Aeneas will hear from Anchises, as Odysseus does from Teiresias, something about his own past and future—that his journey will be personal, like the journey of an analysand into the world below conscious thought.

Unlike Odysseus, however, Aeneas in the underworld hears almost nothing of his future life in Italy or of his death. Odysseus learns from the ghost of the prophet Tiresias that he will make his way to Ithaca and punish the men who are eating up his estate and paying court to his queen; then he will set out on a journey that will take him far inland, to a place where the inhabitants do not recognize even the oar that he must carry with him; finally, death will come to him from the sea, in his old age (*Odyssey* 11.100–137). Aeneas, in contrast, learns a great deal about Rome's future but not much about his own—only that he will have a posthumous son, Aeneas Silvius, by the Italian princess Lavinia (*Aen.* 6.760–765) and will fight wars against "the Laurentine people and the city of Latinus" (6.890–892). This last piece of information comes in reported speech at the very end of Anchises' long account of Rome's future heroes; it feels like an afterthought and tells Aeneas nothing new—he had already learned as much from the Sibyl, before he entered the underworld (*Aen.* 6.86–94).[27]

In any case, there is no sign that Aeneas remembers any of this once he emerges through the gates of horn and begins his wars in Italy; when, in book 8, he receives a divinely crafted shield decorated with scenes from the future of Rome, he does not recognize any of them (*Aen.* 8.730). His failure or inability to remember what he learns about his future provides a key to his character. If Aeneas' journey to the underworld, where he encounters his past in the form of Palinurus, Dido, and Deiphobus and his future in the form of Anchises' prophecies, is a kind of psychoanalytic voyage of discovery, he emerges from it as an imperfect character, who cannot understand who he is because he cannot make sense of what he has experienced.

In psychoanalysis, the working of an event in the future can determine its meaning in our past. A past event can hide itself below the level of memory but continue to act, eventually reemerging in the future as a traumatic recollection. This deferred action, or "belatedness," becomes an important concept in the thought of both Freud and Lacan. In one of his early works, Freud recounts the case of a patient, Emma, who could make sense of childhood trauma only through later experiences, which led her to recover an adolescent memory and the anxiety she connected with it. Her future determined the meaning and significance of her past; as Freud put it, "Here we have the case of a memory arousing an affect which it did not arouse as an experience. . . . We invariably find that a memory is repressed which has only become a trauma by *deferred action*" (Strachey 1966, 356). For Lacan, the act of recollecting earlier trauma, or "rememoration," was an essential consequence of effective analysis; as he put it,

"One does not get better because one remembers. One remembers because one gets better" (2006, 521). Events do not have meaning as they occur but acquire it only after the fact. Aeneas does not and cannot get better, because his future is not available to give meaning to his traumatic past. His future, his *genus*, as revealed by Anchises in the underworld, is not his personal future but the history of Rome, a city that, in Vergil's chronology, will not be founded until three centuries after his death (*Aen.* 1.267–274).[28]

Aeneas is, in Terry Eagleton's memorable phrase, "homesick for a future that he will not live to see" (2018, 14). An empire that he will never experience, cannot remember, and cannot imagine is the meaning of his life and suffering. Vergil makes this clear from the very first sentence of the poem: Aeneas is "an exile by fate" (*fato profugus*), and his fated journey from Troy to Italy, with all its suffering, results in "the walls of lofty Rome," the climactic last words of the epic's first sentence. Yet the prologue also makes clear that between Aeneas' life and the walls of Rome intervene the histories of the Latin race and the rulers of Alba Longa (*genus unde Latinum / Albanique patres atque altae moenia Romae*, *Aen.* 1.6–7). Two hundred and fifty lines later, a speech from Jupiter reinforces both the prologue's message and the idea that the events of Aeneas' life are not what is most important about that hero.

At the low point of Aeneas' fortunes, when he is shipwrecked and cast away on the shores of North Africa, Venus asks her father a simple question: What has her son done to deserve all this suffering? Why is he being kept from Italy, the land promised to him? Has Jupiter changed his mind and reneged on his promise to bring forth from Aeneas' Trojan blood, in the fullness of time, a race of Romans who will hold land and sea in their power? Jupiter answers, but he does not address the emotional point of Venus' question. He says nothing about the sufferings of Aeneas and the Trojan refugees and devotes only three and a half lines of his forty-line speech to Aeneas' individual fate; he promises Venus only that before being deified her son will wage a huge war in Italy, crush fierce peoples, and establish a city (*Aen.* 1.258–259, 263–264).[29] The rest of Jupiter's reply outlines the legendary history and cosmic significance of Rome. Aeneas will rule for three years; his son, Ascanius, will rule for thirty and transfer his kingdom from Lavinium, the city founded by Aeneas, to a new city, Alba Longa; after three hundred years, a queen and priestess, pregnant by Mars, will bring forth twins, Romulus and Remus, the founders of Rome. Jupiter then reveals what destiny has in store for Rome.

To these I set limits neither of space nor time:
I have granted them empire without end. Even harsh Juno,
who now harries them with anxiety on land and sea,
will change her mind, and with me foster
the Romans, lords of the world, the toga-wearing folk.

Aen. 1.278–282

In the fullness of time, the race of Aeneas' ancestor Assaracus, the Trojans, will conquer the homelands of Achilles and Agamemnon (*Aen.* 1.283–285). The Roman conquest of Greece will avenge the sufferings of Aeneas and his people, but only generations after Aeneas' death, at a time when Achilles' Phthia and Agamemnon's Mycenae will have declined into insignificance. Finally, Jupiter announces, history will culminate with the advent of Augustus, "a Caesar of Trojan origin, who will bound his empire with Ocean, his fame with the stars" (1.286–287). Augustus will become a god, and with his reign, the Golden Age—that imagined Eden to which Vergil, Horace, and others turned amid the wars of the dying Roman Republic—will return.[30]

Venus asks about her son in the present of the poem, but Jupiter finds the meaning of Aeneas' life in the far distant future, in Augustus. The meaning of Aeneas' suffering in exile and war stands outside the limits of his birth and death. Aeneas exits through the gates of ivory into a world in which he will be forever and always cut off from the knowledge that would give meaning to his struggle and suffering. He cannot "rememorate" what he experiences in the underworld, because those events cannot be part of his, Aeneas', consciousness. He cannot become, in Lacanian terms, a "subject." The ivory gates are the only way out, and they lead to a world in which Aeneas can only be a deeply flawed human or not quite human.

What's Not to Like?

In Lacanian psychoanalysis, the term *perversion* refers to the clinical position in which someone conflates his or her own desires with those of some other entity—or, as Lacanians would say, with those of the Other.[31] Someone who consistently identifies his or her own desires and pleasures with those of the universe, fate, or the gods, and who believes in the truth of what those seem to be saying, qualifies, in Lacanian terms, as a "pervert." James I. Porter suggests that Aeneas fits this description. "One of the most disquieting features of Aeneas," Porter observes, is "his complete subservience to a divine mission—the founding of Rome and its terrible imperium—in the guise of pious devotion. Does not this behavior fit to a T the Lacanian definition of the pervert?" (2004, 138). Readers who find Aeneas unlikable or wanting as a human being may be responding to something like this implication of his character as Vergil presents it. When Aeneas says to Dido that it is not of his own free will that he seeks Italy, students and other readers may respond with disgust, not because Aeneas is lying to Dido or abandoning her for something that he likes better, but because he seems to have no will, no subject position of his own, and no capacity to make truly free choices. Students have to drill down into the language of the text to support any suggestion that he feels anything at all for Dido. To many readers, Aeneas seems not so much unreal as empty, even inhuman. Fate and *pietas*, Aeneas' much-vaunted "piety," define his character and empty his soul. Yet these are the things that make him heroic.[32]

Fate and History

Fate brackets the extended prologue of the first thirty-three lines of the *Aeneid*. In line 2, Aeneas is *fato profugus*, an exile by fate; in line 32, the Trojans are *acti fatis*, driven across the seas by fate. The second line from the beginning of the prologue and the second line from its end sound the note that will echo through the entire poem. Between these bookends, fate also figures in two ways in the thought of Juno, whose anger will harry Aeneas and the Trojans in their exile. First, Juno proposes to make her beloved Carthage ruler of the world, if the fates allow (*si qua fata sinant*, *Aen.* 1.18). Juno has learned, however, that descendants of the Trojans will, in time, destroy Carthage. That fact allows no conditional: thus the Fates are unrolling their scroll, as she knows (*sic volvere Parcas*, 1.22). From the beginning of the poem, Aeneas and Juno are set against one another, not merely because of Juno's grievances against the Trojans, which Vergil enumerates (1.24–28), but because one is acting as an agent of fate while the other struggles against it.

What is fate in the *Aeneid*? It is tempting to identify it, as Richard Heinze and many other readers have, with the will of God (Heinze 1915, 293). Jupiter's grand, programmatic speech near the beginning of the poem seems to support that view. "Opening the secrets of fate," he says, "I shall set them in motion" (*volvens fatorum arcana movebo*, *Aen.* 1.262). What he then says becomes, in the world of the poem, true. But does Jupiter decide what will happen, or does he merely know what will happen, declare it, and act accordingly? Either view will account for his appearance to Aeneas at Troy, his dispatching of Mercury to order Aeneas to leave Carthage, his sending of Anchises to Aeneas at a crisis in Sicily (5.726), and his final, imperious command to Juno, "I forbid you to make any further efforts" (*ulterius temptare veto*, 12.806). In many other places in the poem, though, fate appears to be an impersonal force, unconnected with Jupiter. There is nothing about Jupiter in the prologue's invocation of the fate that sends Aeneas into exile and opposes Juno. In the underworld, when Aeneas' dead helmsman, Palinurus, begs him to take him across the Styx, even though he is unburied, the Sibyl reproves him: "Stop hoping to bend the gods' fate by prayer" (*Aen.* 6.376). The ordinance forbidding the unburied to cross the Styx is not ascribed to Jupiter or any other divinity; the ghastly ferryman Charon is simply "not allowed" (*nec . . . datur*, 6.327) to take them. Sometimes fate seems to be plural: Venus tells Jupiter that she has consoled herself by "weighing fates against opposite fates (*fatis contraria fata rependens*, 1.239), and as Juno stirs up the forces of Hell against the Trojans in Italy, she rails at the fates of the Trojans that oppose her fates (*fatis contraria nostris / fata Phrygum*, 7.292–294). Characters can have their own individual fates: when Vergil explains that two characters were not to meet in battle, he says, "Their fates await them at the hand of a greater enemy" (*illos sua fata manent maiore sub hoste*, 10.438); and Jupiter tells Hercules that Turnus' destiny is summoning him too (*etiam sua Turnum / fata vocant*, 10.471–472).

In the *Aeneid*, fate cannot be identified with the divine will of Jupiter, but throughout the poem, an impersonal force does work to shape its character's lives, especially the life of Aeneas. That force is history, especially the history that Vergil knew as he was writing the poem. For many in Vergil's generation, the experience of the Roman civil wars left them, like Freud's Emma, struggling to account for what they had become and to explain the incongruities and absences of their life. Their history as Romans seemed lacking in meaning, and as discussed further in chapter 2 below, their poets could imagine escape into the mythical Golden Age of the past or could contemplate the possibility that their Roman nature might be stained by some ancestral curse of fratricide. Vergil offered them a vision of history that was purposeful, rational, and ultimately—in the god's-eye view Vergil allows—intelligible. That view prescribes that once something has happened, it and the events leading up to it can be understood; those events are inevitable. In the *Aeneid*, fate is the sense that history makes.[33]

Throughout the *Aeneid*, Aeneas moves in a world that makes a sense that he cannot know, knows in part, or knows imperfectly. But to Vergil's readers, Aeneas' struggles and sufferings make sense because they tend toward a goal, the reign of Augustus. In Jupiter's reply to Venus in book 1 and in the parade of Roman heroes in book 6, two things happen. First, the events of Aeneas' life are shown to be leading up to a future event, the Augustan Golden Age, which is not mythical, remote, or distant but is just visible in the offing; it is not far from the present of the poem's creation and is manifest in the working out of historical forces. Second, all the events of Roman history, including the trauma of civil war, fall into shape and become intelligible in retrospect.[34] Jupiter interprets history correctly, and his view prevails. Juno interprets it incorrectly, and she must, as Jupiter says, change her view in the end.[35]

Aeneas cannot interpret the history that would make sense of his life, because it lies in the future, beyond his lifetime. Instead of interpretation, he depends on the quality that, as Vergil announces in the tenth line of the poem, marks him out: *pietas*. The word *pietas* and its adjective, *pius*, are notoriously difficult to translate. The English and Romance derivatives—"pious," "piety," *piété*, and the like—suggest that it must have something to do with the gods. But most of its Latin usages refer, as Cicero says (*De inventione* 2.66), to a disposition to do what is right toward other people, especially one's parents, close relatives, or country. It is an easy move to include the gods in this nexus of familial and civic duty, as Cicero does in a theological context when he defines *pietas* as "justice toward the gods" (*On the Nature of the Gods* 1.116.8). Most of the time, however, Cicero and other writers of the first century BC use *pietas* in the former sense, to mean duty toward one's parents, family, friends, or homeland.[36] Vergil gives the connotation of duty toward the gods a new emphasis, because in some ways, it is the only choice Aeneas has.

Pietas in Search of an Object

When he first appears in the *Aeneid*, Aeneas has lost all the conventional anchors of *pietas* except for his son, Ascanius. His father, Anchises, died in Sicily just before Aeneas set sail on the voyage that led him to Carthage (*Aen.* 3.708–713). That loss, as Aeneas later tells Dido and her guests in Carthage, deprived him of the one person on whom he could rely to help and console him in worry and misfortune (*omnis curae casusque levamen*, 3.709). His wife, Creusa, disappeared during the escape from Troy (*Aen.* 2.738–740). All but a few of his comrades have perished in the Trojan War or fallen during the journey into exile. His country, Troy, has ceased to exist.[37] Now a raging storm has driven his fleet off course. Aeneas has no more left to give and no one to help him. He lifts his hands to the heavens and howls in despair.

> O three and four times happy,
> you whose lot it was to meet death at Troy,
> under those lofty walls, before your fathers' eyes!
> O Diomedes, bravest of the Greeks! Why could I
> not have fallen by your hand on the Trojan plain,
> poured out my blood where Hector lies, and huge
> Sarpedon, where the Simois tumbles so many shields of men,
> their helmets and strong bodies, under its waves!
>
> *Aen.* 1.94–101

A character's first appearance and first speech give important clues as to how to read him. It is important to remember what Aeneas is when we first meet him: a refugee, afraid, alone, soaked to the skin, and looking, in what he thinks are his last moments of life, back to Troy, to those who died there, and to the hero's death that, he believes, he will never have. To some extent, everything else that he does and becomes in the *Aeneid* is overlaid on the emotion of this initial outburst. Aeneas will gain—so Jupiter assures Venus (and Vergil assures his readers)—a new home and a new family, but within the *Aeneid*, he will never recover or replace what he has lost. As the poem begins, Aeneas is *pietas* in search of an object.

After Aeneas lands in Carthage, Dido provides a simulacrum of the wife and the country that Aeneas has lost. During that winter in North Africa, he does not know what readers of the poem know: that he will reach Italy, where his descendants will found Rome, and that Rome and Carthage will become bitter enemies. It takes a jolt from Jupiter to set Aeneas back on his destined path. The god sends Mercury, who finds Aeneas directing the work of building Carthage (*Aen.* 4.219–264). Mercury relays Jupiter's message with a question: Has Aeneas forgotten his destiny and the Italian kingdom that is owed to his son, Ascanius?

This epiphany, and the encounter with Dido that follows, shatter Aeneas.

He is speechless, unable to think; his hair stands on end, and his voice sticks in his throat; the gods' unambiguous admonition and their power to command leave him thunderstruck (*Aen.* 4.279–282). The supreme god's order transforms Aeneas' view of the world he has built with Dido: he suddenly burns with eagerness to leave Carthage (*ardet abire fuga dulcisque relinquere terras*, 4.281). But, as Vergil makes clear, Aeneas is no robotic agent of the divine will. The difficulty with which he tears himself away from Carthage appears, like ripples betraying the presence of an unseen reef, in adjectives barely disturbing the surface of the narrative. The land of Carthage, even as he burns to leave it behind, is sweet (*dulcis*, 4.281). Dido, he tells his men, is the best of women (*optima*, 4.291) and does not expect such a great love (*tantos amores*, 4.292) to be broken apart. There is no reason to suppose that the love is all on one side; like the tears that roll down uselessly at 4.449, it belongs to both parties in this tragedy.[38] Finally, one silent action at another emotional crisis shows how deeply Aeneas feels the loss of Dido. When Mercury found him laying out foundations and watching new buildings rise in Carthage, he was wearing a splendid cloak of Tyrian scarlet, which Dido had embroidered in gold for him with her own hands (*tenui telas discreverat auro*, *Aen.* 4.263). That cloak appears again, described with the same words, in book 11, when a grieving Aeneas uses it to wrap the body of the young warrior Pallas (*Aen.* 11.73–75). Details added to Vergil's previous description of the cloak illuminate Aeneas' memories: Dido was happy as she embroidered the cloak for him with her own hands.[39]

Aeneas does what he must do even though he does not want to (*Italiam non sponte sequor*, *Aen.* 4.361). Just as he conceals the pain in his heart while he encourages his hungry and exhausted men on the shore of Carthage, so he cannot or perhaps fails to express to Dido his feelings about her (4.369–370). *Pietas* is the quality that allows him these silences. Nowhere is this connection plainer than in four lines at the end of the agonizing trio of speeches at the center of book 4. Aeneas has tried and failed to explain his decision to leave Carthage, and Dido has responded with passionate anger.

> But *pius* Aeneas, although he yearned
> to ease her agony, turn away her grief with words,
> nevertheless, groaning, shaken at heart with great love,
> follows the orders of the gods and goes to his fleet.
>
> *Aen.* 4.393–396

Stripped of father, homeland, and wife, and now deprived by divine command of the illusion that he created in Carthage, Aeneas has no object for his *pietas* except a future that he cannot know. Enigmatic instructions from the gods let him know that his life has a meaning, but he never learns it. In the underworld, Anchises fires his son's spirit with love of his approaching fame (*Aen.* 6.889), but that blaze remains, like so much else, below the level of Aeneas' conscious thought.

Because Aeneas lacks the human touchstones of *pietas*, he must fall back on trust in the gods who reveal the existence of a future that will give meaning to his suffering. That quality of *pietas* as devotion to the gods marks Aeneas from his first appearance in Greek literature. In book 20 of the *Iliad*, Aeneas encounters Achilles, who is a greater warrior and deadly. As they prepare to engage in a duel that will surely result in Aeneas' death, Poseidon speaks to the other gods.

> Alas for great-hearted Aeneas, who will now
> Be killed by Achilles and go down to Hades
> Because he innocently obeyed Apollo,
> Who will do nothing to keep him from perishing.
> Why should he, a guiltless man, now suffer
> For the woes of others, a man who has always
> Pleased the gods in heaven with his offerings?
>
> *Iliad* 20.293–299, trans. Lombardo

Vergil built his Aeneas out of the elements of Poseidon's description of a man who suffers but is always attentive to the gods. Even before the *Aeneid*, that action made Aeneas an exemplary figure for *pietas* in literature and art.[40] After the *Aeneid*, the association became indissoluble.[41]

In the *Aeneid*, Aeneas is called *pius* twenty times; on one additional occasion, the adjective is applied to his hands (*Aen.* 3.42).). Often when he is described as *pius*, he is performing some kind of religious act or responding to the presence of a god: praying to Jupiter to save the remnant of the Trojan fleet in Sicily (5.685), going to the temple of Apollo at Cumae (6.9), performing funeral rites for a loyal servant (7.5), sacrificing to Juno (8.84), or reinforcing a solemn oath with prayer (12.175). Other characters in the poem describe Aeneas as *pius* (5.418, 9.255, 11.170), and he twice describes himself as *pius Aeneas.*

Those two passages of self-description show Aeneas using *pietas* to construct a meaning for his life.

Toward the end of the teasing, ambiguous encounter with his disguised mother at the beginning of the poem (discussed earlier in this chapter), Aeneas introduces himself to the oddly attired huntress, having recognized her as a goddess of some kind.

> I am *pius* Aeneas. I carry with me my city's gods
> snatched from the enemy—my fame goes beyond heaven.
> I seek a homeland, Italy, and I am descended from Jupiter.
> I set out from Troy with twenty ships, following fate
> with my mother the goddess showing the way.
> Barely seven are left, broken by wave and wind.
> And me? Unknown and in need I wander the African desert
> driven out of Europe and Asia.
>
> *Aen.* 1.378–385

Aeneas' description of himself as *pius* is not arrogance, says Servius, but simply disclosure. Servius sounds as though he is anticipating a frequent objection, and commentators are fond of quoting Charles James Fox's remark, "Can you bear it?"[42] But Vergil has chosen the epithet because it echoes the Homeric question about Aeneas—"Why should he, a guiltless man, now suffer for the woes of others, a man who has always pleased the gods in heaven with his offerings?" (*Iliad* 20.297–299)—and because it reinforces the view that Aeneas now takes of his situation. The bitter anger of his first speech in the poem has given way to despairing irony. Is this, he asks, what *pietas* gets him—to have two-thirds of his fleet destroyed and the rest made unseaworthy, to be a refugee from two continents and wandering in desperation through the wilderness of a third? Aeneas' *pietas* may not have brought him the heroic fame or heroic death that he wants, but it allows him to follow fate as he understands it. It makes him who he is.

The second passage in which Aeneas refers to himself as *pius* comes at another moment when he has nearly lost the quality that gives meaning to his life. This time, he gives way not to doubt but to rage. In the war for Italy that broke out after he made his way there, Aeneas forms an alliance with King Evander, a Greek refugee from Arcadia who established a city on the site of the future Rome. Aeneas develops a close, subliminally erotic bond with Pallas, Evander's son.[43] When Turnus, the leader of the Italian forces, kills Pallas, Aeneas strikes out in a berserk rampage in which he seems to forget the claims of *pietas*. He captures eight Italian youths to sacrifice on Pallas' pyre (*Aen.* 10.517–520); the rumor that Octavian had done something similar (discussed further in chapter 2 below) is not enough to explain this atrocity. Magus, facing certain death, falls at Aeneas' knees and begs him, in the name of Anchises and Ascanius, to spare his life; Aeneas cuts his throat. A priest flees from him; Aeneas runs him down and kills him. Vergil compares Aeneas to a mythological monster.

> Like Aegaeon, who had, they say, a hundred arms,
> a hundred hands, and blazed fire from fifty chests
> and fifty mouths, when he clashed fifty shields
> and fifty blades against the lightning-bolts of Jupiter:
> so Aeneas raged in triumph over the plain
> once his sword had warmed up.
>
> *Aen.* 10.565–570

In the usual version of Zeus' war with the Titans, as found in the Greek poet Hesiod (*Theogony* 617–686), the Hundred-Handers are allies of Zeus. Whether or not Vergil is following a lost variant of the myth, he has, for once in the *Aeneid*, set Aeneas against the ruler of the universe.

Aeneas' rampage ends when he wounds an exiled Etruscan king, Mezentius. The old king is struggling to get away from the battlefield, when his son, Lausus, comes to his rescue. It is a crazy, brave deed, and Aeneas recognizes deluding *pietas* even as his sword rips through the tunic made by Lausus' mother and buries itself in the young man's guts (*Aen.* 10.810–820). As Aeneas looks down at Lausus' dying face, he weeps. His rage drains away, and he remembers his own father.

> Yet as he saw the face and expression of the dying boy,
> how death's mysterious paleness flickered over it,
> Anchises' son groaned and clasped his right hand in pity,
> and the image of his love for his father rose in his mind.
> "What now, pitiable child, in return for your glorious deed,

what will *pius* Aeneas give worthy of such a valiant nature?
Keep your weapons, which made you happy; I return
you to the spirits and ashes of your ancestors, if it matters to you."

Aen. 10.821–828

As Vergil makes clear, Aeneas' *pietas* can never leave him; two seemingly paradoxical appearances of the phrase *pius Aeneas* during his berserk rage reinforce its essential presence and lead up to the triple sequence of *pietas*, *pietatis*, and *pius Aeneas* in the Lausus episode (10.812, 824, 826). In one, *pius Aeneas* taunts a man he has just killed (10.591); in the other, *pius Aeneas* throws the spear that wounds Mezentius (10.783). *Pietas* brought Aeneas to the edge of despair in the first four books of the poem; in the tenth, it pulls him back from the edge of another kind of insanity, the fury (*furor*) that threatens to thwart the purposes of history at every point in the *Aeneid*. Once again Aeneas' *pietas* emerges as his defining characteristic, the quality that restores him to himself and gives meaning to his life.

Beyond Disliking

I venture to guess that most present-day readers of the *Aeneid* have never heard of Lacan.[44] If they dislike Aeneas, it is because he seems to be a defective or incomplete human being—not, perhaps, a Lacanian pervert in thrall to the Other, but a character who conceals his feelings from his most intimate associates; who seems to have no truly satisfying human relationship except, perhaps, with his father; and whose actions, no matter where ultimate responsibility lies, lead to the destruction of the women he loves. Judging Aeneas by the standards that they apply to human beings in their world, recent readers find that he does not seem to be the kind of person with whom they want to spend much time.

Critics who use Aeneas as a moral exemplum or a psychological case study also assume that Aeneas is, in some way, one of us. Exemplary criticism assumes that people in the past are like us, and so that contemplating Aeneas can shed light, as it does for Carol Gilligan, on contemporary moral dilemmas. Psychoanalytic criticism assumes that we are like people in the past and that concepts and methods that work for understanding our contemporaries can help us understand characters like Aeneas.

But the past is notoriously a foreign country,[45] and it may not be reasonable to suppose that the people there will follow the same rules that we do. Hence I return to the question with which this chapter began, but with one modification, to ask not what it means to like or dislike a fictional character but what it could mean to like or dislike Aeneas. This chapter has sketched an answer to that question, in three parts. First, looking at Aeneas through a psychoanalytic and Lacanian lens highlights his alienation from reality and helps to show how his special relationship to fate or history creates a lack of the self-knowledge necessary for full realization of his humanity. Second, his signal virtue, *pietas*, turns out to be a response to that special relationship and lack of knowledge. Finally, when readers form a judgment about Aeneas, when they like or dislike him, their judgment may not be exactly analogous to the judgments that they form about other human beings. Most of the people we meet do not carry a destiny aligned with the track of history or a signal virtue that allows them to realize that destiny. Aeneas may not, in fact, be a human being of a kind that we can recognize in our world. His contact with what Lacan called "the Real" weakens his ties to our ordinary reality.

In a way, no one in antiquity may have been human in the way that people are human in the twenty-first century, because the way that humans imagine themselves has changed. French sociologist Marcel Mauss (1872–1950) recognized this difference by drawing a distinction between the "person" (*personne*, the individual human being conceived as a member of an ordered, collective society) and the "self" (*moi*, the individual understood as an autonomous moral agent). For Mauss, Roman law, family structures, and cult practices constructed the individual as a *personne*, someone who existed as part of a network of clan relationships, public actions, and legal obligations (Carrithers 1985, 14–19). In *The Care of the Self*, the third volume of *The History of Sexuality*, Michel Foucault (1926–1984) developed the idea that the self was not an object of individual self-study, discovery, or practice until the high Roman Empire, long after Vergil's death. More recently, British scholar Christopher Gill and others have developed the concept of the Greco-Roman "structured self," by which Gill means a personality that seeks to shape itself according to an objective philosophical model of the structure of the universe; that structured self is created by participating in social interactions, especially dialogue and argument.[46] Canadian philosopher Charles Taylor sees the modern, autonomous self emerging as early modern ideas about natural law and rights consolidated and secularized moral philosophers' attempts to define the human good.[47] Foucault, Gill, and Taylor have their critics,[48] but their ideas can point the way to understanding Vergil's Aeneas.

Aeneas is a hero in one ancient sense of the word; that is, like Achilles, he has a divine parent and abilities and qualities that separate him from ordinary mortals: prowess in combat and the distinguishing virtue that the Romans called *pietas*. Aeneas is mortal, but like Achilles, Pelops, and other heroes, he will receive worship in cult after his death, as Jupiter confirms at the beginning and end of the *Aeneid* (*Aen.* 1.259–260, 12.794–797). Livy, Varro, Dionysius of Halicarnassus, and some archaeological evidence confirm that even before Vergil, Aeneas was commemorated and received worship as "Jupiter Indiges" at a site near Rome.[49] Some have tried to make him something more, a spiritual figure whose deeds advance him on a death-transcending trajectory toward immortality.[50]

In the rest of this study, I endeavor to discover Aeneas as something else: a "mortal hero," to use Seth Schein's terminology (1984), and a moral hero whose labor and struggles, seen in terms of the Roman "structured self," are human and tragic. In one sense, Aeneas' parentage, exploits, and eventual deification put him on a plane that is beyond the human; in another sense, he remains part of the world of Vergil and his readers—the world of the collapsing Roman Republic, civil wars, and triumviral horrors, as well as the world of readers in the twenty-first century. As he struggles to align his actions with the purposes and structure of a world that he does not understand, Aeneas makes choices, speaks and withholds speech, weeps, and becomes angry (behaviors discussed in chapters 3–6 below). His choices, silences, tears, and anger are part of an ongoing attempt to create his identity through his practice of *pietas*, a virtue that depends on the quality of his interactions with other people. His self is not a post-Kantian, unitary center of will and action. Becoming who he is cannot be a process of self-discovery; it is more like managing an ongoing crisis of misunderstanding and existential vulnerability. In the end, as we shall see, Aeneas fails; the struggle destroys its protagonist. Aeneas belongs to Rome; he is not a man of our world, and to like or dislike him may be to misunderstand him in a fundamental way. But we can learn to admire his struggle and his moral heroism.

CHAPTER 2

The First Three Words

Arma virumque cano. The second word of the *Aeneid*, *virum*, a man, or a hero, or a husband, announces its central character, Aeneas. The first word announces its subject: *arma*, arms, weapons, war. The third word, *cano*, proclaims the presence of an author. I, Vergil, sing this song. It is mine. *Cano* surprises. Epics begin with an invocation of a Muse or a divinity, like the *Iliad*'s "Sing, goddess" or the opening words of Apollonius Rhodius' *Argonautica*, "Beginning from you, Phoebus Apollo." Quintus Ennius, Rome's greatest epic poet before Vergil, may have begun his *Annales* with an invocation of the "Muses who tread great Olympus with your feet."[1] The *Aeneid* begins by announcing its author. It is a poem derived from the *Iliad*, the poem of war, and the *Odyssey*, the poem of the man, hero, and husband Odysseus. *Arma* and *virum* are linked by a conjunction, *-que*. That little particle suggests a closer connection than another word for "and," *et. Arma virumque* ought to belong together, like bacon and eggs, hunger and thirst, or *senatus populusque*, the senate and people of Rome. The subject of the *Aeneid* and its central character ought to be inseparable in reading and in interpretation. We readers want the *Aeneid* to be about Aeneas. Yet it is not entirely.

Aeneas is the central character of the *Aeneid* but not its central subject. The *arma* that open the poem are the wars of Rome, both the legendary wars from which it was founded by Aeneas and the civil wars from which it was refounded by Augustus. The *Aeneid* is about Rome and about its two foundings from the death and destruction of war. There can be no understanding of the poem that does not explain the relationship between its central character and its subject, between *arma* and *virum*, and between those and the poem's creator. Finding

Aeneas, the *vir* at the heart of the *Aeneid*, also means assessing what we know about the author who marked the epic as his own with *cano*, "I sing," and who sang from his own experience about the costs and consequences of war.

Arma Cano: *The Wars and the Author*

For the first forty years of Vergil's life and for two decades before, Roman fought Roman in civil wars, armed insurrections, and urban riots. The story has been told many times, and through time's inverted telescope, it is easy to overlook the savagery of it.[2] Perhaps the Hundred Years' War that filled Europe with slaughter and devastation in the late Middle Ages comes closest to matching the Roman experience.[3] Terrible deaths become vignettes in a broad canvas, overpainted by time like the slaughtered babies in Breugel's *Massacre of the Innocents* or blurred by the rhetoric of ancient writers as they tried to cope with horror using tools no better than tricolon and antithesis. "Neither sanctuary of the gods, nor hearth of hospitality, nor ancestral home escaped," explained Plutarch. "Men were butchered in the embraces of their wives, children in the arms of their mothers" (*Life of Sulla* 31.5). Plutarch's words overlay the distant horrors with rhetorical abstractions. In this chapter, I intend to write not a history of the Roman civil wars but, rather, an impression of them. Three episodes, one from Vergil's childhood and two from his young adulthood, may be enough to show the world that shaped his experience and gave birth to the *Aeneid*.

Catiline

The ancient sources vary as to details but agree that in 82 BC, twelve years before Vergil was born, Marcus Marius Gratidianus died a horrible death. One source says that before his executioners killed him, they marched him across Rome, beating him with vinestocks (the Roman centurion's combination swagger stick and cudgel).[4] Then they broke his arms and legs and gouged out his eyes, "in order that he might expire member by member."[5] Another source says that one of his executioners carried his head halfway across the city, to present it, "still full of life and breath," to Sulla.[6] Some sources present Gratidianus' death as a human sacrifice, carried out by an avenging son at the tomb of a man for whose death Gratidianus may have been responsible.[7] The horror of Gratidianus' death was not exceptional. He was one of many victims of the first

Roman civil war, in which Roman legions led by rival warlords battled each other. After it was over, Lucius Cornelius Sulla was Rome's sole ruler, and his opponents, Gaius Marius (uncle of Marcus Marius Gratidianus) and Cornelius Cinna, Marius' successor, were dead. Lists of names went up in the Forum—80 on one day, 220 the next, and another 220 on the next. A person whose name was on the list was "proscribed" and was fair game for anyone who wanted to betray and murder him. The killer received a reward, the victim's property was sold at auction for the benefit of the strongman and his henchmen, and the victim's family lost civil status and rights. In the late eighties BC, Romans gathered in the Forum to read lists of the names of people marked down for extrajudicial murder; if they lifted their eyes, they could gaze on piles of human heads nearby.[8] Revenge was in the air, and there were no limits on human fury.

The man who may have carried Gratidianus' head to Sulla met a violent death twenty years later, when Vergil was seven years old.[9] Like Sulla, Lucius Sergius Catilina ("Catiline" in English) was a Roman patrician leading an army that, he hoped, would make him the first man in Rome. Unlike Sulla, Catiline failed. Born in 108 (or possibly 106) BC, he belonged to the generation of Caesar, Cicero, and Pompey the Great. Like Pompey, he gained early military experience in the War of the Italian Secession (90–88 BC) and was able to take advantage of the civil war and Sullan proscriptions that followed. Like Caesar and Pompey, Catiline studied Sulla's example; as his ancient biographer puts it, "After Sulla's despotism, immense lust for seizing the commonwealth attacked him."[10] Unlike the cool and calculating Caesar or the deviously inscrutable Pompey, Catiline found the adrenaline rush of battle, slaughter and rape and looting, and the chaotic swirl of civil war irresistible.[11] Caesar and Pompey could play chess with the Roman Republic; Catiline wanted to smash the board and grind the pieces to dust.

Many people became rich from Sulla's proscriptions, and others, such as Pompey, made reputations that helped them move ahead in the uphill race that was Roman aristocratic politics, which had resumed its course after the dictatorship of Sulla ended in 81 BC. Catiline, however, somehow failed to rise. His career after the dictatorship of Sulla gives the impression of a man who was his own worst enemy. Rumors swirled around him, but nothing seemed to stick. Some whispered that he had murdered his first wife and their son so that he could marry a beautiful noblewoman. In 73 BC, he was brought to trial for adultery with a vestal virgin but acquitted. Five years later, he was elected as one of eight praetors, officials who ranked just below the two consuls and held judicial, administrative, and military responsibilities. Following his year of office, a praetor usually went out to govern one of Rome's provinces as propraetor; Catiline was propraetorian governor of the province of Africa (approximately modern Tunisia, with bits of Algeria and Libya) until sometime in 66 BC.

A provincial governor was expected to return to Rome richer than he left. One governor joked that he needed to make three fortunes during his term of office: one to pay the expenses of getting elected, one to bribe the jury that would try him for corruption and extortion, and one to keep as compensation for his services (Cicero, *Against Verres* 1.1.40). Catiline should have returned from his province with money and the prospect of becoming the first of his family to become consul in more than three hundred years.[12] He duly became a candidate in 66, probably for one of the consulships that had become vacant that year after the incumbents had been convicted of electoral bribery, but he was disqualified. He may have missed the filing deadline because he could not get back from his province in time, or the presiding magistrate may have ruled him ineligible because a delegation from his former province had appeared in the senate to indict their former governor on charges of corruption.[13] In either case, Catiline had reason to feel aggrieved. The consular magistrate presiding over elections had considerable discretion in admitting or denying candidates, and Catiline seems not to have yet been a defendant in the court case that was certainly brought against him a few months later, in 65. By 66, however, Catiline had acquired a reputation as mad, bad, and dangerous to know. The senatorial aristocracy was unwilling to take a chance on the bloodthirsty young man, seducer of virgins and vestals, and rapacious propraetorian governor. (Not that there was anything wrong with that, in the view of most senators, but one could go too far; as the emperor Tiberius observed, a good shepherd should shear his sheep, not flay them.)[14]

Catiline probably did not become involved at that point in a conspiracy to assassinate the consuls and take over the state, as some sources allege, but three years later, he tried to follow in Sulla's footsteps. He had been a candidate for the consulship of 63, but the senatorial aristocracy, forced to choose between the dangerously unpredictable Catiline and a man who, though reliable and politically orthodox, was not one of them, united behind Marcus Tullius Cicero, the first in his family to reach senatorial status. They had reason to be nervous about Catiline. His electoral promises, either in that year or the following, called for a financial revolution: cancellation of debts, confiscation of assets, and redistribution of wealth. According to Cicero, Catiline intended his program to appeal to cash-strapped aristocrats, ambitious politicians whose need for funds had led them deep into debt, veterans of Sulla's armies who had poorly managed their war booty and allotments, and all who, for whatever reason, hoped for a fresh start and a way out of their financial difficulties (*Against Catiline* 2.18–20). Catiline's program appealed also to the urban poor, victims of the liquidity crisis that was a recurring feature of Roman life in the first century BC.[15]

Catiline tried again in the elections of 63 for the consulship of 62, and again he failed. Then, in the autumn of 63, he struck back at the republic and at the senatorial nobility that had three times rejected him—him, one of the patrician Sergii, with ancestors stretching back to the dim beginnings of Rome! If, Catiline said, an attempt were made to set his fortunes on fire, he would respond not with water but by pulling down the surrounding buildings.[16] In a city without a fire department, where the best way to deal with a blaze was to isolate it by pulling down the neighboring houses, everyone understood what he meant.

Catiline's plan for a coup d'état depended on synchronizing chaos in Rome with the advance of a military force in Italy. He proposed to raise money from those who remembered Sulla's proscriptions and who could hope to profit from a second wave of killing and confiscation.[17] Then he would recruit an army from the disaffected and debt-ridden, with discontented veterans of Sulla's army providing a nucleus of discipline and experience.[18] His fellow conspirators would assassinate the consuls and set fires in multiple places throughout the city. With the city ablaze and leaderless, Catiline would march in at the head of his troops and do as Sulla had done: reward his friends, proscribe his enemies, vacuum up their estates, and become master of Rome. It is hard to imagine that he would have voluntarily laid down his dictatorship, as Sulla had.

In the end, Catiline's attempt to follow Sulla's path failed because of a combination of bad luck, bad management on the part of the conspirators, and—it must be said, though the consul's lifelong habit of boasting about it can be tiresome—good management on the part of the consul Cicero. The complex coordination broke down: Gaius Manilius, who commanded the main concentration of Sullan veterans encamped near Fiesole, proclaimed open revolt against the government on October 27, but Catiline's agents in Rome were not prepared to act until the night of November 6–7. The conspirators failed to keep their plan under wraps; one of them, Cornelius Lentulus, went around reminding people of an ancient prophecy that three Cornelii would rule at Rome: there had been Cornelius Cinna and Cornelius Sulla, and they might guess the third.

Another conspirator, Quintus Curius, hinted to his lover Fulvia that he would soon be in a position of great power; she went to the consul, and Cicero turned her into a source of intelligence from within the conspiracy. Finally, the conspirators made a clumsy attempt to suborn a group of Allobroges, Gauls who were visiting Rome; the Gauls, recognizing a losing prospect when they saw it, went immediately to the authorities and provided them with written proof of the conspiracy's plans.

Faced with the collapse of his plans, Catiline decided to trust his army, as Sulla had trusted his. On the night of November 8–9, Catiline left Rome with the pomp of a departing proconsul, attended by an escort of lictors carrying fasces, bundles of rods and axes that symbolized *imperium*, legal power to command.[19] In his mind, he should have been consul, if not in 65, then in 63 or 62; now, he thought, he and the army he commanded would act where elections, bent by the influence of a corrupt senatorial aristocracy, had failed. That Catiline felt the need for visible symbols of legitimate authority as he set out to lead a military coup d'état testifies to the essential conservatism of the Romans. Catiline may also have been anticipating the success of his plans, according to which the consuls were to be assassinated as he began his military takeover.

As Catiline moved toward his army at Faesulae (modern Fiesole, about 278 kilometers from Rome), his plans for an uprising in Rome were falling apart. The consul Cicero, armed with information from his network of informants, summoned the senate and secured authority to round up the leading conspirators. They were taken to the Mamertine Prison near the Forum and garroted. When the news of their deaths reached him, Catiline abandoned his plan to march on Rome and headed north toward Gaul. He had perhaps as many as twenty thousand troops under his command, which he managed to organize into two legions, but only a quarter of them were trained and equipped; the rest armed themselves with what they could find, hunting spears and even sharpened stakes (Sallust, *Catiline* 56). Catiline was also short of cavalry; he may have hoped to make up the deficiencies in Gaul.[20] In hot pursuit was a Roman army, nominally led by the consul Antonius, but actually commanded by his legate, Petreius; Cicero and his allies in the senate may have felt that Antonius was not entirely trustworthy where Catiline was concerned.

Petreius caught up with Catiline at Pistoria, in what was then Cisalpine Gaul, about 140 kilometers from Vergil's birthplace, which was in Mantua. By then, Catiline's forces had begun to melt away, as uncommitted enthusiasts and those who hoped for easy plunder vanished into the hills. Once again it was civil war, with legion against legion, and the memory of what had happened in the times of Sulla deterred all but those firmly committed to Catiline's revolutionary program or inspired by his leadership. Sallust gives Catiline a speech before the final battle; in it, Catiline urges his soldiers to contrast themselves, fighting for homeland, liberty, and their lives, with their opponents, fighting only to preserve the power of a few (Sallust, *Catiline* 58).

Faced with dwindling supplies, a Roman army in his front, and another blocking his retreat across the Alps into Gaul, Catiline led his army down into the plain and improvised a battle line. He arranged his first legion, made up of veterans and the best-trained and best-equipped of the newcomers, into a front of eight cohorts, perhaps a little more than four thousand men;[21] he kept the rest, with their sharpened stakes and hunting spears, in reserve. Since he had pulled the veterans and centurions from that nominal second legion, its effectiveness was doubtful at best.[22] Everything depended on the single, understrength legion that he had cobbled together.

Petreius also put his experienced troops in the front line; he had spent more than thirty years in military life and knew many of his soldiers well enough to remind them of their past courageous acts (Sallust, *Catiline* 59.6). Unlike Catiline, though, Petreius could count on a reserve line made up of equipped and trained regular troops. The two armies moved toward each other, the skirmishers hurled their javelins and withdrew, and the butchery began. The legionaries did not bother with the usual volley of spears but moved straight to hand-to-hand combat with the *gladius*, the Roman infantry's short sword. When it was over, Catiline's veteran legion lay dead in its ranks; each man's body, Sallust says, lay covering the place where he had been stationed when he was alive. They found Catiline at some distance from his men, dying but still showing, with his last breath, the combination of bravery and madness that had been the keynotes of his life. The front of his body was covered with wounds; there were none on his back (Sallust, *Catiline* 61.1–5).

Catiline's attempt to emulate Sulla is often cast as a conspiracy or as the attempt of a decayed aristocrat to assert his *dignitas*, his personal standing and right to count among the rulers of Rome. It makes more sense to see it as another civil war, but one that lacked the critical mass necessary to explode as had the conflicts between Sulla and Gaius Marius or Cornelius Cinna or as would the one between Caesar and Pompey. Civil war was always lurking beneath the surface of late republican Rome. Vergil grew to manhood in a world where rage (*furor*), the expression on dying Catiline's face, glowed like volcanic fire under a thin crust of earth.[23]

The Rubicon

In 56 BC, few people expected an immediate eruption. If the fourteen-year-old Vergil, though, had paid attention to Rome's governing class, he might have sensed seismic foreshocks. Caesar, proconsul of the Gauls (both the barely subdued territory across the Alps and the almost-Roman province that included Vergil's birthplace), was following his usual practice and spending the winter on the Italian side of the Alps, so that he could keep an eye on things in Rome. Proconsuls and their suites take up a lot of room and impose on local notables; the father of one of Vergil's slightly older contemporaries, the poet Valerius Catullus, was important enough to entertain Caesar at the Valerian estates in Transpadane Gaul (Suetonius, *Julius* 73). Vergil's family does not seem to have been as important as that of Catullus, but perhaps the proconsul's progress touched on Vergil's life.

We know next to nothing about Vergil's early years. In 56, he was probably living peacefully in or near his birthplace outside of Mantua, in the part of northern Italy that the Romans called Gallia Transpadana (Gaul across the Po) or Gallia Togata (Toga-Wearing Gaul). Vergil, the poet who shaped the mind and soul of Rome, was in a legal sense born not in Italy but in a part of the Italian peninsula ruled by Rome as one of its Gallic provinces. Transpadanes did not become fully Roman until 49 BC, when one of Julius Caesar's agents, the praetor L. Roscius, carried a bill granting them citizenship.

In that winter of 56, Cisalpine dignitaries like Catullus' father were lining up to see and be seen with one of the three most powerful men in Rome. Four years earlier, in 60 BC, Caesar, Pompey, and Marcus Crassus had agreed to form an alliance. If asked, they might have called it *amicitia* (friendship). Their political opponents would have used harsher words: *dominatio* (tyranny) or *factio* (faction). Modern historians call it (not quite accurately) the First Triumvirate.[24] When historian Asinius Pollio looked back from the Augustan principate to contemplate the end of the Roman Republic, he began his history with 60 BC, when three men colluded to dominate political life in Rome.

By 56 that alliance was in trouble. Pompey had risen to prominence as a young officer in the War of the Italian Secession, in the early eighties BC, and had continued to one military triumph after another; now, he found himself vexed by political life. Pompey's rivals in the senate, inspired and sometimes led by Cato the Younger, combined to frustrate the triumvir's geopolitical designs for the East, where Pompey had held a series of extraordinary commands since 67 BC, and to detach Pompey from Caesar, whose conquests in Gaul threatened to give him enough wealth and influence to replace Pompey as the dominant partner in the triumvirate. Not only rabid conservatives like Cato the Younger but also moderates like Cicero feared a single dynast dominating Roman politics; they remembered dreadful times barely three decades in the past: Sulla marching on Rome at the head of an army more loyal to him than to the republic, and then Sulla's dictatorship, with its quasi-legal murders, rigged trials, and confiscations. Perhaps worse in the eyes of the Roman senatorial class was dictatorship's elimination of competition for office; the struggle to climb the greased pole from minor magistrate to consul was all they knew and often all they cared about. Sulla had resigned, retired, and died, and the mechanism of the republic—elections, competitive politics, and corruption—recovered. But perhaps the next time Rome would not be so lucky.

Thus Cicero and others were delighted when, in the spring of 56, an inveterate opponent of Caesar declared his candidacy for one of the two consulships for the following year. If elected, L. Domitius Ahenobarbus, Cato's son-in-law, might be able to drive a wedge between the two dominant triumvirs. Ahenobarbus hammered away. As praetor in 58 BC, he had proposed legislation to deprive Caesar of his proconsular command. Ahenobarbus announced his intention of reviving that legislation if he was elected consul for 55. Cicero did his best to detach Pompey from Caesar and to guide the former along the right path: the best form of government for Rome, he argued in 56, was that established by the ancestors, a state directed by a senate chosen from citizens notable for industry or virtue, who would be guardians, defenders, and champions of the commonwealth, charged with guiding the annually elected magistrates who converted its wisdom into action (*In Defense of Sestius* 137).

Pompey seems not to have been persuaded by Cicero or anyone else; his motives are often hard to read, but his career offers glimpses of a persistent drive for power and what the Romans called *auctoritas*, the personal prestige that lets you compel others to do what you want without resorting to force or law.[25] On the Campus Martius in Rome, a huge complex—with a theater, porticos, public gardens, and a hall for meetings of the senate—was being built to advertise Pompey's wealth, generosity, and influence. In it, the people of Rome could be entertained by Pompey's games and shows, enjoy leisure made possible by the imperial wealth gathered by Pompey, and admire statues representing fourteen nations that Pompey had conquered.[26] The senate could meet there under the watchful eye of the conqueror's statue. Pompey did not succumb to the constitutional blandishments of Cicero. He left Rome to meet with Caesar.

At Luca, modern Lucca in Tuscany, just inside the borders of Caesar's province, the triumvirs met and patched things up. Pompey and Crassus would be consuls for 55 BC; then Pompey would get a proconsular command in Spain, and Crassus, the unmilitary triumvir, would get Syria and a chance to take on the Parthians on Rome's eastern frontier. Caesar's command in Gaul would be extended for another five years.

Then in rapid succession two deaths doomed the triumvirate and made civil war easier, if not inevitable. Julia, Caesar's daughter, had been married to Pompey since 59 BC, shortly after the triumvirate was formed. Such arranged political marriages were routine in Rome; women were the adhesive of aristocratic alliances, and a marriageable daughter was a political asset. Pompey and Julia seem to have genuinely liked each other, and Pompey, like some love-besotted teenager (he was fifty years old; she was about twenty) preferred strolling through gardens with Julia to the rough-and-tumble interactions of the Forum and the senate house (Plutarch, *Life of Pompey* 48). Pompey's affection for his young wife did not extend to his father-in-law (his junior by half a dozen years), and Julia's death in 54 BC broke the last link between the two most important members of the triumvirate.

The alliance might have endured, with its third member as counterweight and peacemaker, if Crassus' search for military glory had not ended a year later, at Carrhae in northern Iraq. The Parthians' mounted archers and heavy cavalry caught his forces in the open and surrounded his legions. The legionaries hunkered down behind their shields and waited for the Parthians to run out of arrows, but the Parthian commander Surena arranged for relays of camels to resupply his archers. The big legionary shields grew heavier and heavier, the Romans dropped one by one, and soon only a few were standing.[27] Crassus was butchered while attempting to negotiate a surrender; twenty thousand Romans were killed, ten thousand were captured, and another ten thousand—perhaps the equivalent of two or three of the seven legions who had set out toward the Euphrates—straggled back to Syria.[28] The Parthians took away the legions' sacred standards, silver gilt eagles, and kept them until 20 BC, when Augustus negotiated their return.

With Crassus dead, it was left to Pompey and Caesar to manage their ambitions in an increasingly dysfunctional commonwealth. It did not take long for the fault lines to rupture. Pompey, who had been Rome's foremost general for a generation, had no need for military glory; instead of taking command of the legions in his Spanish province, he stayed at Rome. There he could influence events without the need to dirty his hands in retail politics. (When elected consul for the first time in 70 BC, Pompey knew so little about senatorial protocol that he had the scholar Varro write up a handbook on the subject, and the general seems to have disliked the open debate that surged through Roman political life.)[29] Caesar remained with his legions in Gaul. From there, he moved to acquire the things that he needed to become preeminent at Rome: wealth, like Crassus, and military reputation, like Pompey. Caesar's backers and agents in Rome held him up as a counterweight to an influential group of senators whose most outspoken member was Cato. Those aristocratic constitutionalists (*optimates*, as they are sometimes called) saw themselves as entitled to continue their families' long service in Rome's highest posts and to compete for a share of the rewards of that service: provincial governorships, influence in the courts, a retinue of clients, and the wealth and power that all these brought. As the surviving triumvirs became increasingly alienated from each other, the *optimates* began to see Pompey as a manageable strongman, someone who could oppose Caesar militarily without overthrowing the republic and becoming another Sulla. Cicero began to speculate about a commonwealth guided not by a wise and just senate, as he had suggested in 56, but by a dominant citizen, a "helmsman and director of the state."[30]

The *optimates* are often characterized as conservatives and set in opposition to a popular or democratic faction, the *populares*, represented by Marius and his kinsman Caesar. That characterization is both overly simple and anachronistic.[31] The senatorial aristocracy of Rome was united in its belief that political life had one goal: to struggle up the ladder of office from quaestor to praetor to consul, accumulating influence and reputation along the way and surpassing as many of one's peers as possible. But the competition to be one of twenty quaestors led to the competition to be one of eight praetors and then one of only two consuls. The greasy pole grew slipperier the higher one climbed. A consulship was not the end. Could you amass enough influence to be elected consul a second time or (as rarely happened) a third, or even seven times, like Marius? The senate assigned provinces to ex-magistrates, but not all provinces afforded an equal opportunity for their governor to extort or acquire wealth and influence. Could you influence or outmaneuver fellow senators to get a prime assignment? Or could you somehow bypass the entire system—as Sulla had done and as Catiline had hoped to do—and become the first man in Rome, the princeps? The *optimates* and the *populares* formed a single governing class united by a single set of political instincts and values. They differed over means, not ends. Someone who used the popular assemblies and perhaps a touch of mob violence to climb the greasy pole was a *popularis*. Someone who depended on the force of tradition, the wealth and influence of noble peers, and perhaps a touch of violence from his own mob was among the *optimates*.

At the heart of politics lie three things: power, money, and violence. If a state is lucky, only the first two will come into play. If it is not, then the third is decisive. So it was for Rome in 49 BC. From Gaul, Caesar found himself facing a narrow range of choices, given his die-hard opponents at Rome, Pompey's ambiguous stance, Caesar's own keen sense of his standing in the ultracompetitive milieu of senatorial politics (his *dignitas*, as the Romans called it), and especially his ambition.[32] There was no such thing as second place for Caesar. Once, while traveling through some godforsaken Gallic hamlet high in the Alps, his entourage smiled at the thought that even miserable places like that knew ambition and concern for status. "I'd rather be the first among these people," Caesar said, "than second at Rome" (Plutarch, *Life of Caesar* 11.2). Caesar felt that he had few options as his proconsular term drew to a close in 50 BC. If he returned to Rome, it would have to be as consul. But if Caesar left his province and entered Rome as a private citizen, as the law required, he would be open to prosecution by the optimate faction that had opposed his actions in Gaul and the machinations of the triumvirate. He would somehow have to arrange to be elected consul in absentia instead. If he could not, open conflict with Pompey, the champion of the *optimates*, was inevitable. That meant civil war, again.

While Caesar was in Gaul, his agents in Rome looked after his political interests. The most important of those agents were the tribunes of the plebs. That office had begun during the early years of the republic, when the plebeians of Rome struggled for rights against an entrenched, hereditary nobility, the patricians. In the early years of the fifth century BC, the plebeians used strikes, demonstrations, and other means to secure fundamental civil rights: to assemble and pass resolutions (*plebiscita*, or plebiscites), to petition for redress of grievances, to appeal against the unjust actions of a patrician magistrate, and, eventually, to hold all the offices of state, including the consulship. Their leaders in that movement were the tribunes. By the days of Caesar and Cicero, the distinction between patrician and plebeian had ceased to be important; being a patrician was a bit like being in the *Social Register*—of interest to others who are and perhaps to a few who are not, but no longer synonymous with power and influence. The ten tribunes, however, retained the powers that they had won centuries earlier: the right to preside at assemblies of the plebs, where tribunes could put forth motions that could turn into laws; personal sacrosanctity, which in theory secured the tribunes against violence; and, most important, the power to veto any act of a magistrate or resolution of the senate. The veto was the key to the power of the tribunes. They could oppose, obstruct, and prevent any action in the working of the Roman state. The tribunate had become a rung on the ladder of political ambition, and it was worth resigning patrician status to be elected to it.[33] Tribunes came from the same class and families as the rest of the senatorial nobility and played the same high-stakes game of ambition and power.

Caesar's opponents in Rome, led by Cato and Domitius Ahenobarbus, had kept up a steady barrage of obstructive action. Ahenobarbus' attempt to recall Caesar from Gaul came to nothing when, strengthened by the reconciliation at Luca, the triumvirs installed Caesar and Pompey as joint consuls for 55. In that same year, Caesar took advantage of the fortuitous violation of a truce to attack and massacre a German tribe, the Usipetes, and he did not spare their women or children. In the senate, Cato proposed that for that act of genocide, which even the Romans recognized as a war crime, Caesar should be handed over to the remaining members of the tribe. That motion, too, came to nothing, but the *optimates* succeeded in prosecuting one of the triumvirs' agents, Aulus Gabinius, in 54, for malfeasances during his governorship of Syria. Could they do the same against Caesar himself once his proconsulship ended? Perhaps, but they would have to disarm him first.

Caesar expected to serve again as consul in 48, but to be elected, he had to return to Rome as a candidate during the elections held in 49. His command in Gaul, which had been extended for five years at the conference at Luca, would expire at some point in 49, so he faced a gap of months when he would be without the protection of his army or the immunity to prosecution conferred by proconsular or consular office.[34] Sometime in 51, he asked the senate for permission to run for consul in absentia and for an extension of his command until the end of 49, so that there would be no gap in legal immunity between the end of one office and the beginning of the next. The senate refused, and Pompey kept an ambiguous silence. Was he for Caesar, for the *optimates*, or for something or someone else entirely? Pompey's legions in Italy and Spain were the armed power behind what was left of the republic; Caesar's forces in Gaul were his trump card to protect his *dignitas* and, very likely, his life and property.

A period of tense negotiations, proposals, counterproposals, and tribunician vetoes filled most of 50 BC. A motion was put forward to recall Caesar immediately from Gaul; one of the tribunes in Caesar's pocket, Scribonius Curio, vetoed it. Proposals were made for mutual disarmament; on December 1, 50 BC, Curio moved that Pompey's military command should end when Caesar's did and that both triumvirs should be disarmed. Three hundred and seventy senators voted for the motion; 22 opposed it. Crowds in Rome cheered Curio as peacemaker and garlanded him with flowers, celebrating peace because their blood would be shed if it came to civil war. The die-hard *optimates* could not accept this overwhelming vote for peace. On December 2, the presiding consul, without authorization from the senate or the support of his fellow consul, went to Pompey and in the name of the republic offered him a sword and command of the home forces in Italy. Pompey accepted. When Caesar heard, he countered by moving one of his legions to Ravenna, just beyond the border separating his province from Italy.[35] Although both triumvirs made stabs at negotiating an armistice, the *optimates* sensed blood and appointed new governors for Transalpine and Cisalpine Gaul. Caesar's tribunes again vetoed the moves of the *optimates*, until it became clear to the tribunes that they had better leave Rome for their own safety. They fled north to join their patron.

The die was cast. *Alea iacta est* is probably not quite what Caesar said when he led his troops across the Rubicon River a few weeks later. According to Plutarch (*Life of Caesar* 23.6), he quoted the poet Menander, in Greek: "Let the die be cast." After the war with Pompey was over, Caesar wrote that he had acted in defense of his *dignitas* and of the rights of the people of Rome, as represented by their tribunes (*Civil War* 1.7). There may have been some truth in that justification, but Plutarch probably gets nearer to the reality of the situation.

> Caesar had long ago resolved upon the overthrow of Pompey, as had Pompey, for that matter, upon his. For once Crassus, the fear of whom had hitherto kept them in peace, had been killed in Parthia, if one of them wished to make himself the greatest man in Rome, he had only to overthrow the other; and if he again wished to prevent his own fall, he had no choice but to be beforehand with him whom he feared.
>
> Plutarch, *Life of Caesar* 28.1–2

Caesar threw the dice, and Rome was once more embroiled in civil war.

This time was different, though. Sulla, Marius and Cinna, and then Sulla again had made themselves masters of the republic by making themselves masters of Rome, and Catiline's plans hinged on an uprising in Rome and his ability to take control of the city itself. The civil wars of the eighties and Catiline's abortive attempt to follow Sulla's example had been local affairs, focused on the urban center of what was still, in some ways, a city-state, despite its Mediterranean-wide network of provinces, allied states, and client kingdoms. Caesar understood a new reality: that Rome was a world power and that the object of a Roman civil war was the world from Britain to North Africa and from Gibraltar to Syria. He bypassed Rome and swept down the northeast side of the Italian peninsula, forcing Pompey to abandon Rome and race for Brundisium, the main port of embarkation for the eastern half of the world that was now Rome's.

Nearly three years after a decisive defeat for the Pompeians at Pharsalus in northern Greece, followed by Pompey's death in Egypt and campaigns in Africa and Spain, Caesar returned to Rome in March of 45 BC. A year later, he was dead, assassinated at the foot of Pompey's statue in the theatrical complex that Pompey had built to advertise his conquests. The assassins, the same kind of aristocratic constitutionalists who had opposed Caesar and his fellow triumvirs since 60 BC, believed that removing the tyrant would bring back the old days of limitless ambition and free competition, the struggle to climb the greasy pole and become first at Rome. Instead, Caesar's assassination brought another fifteen years of civil war and political chaos.

The world that a person knows in his twenties and thirties often shapes his or her political views and moral and ethical outlook. Vergil was twenty when Caesar crossed the Rubicon, twenty-five when Caesar was assassinated. Vergil's boyhood and adolescence had been marked by the stamp of Sulla: the threat that some rogue senator, some Cinna or Catiline, might stage a coup, become all-powerful, and fill the Roman Forum with the heads of his proscribed enemies. To a boy growing up in Transpadane Italy and from a family innocent of political ambition, it might have been possible to put such things in the background or to dismiss them as affairs of a remote governing class in the city of Rome. But Caesar made things different. Caesar's civil war was a world war, and there was no escape. What followed his assassination was far worse.

Perusia

Between Vergil's twenty-sixth and fortieth birthdays, the Roman Republic imploded and disappeared. After Julius Caesar's assassination, his right-hand man, the former tribune Marcus Antonius (better known in English as Mark Antony) and his great-nephew and adopted son, Gaius Octavius (known to modern historians as Octavian) struggled with each other and with the assassins, who claimed to represent the republic.[36] Antony, then about forty years old and an experienced soldier and politician, had power. Octavian wanted it. In March of 44 BC, Octavian was eighteen, and by adopting him in his will, Caesar had proclaimed him as his successor. In a few months, Octavian had raised an army at, as his official autobiography says, his "personal decision" and "personal expense," and his soldiers had made him consul.[37] In 43 BC, Antony, Octavian, and a third warlord, Marcus Aemilius Lepidus, met, safe from each other's armies, on an island in the Lavinus River near Bononia (modern Bologna). Once again, as in 56, three men made an agreement to share power, but this agreement was different. On November 27, 43 BC, the tribal assembly at Rome passed a law naming Antony, Octavian, and Lepidus as "Members of a Commission of Three for Establishing the Republic" (*Triumviri Rei Publicae Constituendae*), with the power to appoint magistrates, make laws, and designate provincial governors.[38] The law specified a five-year term for the commissioners to do their work, but few can have expected them to abide by it. The death warrant of the republic had been signed into law. Its dying was bitter and bloody.

The triumvirs' first acts brought back the horrors of Sulla and Marius, which older people remembered all too well. Once again, lists were posted in the Forum. As had happened a generation before, those who were proscribed were subject to death, and their estates were confiscated.[39] The end of the triumvirs' decree announcing the proscriptions, with its merciless call for informers and appeal to human greed, invokes a terror that is all too familiar from dictatorships before and since.

> Let no one harbor any one of those whose names are hereto appended, or conceal them, or send them away, or be corrupted by their money. Whoever shall be detected in saving, or aiding, or conniving with them we will put on the list of the proscribed without allowing any excuse or pardon. Those who kill the proscribed and bring us their heads shall receive the following rewards: to a free

> man, 25,000 Attic drachmas per head; to a slave, his freedom and 10,000 Attic drachmas and the master's right of citizenship. Informers shall receive the same rewards. In order that they may remain unknown, the names of those who receive the reward shall not be inscribed in our registers.
>
> Appian, *Civil Wars* 4.11

Lepidus proscribed his own brother, and Antony proscribed his uncle. Cicero got as far as Formiae before the soldiers caught up with him; the centurion commanding the force sawed off Cicero's head and hands and brought them to Rome, where they were displayed on the speakers' platform in the Forum. People hid in sewers, chimneys, and anywhere they could. Slaves betrayed masters, wives turned in their husbands; a praetor's son betrayed his father and was rewarded with a magistracy of his own (Appian, *Civil Wars* 4.18). Others, like the woman commemorated in the long inscription called the "Laudatio Turiae," acted with courage and loyalty, often at the cost of their own lives.[40] Such isolated and admirable acts are not enough to alter the conclusion that Roman civil war, which had been confined to armed conflict between armies led by aristocratic politicians, had now turned to civil near anarchy. Roman society depended on preservation of hierarchical relationships and personal loyalties, all that the Romans summed up with the words *pietas*, *fides*, and *amicitia*; now society was breaking down. The proscriptions were a chance to settle scores, hasten an inheritance, or dissolve a marriage. You could tell the private murders from the quasi-legal executions, Appian says, because privately murdered corpses still had their heads (*Civil Wars* 4.15).

Antony, Octavian, and Lepidus needed money. They reached far down into the class of financiers and businessmen, the *equites*, who had largely been spared in earlier proscriptions; this time, hundreds of senators and perhaps as many as two thousand *equites* were marked for death.[41] In their struggle against the assassins of Caesar, the triumvirs controlled Roman forces from Spain to Greece, more than twenty legions; against them, Brutus and Cassius pitted the armies of the Roman East, equally strong. Those forces met at Philippi in northern Greece in 42 BC, where the tyrannicides were defeated. Some of the losing side's strength could be absorbed into the victors' army, but now the veterans of something like twenty-eight legions, perhaps as many as sixty thousand men, had to be paid or paid off.[42] At the end of his service, a legionary soldier expected to be given a farm big enough to support him, and the triumvirs took the land they needed from communities all over Italy. The region across the Po,

Vergil's homeland, was especially hard hit, and if ancient tradition is to be believed, Vergil lost his ancestral lands, only to have his finances restored by Octavian.[43]

The Mediterranean-spanning wars of Roman against Roman did not end with the defeat of Brutus and Cassius at Philippi. After that battle, the triumvirs redivided their world; Spain and Sicily, along with authority in Italy, went to Octavian, and Antony was assigned Gaul, along with the task of mopping up the mess that the tyrannicides had left in the East. Lepidus was left with Africa. In Sicily, Sextus Pompey, son of Pompey the Great, was continuing his father's war against Caesar by battling Caesar's heir. Sextus gained strength from those fleeing the reign of terror in Italy. Since Octavian and Antony were distracted by their growing hostility toward each other, Sextus held out until Octavian finally defeated him in 36. Antony became increasingly involved with the eastern part of the Roman world, including Egypt and its ruler, Cleopatra VII.

In 41 BC, a fresh internecine war in the heart of Italy threatened the precarious triumvirate.[44] Mark Antony's brother, Lucius Antonius, was one of the consuls for 41. As one of the two nominal heads of the Roman state, he faced the challenge of maintaining the forms of legality against the rapacity of the triumviral commission while supporting his absent brother's interests. Refugees began to appear in Rome, first a trickle and then a flood of displaced Italians whose farms had been appropriated by the triumvirs for distribution to demobilized soldiers. In many cases, soldiers discontent with their official allotments had encroached on adjacent land or taken the best lands by force.[45] As Appian explains, it did the refugees no good to appeal to Octavian (who had returned to Rome by then).

> They [the soldiers] were contemptuous in the knowledge that their rulers needed them to confirm their power, for the five years' term of the triumvirate was passing away, and army and rulers needed the services of each other for mutual security. The chiefs depended on the soldiers for the continuance of their government, while, for the control of what they had received, the soldiers depended on the permanence of the government of those who had given it.
>
> Appian, *Civil Wars* 5.13

In desperation, the refugees turned to the only other legal authority in Rome, the consul Lucius Antonius.

Antonius appears to have been sympathetic to the claims of the displaced

Italians and suspicious of the way in which Octavian was flouting even the frail legal parameters of his commission, but he also had more personal reasons for his next actions. It was becoming clear that the two dominant triumvirs, Octavian and Antony, distrusted each other and would sooner or later come to blows. Antonius loyally supported his brother and sought ways to promote Antony's interests at Rome. In this he was abetted by Antony's wife, Fulvia. Ancient sources claim that Fulvia was motivated by jealousy of her husband's mistress, Cleopatra, and hoped to get her husband back to Italy by provoking a split between the triumvirs; it is just as likely that Fulvia, like many political wives at Rome, saw her task as promoting her husband's agenda.

At this point in his life, Octavian was not yet the future emperor Augustus, the Revered One. He was twenty-one years old, prone to bouts of ill health, and utterly ruthless. To call him a terrorist is only slight exaggeration. After Philippi, he was merciless to his aristocratic captives; when one begged his conqueror for a proper burial, Octavian replied that the birds would take care of that. A father and son asked him to spare them; Octavian told them to draw straws or play *mica*, the Roman version of rock-paper-scissors, to decide who would live. The father chose to face execution, and the son killed himself as Octavian watched (Suetonius, *Augustus* 13). Octavian's frightening lack of regard for the senatorial aristocracy from which Antonius and his brother came, his dependence on a brutal and licentious soldiery, pressure from Fulvia, and perhaps sympathy for the dispossessed Italians converged to drive Lucius Antonius to a decision: he would raise an army of his own and march against the young triumvir in Antony's interest. There were enough active and recently retired soldiers loyal to Antony to make it possible. The armies themselves had little enthusiasm for another round of civil war and made efforts to broker peace between consul and triumvir, to no avail.

Within a few weeks, armies were once again marching in and around north-central Italy. Legions loyal to Antony and led by Asinius Pollio, Ventidius Bassus, and Fufius Calenus were moving down from Antony's official province of Gaul. Forces loyal to Octavian and led by Salvidienus Rufus were in northern Italy, where they stood between the Antonine troops and Rome. Octavian's right-hand man, Marcus Agrippa, was raising an army in southern Italy. Octavian himself headed an army of four legions, and he and Lucius Antonius, who may have had a slightly larger force, began to maneuver around Rome, dodging and feinting at each other. When Lucius marched toward Rome, Octavian retreated northwards, and Lucius followed. Lucius may have hoped to link up with his brother's troops moving down from Gaul, but Salvidienus and his army stood in the way. Meanwhile, Agrippa had gathered an army and moved into Tuscany to block Lucius' other routes north. Lucius finally turned toward Perusia (modern Perugia) and settled in to try to make sense of an increasingly complex military and political situation. Octavian and Salvidienus converged on the hilltop town, and the Roman army began to do what it did best: dig. Within a few weeks, Perusia was surrounded by miles of siege works in a double ring, one to keep Lucius Antonius in and the other to keep the Antonian forces from coming to his relief. Winter was on its way.

After a few months, the besieged at Perusia were starving. Lucius Antonius looked out at the forces of Octavian, assessed the remaining supplies, and made a decision: the slaves would not be fed. And they would not be allowed to leave, lest the enemy learn that food was short inside the walls. Appian tells what happened next: "The slaves wandered about in crowds, threw themselves upon the ground in the city and between the city and their forts, and ate grass or green leaves wherever they could find them" (*Civil Wars* 5.35). When the leaves and grass ran out, the slaves died. Lucius had them shoveled into long trenches so that the smoke of funeral pyres would not alert Octavian to how bad things were.

Later, after the city surrendered, Octavian pardoned Lucius Antonius and the governing class of Perusia. His soldiers sacked the city and slaughtered the remaining population. He may have executed some prisoners from Rome who were his opponents and enemies. There is no need to believe his ancient biographer's statement that he chose three hundred senators and Roman knights from the prisoners and sacrificed them like cattle on the altar of his adoptive father, Julius Caesar.[46] But people could believe that he had; the civil wars following Caesar's assassination were very much about vengeance, and vengeance demanded blood. Long after Octavian became Augustus, the Revered One, he completed a temple and forum dedicated to Mars the Avenger. He had promised to build it much earlier, before the siege of Perusia.

Furor impius intus: *The Precarious World of the* Aeneid

Near the beginning of the *Aeneid*, Jupiter reassures Aeneas' mother, the goddess Venus, that her son's struggle and suffering will be worthwhile (discussed in chapter 1 above). The father of gods and men reveals the future: under the emperor Augustus, Rome's old gods and founders will return to earth, justice will prevail, and war will be no more.

> Then hard times will grow gentle as war is laid aside:
> white-haired Trust and Vesta, Remus with brother Quirinus
> will hand down justice; the grim gates of War will be locked
> with tight iron locks.
>
> *Aen.* 1.291–294

This vision of a future Golden Age forms part of a dialogue between two poets, Vergil and Quintus Horatius Flaccus, whom English speakers know as Horace. Born five years apart, Vergil and Horace lived through the near anarchy of the fifties BC, the wars between Caesar and Pompey, the triumviral proscriptions, the Perusine War, the triumvirs' war with Sextus Pompey, and the final, drawn-out struggle between Octavian and Antony. They witnessed the collapse of the republic and saw how easily the ties that bound friend to friend, father to son, brother to brother, and husband to wife could dissolve. Horace fought, briefly and ingloriously, on the side of Caesar's assassins against the forces of Octavian and Antony.[47] He and Vergil knew what a world without Trust (Fides) and Vesta, goddess of hearth and home, was like. In their poems from the thirties and early twenties BC, they tried to imagine a way beyond that world. Their attempts reveal the despair, pessimism, and anxiety from which Vergil's Aeneas was born.[48]

Vergil opened the conversation in *Bucolics* 4. In 40 BC, a brokered peace between Octavian and Antony, sealed by marriage between Octavian's sister and Antony, prompted him to write a pastoral vision of a coming reset of history. He may even have invented the idea of a returning Golden Age.[49] Astraea, the Maiden (and the constellation Virgo), Justice personified, who was the last divinity to leave earth when the gods fled in disgust at sinful humankind, will return, and the golden age of Saturn will be once more.

> The final age of the Sibyl's song has come;
> the great order of the ages is born anew,
> now the Maiden too returns, Saturn's reign returns,
> now a new offspring descends from heaven above.
>
> *Buc.* 4.4–7

Not surprisingly, the "new offspring" foretold in *Bucolics* 4 led some Christian readers in later times to see the poem as a prophecy of Christ. Vergil was anticipating not a divine redeemer, however, but a child of Octavia's marriage to Antony who would somehow preside over a world at peace. That resolution was not to be; Antony's simmering rivalry with Octavian finally boiled into open conflict, and in 29 BC, Octavian emerged as the last man standing in Rome's civil wars.[50]

Some may have thought that peace had come at last. Wiser observers would have had reason to be skeptical. Roman had been killing Roman for half a century, since the days of Sulla. The republic had been descending into chaos for longer than that, perhaps since a mob of senators murdered the tribune Tiberius Gracchus in 133 BC. Younger men could remember nothing but civil war or the threat of civil war; old men had been born into a dysfunctional political system and seen even that collapse. Who could say whether peace would last or whether another warlord would come out of nowhere, as Octavian had, and bring another round of proscriptions and slaughter?

Vergil's two visions of the Golden Age, one in the *Bucolics* in about 40 BC and the other in the *Aeneid* sometime after 29, show the psychological toll of that century of political chaos and internecine savagery. The fourth *Bucolic* only hints at the anxiety underneath its messianic, slightly breathless picture of a future earth that spontaneously yields crops, where there will be no need for work or commerce—a place where the sheep will even produce pre-dyed wool. At the exact center of the poem, Vergil places a note of qualification.

> Still, a few traces of our ancestral deceit will remain,
> to bid us try the sea in ships, gird with walls
> our towns, cut furrows into the earth.
> Then there will be another Tiphys, a second Argo
> to carry its band of heroes; there will be wars again
> and a second time will great Achilles be sent to Troy.
>
> *Buc.* 4.31–36

Even in the second Golden Age, there will be no escape from the traces of ancient deceit or deception (*priscae vestigia fraudis*). "Deception," *fraus*, is an odd choice of word here. It seems to gloss an earlier line in the same poem; with his patron Asinius Pollio, consul of 40 BC, in charge, Vergil says, any traces of wickedness (*sceleris vestigia nostri*) will have no effect, and the earth will be released from perpetual fear (*Buc.* 4.13–14). *Fraudis* may simply elaborate the meaning of *sceleris* (wickedness), with the order of noun and adjective reversed, but it also reflects the moral crisis of the triumviral period. *Fraus* highlights the breakdown of the social compact during the civil wars, when hierarchical relationships and family loyalties, everything the Romans meant by *fides* and *pietas*, crumbled into a Hobbesian state of each against all.[51]

The traces of ancient wickedness in *Bucolics* 4 disrupt the perfection of the Golden Age, but their only stated effect in the poem is to produce a second age of heroes, a new voyage of the Argonauts and a new Trojan War. Mythic heroism, however, has a dark sequel. In the Greek poet Hesiod's account of human development, the age of heroes gives way to the poet's own age of iron, when humans toil and suffer and die, family ties become meaningless, and might makes right (Hesiod, *Works and Days* 174–201). In his influential astrological poem *Phaenomena*, the Hellenistic poet Aratus revived the Hesiodic scheme and made it popular at Rome—Cicero, among others, translated it.[52] Vergil's hoped-for earthly paradise contains a hint of the seeds of its own destruction, and the reborn "great order of the ages" may lead inevitably to a repeat of the present age of civil bloodshed and legalized murder. This "further voice," as one critic calls it, whispers an anxiety of Vergil's age: Rome may be doomed to an endless cycle of fratricide and anarchy.[53] The peace between the two warlords may yet prove an illusion. It has all happened before and may happen again. Against the harmony of Saturn's return sounds a faint, disquieting overtone.

That feeling of being doomed to an eternal return of civil war comes to the surface in another vision of the golden age written at about the same time as Vergil's fourth *Bucolic* and in dialogue with it.[54] The poet Horace opens his sixteenth *Epode* by contrasting the grim present with Rome's glorious past. Rome has withstood every attack, but now she faces an enemy that she cannot defeat: herself.

Another age is ground away
    by civil war,
and Rome herself is collapsing
    from her own strength—
our city, whom neighboring tribes
    could not prevail to destroy,
nor the Etruscan hand of Lars Porsena.

Rome, whom the rival power of Capua,
  fierce Spartacus,
the Allobroges, disloyal amid our revolution,
wild Germany with its woad-painted youth,
Hannibal hated by our parents,
  did not subdue.
We Romans, a wicked age of blood accursed,
  will destroy her,
and the site of Rome will again be occupied
  by wild animals.

Horace, *Epodes* 16.1–10

Horace begins his review of Rome's would-be conquerors with the earliest days of the Roman Republic as it broke away from its Etruscan kings, and ends with Hannibal, whose power over the Roman imagination, like Hitler's in our time, lingered long after his defeat in 202 BC, at the end of the Second Punic War. I have translated *novis rebus* in line 6 as "amid our revolution"; if my understanding of the phrase is correct, there is one seeming anomaly in Horace's list: he includes a glancing reference to recent events, either the Catilinarian conspiracy or an episode in the civil wars. The Allobroges were the Gauls who betrayed the names of Catiline's coconspirators to the Roman authorities; in 48 BC, a small group of them had defected from Caesar's army to join the Pompeians.[55] By bringing an incident from civil strife in the fairly recent past into his catalog of Rome's enemies, Horace assimilates minor players in an aborted civil war to the external threat of Gallic invasion. Like the wars with Carthage, the possibility of a Gallic incursion shaped Romans' sense of historical dangers to their republic. The ability to reframe internecine conflict as foreign war was essential during the civil wars; Octavian—along with Horace, Vergil, and others—spun his final conflict with Antony into a war of all Italy against the forces of Egypt and the East, and the triumph of one warlord over another had to be presented as a victory over a non-Roman enemy.[56]

Assuming the persona of a Roman magistrate addressing an assembly of the people, Horace offers his fellow citizens the prospect of an end to civil war and a turn to a prelapsarian paradise like that in Vergil's fourth *Bucolic*. But paradise comes at the price of abandoning Rome and leaving fields, shrines, and household gods to boars and wolves, just as the Phocaean Greeks did when they abandoned their city to the Persians in the sixth century BC. In Horace's prescription, there is no cure for being Roman; civil war will end only when Romans become someone else, somewhere else. Exile and reinvention are the alternative to self-destruction.

The Romans, Horace advises, are to seek the Isles of the Blessed,

> where the earth unplowed, year after year,
>   yields up grain,
> unpruned vines are ever in bloom,
> the shoot of never failing olive
>   puts forth buds,
> the dark, ripe fig adorns its tree,
> honey drips from the hollow oak,
>   from high mountains
> water lightly leaps with splashing step.
>
> Horace, *Epodes* 16.43–48

Horace counters Vergil's Golden Age in time with a golden place untouched by time. Vergil imagined time recycling, so that the reborn age of Saturn led, in turn, to a second heroic age, another voyage of the Argonauts, and another Trojan War. But if a renewed age of gold leads to an age of heroes, will a new age of heroes lead to another age of iron? Horace responds to Vergil's barely implied pessimism by imagining a refuge outside mythic history.

> Here no loom of Argo's oar has fared,
>   no Colchian hussy set foot;
> here no Sidonian crew has turned its yard,
>   no toiling squadron of Ulysses.
> No contagions harm the herd, no evil star's
>   torrid rage parches the flock.
> Jupiter set those shores apart for a godly race,
>   when he stained the golden age with bronze;
> with bronze, then with iron he made times hard,
>   but from them—trust your poet—escape
> is granted to the godly.
>
> Horace, *Epodes* 16.57–66

Horace answers Vergil's veiled, cautionary overtone of pessimism with a full-throated jeremiad on Rome's self-destructive degeneracy and with a rejection of Rome's history and location beside the Tiber.

Horace's Roman readers would have recognized his advice as a counsel of despair and a fantasy. For them, Rome was a site that could not be abandoned, their *patria*, a place made holy by tradition and memory.[57] They would have remembered that Romans from centuries before had debated leaving their home beside the Tiber. In the early fourth century BC, Gauls defeated a Roman army at the confluence of the Allia and Tiber Rivers and then moved south to sack the city. After the Gauls were driven off, the stunned Romans contemplated moving their city to the site of Veii, a recently conquered neighboring city. According to the historian Livy, Marcus Furius Camillus, who had led their campaign against Veii and driven off the Gauls, then appeared in the Forum and addressed the citizens.

> Can you not understand the heinousness of the sin which, though we have barely as yet won to shore from the shipwreck brought on us by our former guilt, we are preparing to commit? We have a city founded with all due rites of auspice and augury; not a stone of her streets but is permeated by our sense of the divine; for our annual sacrifices not the days only are fixed, but the places too, where they may be performed; men of Rome, would you desert your gods—the tutelary spirits which guard your families, and those the nation prays to as its saviours? Would you leave them all?
>
> Livy 5.52, trans. de Sélincourt

Livy was a contemporary of Horace and Vergil and, like Vergil, a native of northern Italy. His Camillus transposes onto the fourth century BC the anxiety and guilt of the third quarter of the first. Rumor had it that Julius Caesar planned to move the seat of government to a rebuilt Troy or to Alexandria, and Pompey's decision to abandon Rome in 49 BC and take the senate with him perturbed Cicero; in response to Pompey's offhand remark that "the commonwealth isn't walls," Cicero retorted, "No, but it is altars and hearths."[58] The proposal to migrate to Veii came from the leaders of the plebeians, who were engaged in a long struggle with the patrician senate that, in Livy's telling, prefigures the civil strife of the late republic. Livy's Camillus and Horace in *Epode* 16 reflect anxieties that arose during that strife, concerns about the permanence of the city of Rome itself.

When Horace assumes the persona of a magistrate putting before the Roman people the question of emigrating to the Isles of the Blessed, his proposal could be recognized as controversial, and at the same time as a fantasy. As the son of a freed slave, Horace belonged to a class excluded by custom from political office, and his ventriloquizing of a magistrate corresponds to the impossibilities, *adynata*, that color the oath that he imagines administering to the people in lines 25–34.[59] The fundamental point of Livy's account of Camillus was embedded in Roman consciousness: the idea of Rome was inseparable from the site of Rome. Moving Rome to the Isles of the Blessed is yet another impossibility, an implied *adynaton* greater than any explicit in the poem. So is freeing Rome from its ancestral curse, self-destruction in civil war.

Epode 16 sets out a deeply pessimistic answer to Vergil's fourth *Bucolic*. There would be no return of the reign of Saturn. If time cycled back to a past Golden Age, it would also cycle forward again to an age of iron, like that in which Horace and his contemporary Romans lived. Escaping from the prison of time and history meant escaping from who the Romans were; Rome would no longer be Rome or inhabited by Romans. It was a fantastic idea, a dream to take Romans of the early thirties away from the grim reality of Octavian, Antony, and the ever-present prospect of a return to well-remembered horrors. What David Porter called the "downward movement" of the *Epodes* reaches its political nadir in the penultimate poem of the collection.[60]

A decade later, in 29 BC, when Vergil began work on the *Aeneid*, there may have seemed to be grounds for hope. In 31, Octavian had defeated Antony and his ally Cleopatra in a naval battle off Actium in northwestern Greece. A year later, Antony and Cleopatra were dead, and Egypt, with all its wealth and agricultural resources, became a special province governed by a prefect responsible directly to Octavian.[61] In 29, Octavian took a victory lap. He became consul for the fifth time, had his administrative actions retroactively approved by the senate, and ordered the doors of the temple of Janus closed, symbolizing that Rome was at peace. In August (or Sextilis, as the Romans called it until 8 BC), Octavian returned to the city and celebrated a triple triumph, for victories in Illyria, at Actium, and in Egypt. Poets and other makers of opinion tried hard to overlook the fact that the last two of those victories were arguably part of Octavian's war with Antony and were thus over fellow Romans; Antony's personal and political alliance with Cleopatra allowed those victories to be reframed as conquests of a foreign enemy.[62] General relief over the end of civil war made it easy to agree as Octavian paraded along the ancient route of triumphant generals, flanked by his nephew Marcellus and his stepson Tiberius. Less than two years later, Octavian felt secure enough to stand before the senate and renounce his triumviral special powers and provinces; the republic, he proclaimed, was restored. Alarmed by the thought that he might actually mean what he said, the senate immediately granted him a package of new powers and honors and a new name, Augustus.

If the Romans had had an index for hope and anxiety, like the popular "fear and greed index" that purports to track the stock market, its pointer would have dipped from hope toward anxiety less than a year after Augustus received his new name. Spain, the old stronghold of Sextus Pompey, was still restive, and the Cantabrian tribes in the northwest rose in revolt.[63] Augustus led the armies west, and Romans thought there would surely be another triumph. Then disquieting rumors began to filter back to Rome: Augustus was ill, and the war was not going well. Augustus recovered and managed to settle the Cantabrians for the time being, but he was not back in Rome until 24 BC. After more than two years away, he returned to find his new status threatened. He fell ill again, so ill that he entrusted the financial records of the empire to Calpurnius Piso and gave his signet ring to Agrippa.[64] People began to wonder what would happen when Augustus died, as seemed likely sooner rather than later; he was now forty years old, and his health had never been good. In partial answer, Augustus had arranged a marriage in 25 BC between his nephew Marcellus and his daughter Julia; the alliance would secure the continued dominance of the family of Caesar. Barely two years after the marriage, the young nephew, not the middle-aged autocrat, fell ill and died. Marcellus' death in 23 BC shattered confidence in the stable continuity of the new Augustan regime. The senatorial aristocracy began to think their own thoughts about succession. Conspiracy was discovered, and members of Augustus' inner circle paid with their lives.[65] In the winter of that same year, the Tiber flooded Rome, and that year and the next brought food shortages and many deaths from disease and hunger.[66]

The decade from 29 to 19 BC—one not of settled peace but of uncertainty over the viability and survival of the Augustan regime, unrest in Spain and elsewhere, the very real chance that civil war might erupt once again, and signs that the gods were at best ambivalent about Rome—gave birth to the *Aeneid*.[67] When Vergil imagined a future Golden Age for a second time, he responded to Horace's critique of the fourth *Bucolic* by placing the future paradise firmly in history. His Golden Age in the *Aeneid* is a recognition that Augustan hope must be tempered by the reality of Rome's ineradicable propensity to self-destruction;

in the *Aeneid*, the *Bucolics*' muted pessimism and Horace's despairing fantasy become a grim image of the need to restrain the force that might carry Rome back into Hobbesian chaos.

> There will be born a Trojan Caesar from beautiful family,
> one to bound his empire with Ocean, his fame with the stars,
> Julius, a name derived from Trojan Iulus.
> Someday, Venus, you will receive him into heaven
> laden with the spoils of the East, and he,
> like you, will be summoned with prayers.
> Then hard times will grow gentle as war is laid aside:
> white-haired Trust and Vesta, Remus with brother Quirinus
> will hand down justice; the grim gates of War will be locked
> with tight iron locks. Inside, wicked Rage,
> crouched on a savage heap of weapons, hands bound
> behind his back with a hundred brazen knots,
> will snarl horribly from gore-spattered mouth.
>
> *Aen.* 1.291–296

The "Trojan Caesar" is Augustus (whose name was officially Julius Caesar until 27 BC), and Vergil predicts that the gods who abandoned mankind will return with his coming.[68] Vesta and Fides (Trust)—whose name covers honesty, loyalty, and all that makes one person rely on another—represent the essential humanity lost in the years of civil war; most tellingly, Rome's deified founder, Romulus, here called by his divine name Quirinus, will return with his brother, and they will jointly dispense justice. Rome's foundational myth told how Romulus killed his twin brother, Remus, in a dispute over the new city's walls. Vergil reunites those archetypal brothers in his imagined Augustan future; their reconciliation stands for what had to happen, the erasure of the passions and ambitions that set Roman against Roman in half a century of civil wars.[69]

One of those passions refuses to be erased. The "grim gates of War" were the doors of the temple of Janus, which Augustus had closed during his victory lap in 29 BC to symbolize that the Roman world was at peace. The gates were opened almost immediately thereafter and would close once more during Vergil's lifetime, in 25, to celebrate the supposed end of the Cantabrian revolt in Spain.[70] Romans could not agree on what the closed doors meant: was war or peace locked in, or was Janus himself kept inside to protect the city?[71] Vergil's version of the temple is a prison for monsters of the Roman soul. Inside sits Rage (Furor), chained atop a pile of weapons, hissing and roaring from a mouth that drips blood.[72] Goya might have found a subject here, although Vergil took his image from a painting by Apelles that Augustus displayed near the temple of Mars the Avenger, which Augustus vowed during the civil wars.[73]

Vergil thus ends Jupiter's prophecy with an image that is far from reassuring.[74] Rage is imprisoned but still dangerous. How long will the chains and locks hold? The disquiet and anxiety that were heard as faint overtones in the fourth *Bucolic* now become the crashing finale of one of the *Aeneid*'s most important programmatic passages. With it Vergil rejects Horace's improbable fantasy of removing Rome from the contingent agonies of place, time, and history. Instead of escape to a return of Saturn's mythical, golden time (as in *Bucolics* 4) or unimaginable removal of Rome to an equally mythical place (the Isles of the Blessed), Vergil situates his perfected future firmly in recent history and at Rome. The fulfillment of history will come in a recognizable future, when Augustus, the Trojan Caesar descended from Aeneas, extends his fame until he, like his ancestor Venus, is invoked in the prayers of the Roman people. Under the divine guidance of Romulus and his brother, this culmination of Roman history will see an end to civil strife. It will not, however, be free of the rage that showed on Catiline's dying face or drove Octavian's soldiers as they butchered the inhabitants of Perusia. The monster Rage, *Furor*, can be chained and imprisoned, but never driven out.

Moral History and Moral Heroism

When Vergil and Horace tried to understand and escape the horrors of civil war, they looked first to mythological and moral ways of thinking, to Saturn's long-ago Golden Age or to the equally mythical Isles of the Blessed, to the loss of and need for moral ideals (mythologized into divinities like Fides and the maiden Justice) or the *pietas* evoked at the close of *Epode* 16.[75] In *Bucolic* 4, Vergil imagined Rome's history recycling through a new sequence of ages, a *saeclorum ordo*.[76] In *Epode* 16, Horace envisioned Rome's history as something to escape. In the *Aeneid*, Vergil embraced it. His vision of Roman history, as set out in Jupiter's speech early in the *Aeneid*, begins with the Trojan War and ends with Vergil's own time, when a Trojan Caesar will at last bring peace—and, since this is Rome, glorious conquest and plunder.[77]

In the Greek and Roman world, there was nothing very unusual about understanding civic history and politics in mythological or moral terms. The Athenians imagined that their city-state had been inaugurated in a contest between the divinities Athena and Poseidon and that the Athenian people descended from a line of mythical, half-divine kings who grew from the earth of Attica and sometimes took on the form of snakes. Thucydides makes Pericles attribute Athens' success to the virtue (*aretê*) of its citizens, and the Athenian admiral Nicias, facing defeat during the siege of Syracuse, ends a speech to his men by exhorting, "The city is men, and not walls or ships without men in them."[78] At Rome two centuries before Vergil, the poet Ennius proclaimed, "By ancient morals stands the Roman state, and by its men."[79]

The achievement of Vergil, Horace, and other writers who lived through the barely legalized terror and civil war of the forties and thirties BC was to imbue mythological and moral understandings with a sense of original guilt. Horace sums it up at the end of *Epode* 7.

> It's this way: bitter fate drives the Romans,
> and the crime of fratricide
> ever since the blood of innocent Remus
> poured into the ground,
> a curse to his descendants.
>
> Horace, *Epodes* 7.17–20

Within a framework of mythological and moral meaning, something as long-lasting, bloody, and tinged with déjà vu as the civil discords and armed conflicts that destroyed the Roman Republic could be explained only as the result of something very like original sin. Unlike the Athenians of the fifth century, who could appeal to mythical events and moral excellence to account for their successes, the Romans of the first century had to explain self-destructive failure. Fratricide marked the founding of Rome, and only its curse could explain the terrible sense of doom as Sulla turned into Caesar and Caesar into Octavian. *Furor* could be controlled, chained up in the temple of Janus, but the threat that the monster might escape was always there. The Romans were fatally flawed, and there was no redemption.

The world of the *Aeneid* demands a rethinking of the moral universe. Great deeds are possible: one man can emerge from conflict as ruler of the Mediterranean world. That greatness, though, comes at a cost: lives lost, ties of love and kinship tested or broken, and, above all, the constant struggle against the forces, internal and external, psychological and natural, that always threaten to unchain the fury. What does it mean to be a hero in such a world? Can self-destructive failure somehow be redeemed? How does one choose, when the constants upholding choice have vanished?

CHAPTER 3

The Choices of Aeneas

Like most people, Aeneas sometimes wonders what he ought to do. After Jupiter sends Mercury to tell Aeneas to leave Carthage and Dido, he looks to the pain ahead.

> Ah, what should he do? Dare what approach to win around
> the raging queen? How should he begin his speech?
>
> *Aen.* 4.283–284

The speech that Aeneas comes up with may not be the best choice in his situation, but it is what Aeneas chooses, and the choice is his, even though the occasion and topic are not. More often, Aeneas has help in making choices, especially in the first half of the *Aeneid*.[1] Some of his choices, as well as the direction of his life as a whole, seem to be altogether out of his hands—fated. This chapter briefly touches on one of those choices and explores the issues at stake in the idea that Aeneas' choices are in some sense foreordained. It then focuses on another of those choices, the complex cluster of decisions that lead Aeneas to leave Troy.

After he sails from Carthage for Italy, heavy weather forces Aeneas to stop over in Sicily, where a distant relative, Acestes, welcomes him to his kingdom. There Aeneas celebrates funeral games on the anniversary of his father's death. The games go well, but many of the Trojan refugees are weary and dispirited and would be just as happy to end their voyage and settle in Acestes' friendly territory. Juno, hostile as ever, contrives to exploit the human situation and put difficulties in the way. Her messenger, Iris, disguised as an old Trojan woman,

Beroë, incites the Trojan women to set fire to the fleet. Many of the ships have been consumed by the time a rainstorm puts an end to the damage. Aeneas is in despair.

> His people's father, Aeneas, shattered by bitter misfortune
> turned huge cares over and over, this side and that,
> and weighed alternatives. Should he forget his destiny
> and settle in Sicilian territory, or keep making for Italian shores?
>
> *Aen.* 5.700–704

One of his men, old Nautes, advises him to consult Acestes and proposes leaving behind the crews of the burnt ships, the women and children, and anyone else who is unfit or unwilling to continue. That night, a vision of his father, Anchises, appears to him, confirms Nautes' recommendation, and gives him information about what lies ahead: a journey to the underworld, and war in Italy. In the morning, Aeneas goes to Acestes and "explains the command of Jupiter, the instructions of his dear parent, and the decision [*sententia*] that now stands firm in his mind" (*Aen.* 5.747–748). He has made up his mind to go on, but his individual decision is only one of three factors in the choice he makes. Just as he did in his self-justification to Dido (4.333–361), Aeneas reports something that has not appeared in the narrative, and he neglects to mention something that does; no "command of Jupiter" appears in this episode, and Aeneas does not mention Nautes' recommendation.

But sometimes, as we saw in chapter 1, Aeneas seems to have no choice. He tells Dido, "Italy—I go against my will!" (*Aen.* 4.361). In dreams or omens, in visions or in person, the gods instruct him in his destiny, and he obeys.[2] His will, what he wants, appears insignificant. Aeneas' distinguishing quality, his *pietas*, consists partly of his obedience to these divine commands. The gods' instructions align his actions with fate, with what will most certainly happen—as Vergil's readers know because, for them, it already has. Rome has been founded, and the new Golden Age under Augustus is just visible on the horizon.[3] If what will happen must happen, it might seem to make no difference whether Aeneas chooses one action over another.[4] How, then, can Aeneas be a moral agent? How can he be responsible in a moral sense for what he chooses to do? How can he choose at all? If he can choose, what kind of moral agent is he?

Vergil, Philosophy, and Some Philosophers

Ancient literary and philosophical ideas on moral agency, compulsion, necessity, and fate can illuminate questions like these about Aeneas' choices. Vergil is a poet, not a philosopher, but like his Greek and Roman predecessors and models, he drew on and responded to contemporary philosophical debates, associated with professional philosophers, and was a serious amateur student of philosophy.[5] The ancient biography compiled by Aelius Donatus in the fourth century AD affirms Vergil's philosophical credentials. As it happens, those are almost the only facts about Vergil's life that we can confirm from independent, contemporary sources and from his own words.

When Mount Vesuvius erupted in AD 79, a tidal wave of hot mud and gas buried the town of Herculaneum and, with it, a luxurious villa that may have belonged, years before, to Julius Caesar's father-in-law, Calpurnius Piso. In it was a library containing works associated with an Epicurean philosopher, Philodemus of Gadara, who was Piso's house philosopher. Carbonized scrolls from that library, first discovered in 1752, have been painstakingly opened and deciphered in a process that still continues.[6] Philodemus, who was born toward the end of the second century BC, was active in Rome and around the Bay of Naples during Vergil's lifetime, and in 1988, a papyrus fragment of one of his works revealed a list of his associates or pupils: Plotius, Varius, Quintilius—and Vergil.[7] Another papyrus from the same collection may also contain Vergil's name, as has been suspected since the end of the nineteenth century (Körte 1892).

At the end of the *Georgics*, written immediately before the *Aeneid*, Vergil signs his name and locates himself at Naples, "prospering in the studies of an obscure leisure" (*Georgics* 4.564). It would be nice to think that when the author of *Catalepton* 5 declares his intention to study with an Epicurean philosopher, Siro, we have another firm, first-person declaration by Vergil of his philosophical studies. But it is impossible to be certain that *Catalepton* and other works in the so-called *Appendix Vergiliana* are youthful works of Vergil, as tradition claims. With the Herculaneum papyri and the end of the *Georgics*, we do not need the *Appendix*, the ancient biographical tradition, or any of the other bits and pieces of evidence about Vergil's life to justify using ancient literary and philosophical idea about moral agency to shed light on Aeneas' choices.

Praise and Blame

For modern readers, to say that Aeneas is responsible for what he chooses to do has often amounted to saying that he can be meaningfully praised or blamed for his choices and actions. We describe praiseworthy choices and actions as good, blameworthy choices and actions as bad. When readers of the *Aeneid* profess to dislike Aeneas, they are often blaming him for what he chooses to do or for what he does; in effect, they are making a judgment about his use of moral responsibility. Ancient readers may have taken a somewhat different view of the relationship between moral responsibility, on the one hand, and praise and blame, on the other. For them, praise and blame may have been directed not at uses of moral responsibility—choices and actions—but at the qualities or virtues that underlay such uses. Although that difference is slight and hard to see in practice, it points the way to an understanding of Aeneas' heroism.

The association of moral responsibility with praise and blame appears very early in classical thought. When the Greek poet Pindar (ca. 522–ca. 443 BC) imagines the life of a socially engaged citizen, he equates moral judgment with appropriate assignment of praise and blame.

> Zeus father, may such never be my way;
> let me, walking always in the path
> of simplicity, make my life, and die thus, leaving
> to my children fame without reproach. Some pray for gold, some for lands
> without limit, but I to lay my limbs in the ground as one who gladdened
> his fellow-citizens,
> praising that which deserves it, scattering blame on the workers of evil.
>
> *Nemean* 8.35–39, trans. Lattimore

Although several characters in the *Aeneid* blame Aeneas for what he has done or fails to do, he also gets his share of praise. Those who praise him focus not on his deeds but on his qualities: not only his courage, *pietas*, and trustworthiness, but also his ancestry and physical appearance. In the first book of the *Aeneid*, the Trojan captain Ilioneus describes his absent leader to Dido shortly after the landing at Carthage: "We had a king, Aeneas, than whom no one exists / more just or greater in goodness [*pietate*] and in war" (*Aen.* 1.544–545).[8] At the beginning of the second half of the poem, Ilioneus again speaks to a ruler on whose shores the Trojans have landed. He addresses Latinus, the ruler of Latium in Italy, and makes the case for granting the Trojans land for a settlement: "Our king is himself from the exalted race of Jupiter. . . . I swear by the destiny of Aeneas and by his right hand, powerful / whether felt in trust or tested in war and battle" (7.220, 234–235).

Ilioneus praises Aeneas for moral qualities: justice, *pietas*, and valor—his "powerful right hand" in war. Few readers would deny that Aeneas shows, at least sometimes, the moral qualities for which he is praised: courage, honor, and devotion (*pietas*). Many would also point out that he sometimes fails to demonstrate them when he might have. Aeneas is not consistent in those or any other qualities—as Agnes Michels notes, few characters in the *Aeneid* are "consistently presented as wholly good or wholly bad" (1997, 399)—but he does act, and when characters in the epic praise him for those qualities or blame him for his actions, they imply that he is, in some sense, a moral agent.

Can we share their judgment? Are praise and blame the same for us as they were for Vergil and, before him, Pindar?At the conclusion of chapter 1, I argued that being human in antiquity was different from being human in the twenty-first century, because the way that humans imagine themselves has changed. That difference, I suggested, has come about because we live under the waning influence of a post-Renaissance conviction that to be human means having a unitary, autonomous center of intellect and will directing the actions of an unconscious, physical body. According to that model, we cannot be praised or blamed for that for which we are not ourselves responsible. Only, for example, when being homosexual began to be thought of as an involuntary disposition, not a voluntary choice, could it cease to be a sin in many Americans' eyes. To be fully subject to moral judgment in our world, a thought or action must be the result of a conscious act of will. Actions done under compulsion or out of ignorance do not expose the one who does them to the same degree of moral culpability as acts done freely and willingly, any more than having a horse thief in the family tree or a physical disability diminishes a person's moral worth.

In contrast, people in Aeneas' world saw themselves as personalities created by ongoing interactions with their social environment, including their family and ancestry. As Martha Nussbaum points out (2001, 1–3), immediately after Pindar expresses a wish to gladden his fellow citizens by bestowing praise and blame appropriately, he expands and complicates his picture of moral judgment by comparing human excellence to an organic, growing thing.

> But excellence waxes as the vine
> growth in the young green tendrils,
> raised up among the men who are righteous and wise into the
> limpid sky.
>
> *Nemean* 8.40a–42, trans. Lattimore

Such excellence does not result only from the voluntarily chosen, praiseworthy acts of individual men and women. It is, as Nussbaum says, "like a young plant: something growing in the world, slender, fragile, in constant need of food from without" (2001, 1). In one of his last works, Cicero describes our moral agency and our very humanity as partly created by other people through our connections with them; being good and human, in turn, depends on our participation in those connections,

> because, as has been brilliantly written by Plato, we are born not only for ourselves, but our country claims one share in our upbringing, and our friends claim another. Moreover, as the Stoics like to say, all things which the earth bears are created for the use of humans, but humans are created for the sake of humans, so that they themselves can be of benefit to one another. In this matter we ought to take nature as our guide, contribute our part to the common good, and by the exchange of obligations, by giving and receiving, now by arts, now by labor, now by talents, bind tight the social union of human with human.
>
> *De officiis* 1.7.22

In Pindar's and Vergil's world, matters over which a person had no control could play a part in determining his or her moral responsibility, and moral agency was a matter not only of consciously willing to perform good or bad actions but also of acting in conformity with a good or bad moral identity. Moral goodness consisted not only in willing praiseworthy things and acting on that will but in accurate evaluation of social bonds and in understanding and responding appropriately to the world in which moral choices happen. For a person in that world, choices that are not entirely voluntary and qualities that do not result from conscious choices may still be subject to moral evaluation.

Aeneas has a moral identity: he is *pius Aeneas*. His *pietas* and identity depend on his ongoing evaluation of the social bonds that make *pietas* possible. When the ground of those social bonds—his life in Troy, his family, and Troy itself—is swept from under his feet, he finds himself thrust into an ongoing crisis of identity. In the end, his struggle to preserve and redefine *pietas* in a changed world destroys his humanity and creates his heroism.

Stoics and Epicureans

Some ancient philosophers—the ones that Vergil studied and took seriously—gave serious thought to the connections among fate or necessity, voluntary choices and decisions, and moral responsibility. Epicureans like Vergil's teacher Philodemus shuddered at the idea that fate determined human choices. For them, believing that all things happened by necessity and that moral choice was meaningless was even worse than believing tales of arbitrary, anthropomorphic gods who meddled in human affairs; Epicurus said, "It would be better to follow the mythology about gods than to be a slave to the 'fate' of the natural philosophers: the former at least hints at the hope of begging the gods off by means of worship, whereas the latter involves an inexorable necessity."[9] Thanks to another papyrus from Herculaneum, we know of Philodemus' argument against the idea that we bear no responsibility for our fate-determined decisions and choices; the idea refutes itself, he contended, because by the very act of arguing against an opponent who maintains otherwise, we acknowledge that the opponent bears some responsibility for his or her ideas.[10] The Epicurean universe of atoms and void has no room for fate, destiny, or determinism. Everything that exists or happens in it comes about through the collision, combination, and recombination of eternal, indivisible particles called, in Greek, *atoma*, "uncuttables." As Vergil's Epicurean contemporary Lucretius asserted, those atoms have their own kind of freedom, an uncaused movement called the "swerve."[11] No mind or intelligence guides those particles, and the gods of this universe exist in a distant, Olympian paradise of uncaring calm; they neither care nor intervene in human affairs.

Yet in the *Aeneid* they do, again and again. Jupiter unrolls the secret scrolls of the fates and sends Mercury to Carthage; Juno stirs up a storm, and Poseidon calms it; Venus appears to her son; Apollo cautions Ascanius. The second and third lines of the poem proclaim that Aeneas is an exile by fate, buffeted on land and sea by the violence of the gods and the remembering anger of Juno. Vergil's vision of a world mapped out by fate and directed by divinity amounts to a rejection of the Epicurean worldview of his teacher Philodemus. Some have even spoken of Vergil's "conversion" to another philosophical school, Stoicism, and suggested that Aeneas is a Stoic hero.[12] Vergil was a poet, not a philosopher, and his exploitation of philosophy in the *Aeneid* cannot be reduced to make him an adherent of any school. The Stoics' ideas on fate, necessity, and personal responsibility, however, appear throughout the poem, and Aeneas cannot be understood without them.

For the Stoics, everything that happens has a cause and in turn causes something else to happen, and that chain of cause and effect equals fate. We can get a sense of how Stoic doctrines looked to Vergil by examining the reports of them by his older contemporary Cicero. In his dialogue *On Divination*, written in the months around the assassination of Caesar in 44 BC, Cicero has his brother Quintus explain the Stoic outlook.

> By "fate," I mean what the Greeks call *heimarmenê*—an ordering and sequence of causes, since it is the connection of cause to cause that out of itself produces anything. It is everlasting truth, flowing from all eternity. Consequently nothing has happened that was not going to be, and likewise nothing is going to be of which nature does not contain causes working to bring that very thing about. This makes it intelligible that fate should be, not the "fate" of superstition, but that of physics, an everlasting cause of things—why past things happen, why present things are now happening, and why future things will be.
>
> *On Divination* 1.125–126

Unlike the Epicurean world of random atomic motion, the Stoic world makes sense, and Stoics liked to imagine it as having its own mind, soul, and body, which related every part to every other and gave the whole cosmos order and unity.[13] The problem was to find room in that world for individual choice and action and for moral responsibility.

Chrysippus (ca. 279–206 BC), the third head of the Stoic school, found a way to preserve individual choice and responsibility in the Stoics' universe of interconnected causes and effects. According to another treatise of Cicero, *On Fate* (also written in 44 BC), Chrysippus wove human decisions into the web of cause and effect by arguing that events have different kinds of causes. Some causes, Chrysippus argued, are "perfect and principal"; that is, they are built into the nature of things. A cylinder, for example, rolls because it is round; in that sense, it is fated to roll. But it needs another kind of cause to set it on its way. Something in the environment, some sense impression, may give a person the idea of pushing the roller downhill. That is an "auxiliary and proximate" cause. It is in that person's power, Chrysippus argued, to accept or reject the sense impression and decide to push the roller or not. Philosopher Dorothea Frede sums up the Stoic view as follows:

> This much seems clear; the Stoics relied on a distinction between the antecedent or external and the principal or "inner" cause to explain how human beings are part of the web of causal interconnections in such a way that there is room for personal responsibility. The Stoic justification consists in making the internal but not the external causes the principal causes of human actions. Though the environment acts on us in a way that is not subject to our control, our reactions are "up to us" since they depend on our inner state.
>
> Frede 2003, 191–192

According to that view, fate makes the road. We travel on it and can go nowhere but where it leads, but what kind of traveler we are and how we make our journey is up to us.

I believe that Vergil's Aeneas makes decisions from something like that Stoic position. If everything that Aeneas does is part of a chain of cause and effect whose result we know, saying that Aeneas' actions are determined by fate is the same as saying that his actions are determined by history—a history that the *Aeneid*'s readers have always known but that he cannot. It is not the same as saying that he is a mere puppet of the gods, or that all his choices and actions are determined and beyond his control. Old Nautes' advice needed to be supplemented and clarified precisely because it was based on a misunderstanding of the Stoic position. "Let us go," he said to Aeneas, "where Fate drags us forward or drags us back" (*Aen.* 5.709). At that point, Aeneas needs a vision of Anchises, because he knows that Nautes' advice is unsatisfactory. Aeneas' success or failure as a moral agent will depend on his ability to travel his road in the right way, not by being dragged, but by aligning his choices with their outcomes in a future that, from a reader's point of view, has already happened. Aeneas' status as a person on whom the future is already acting makes his moral choices unlike those of ordinary mortals, but they are still choices (at least some of the time), and in the world of the *Aeneid*, he is in some sense responsible for them.

We are all, in a way, either Epicureans or Stoics; either we try to be content in a world that does not, ultimately, make sense, or we create one that does. Vergil himself was born and came to adulthood in a world where people seemed powerless in the face of the inescapable violence, pain, and suffering of civil war, where the collapse of the old structures of kinship and civic bonds made people long for the return of a lost golden age, and where there sometimes seemed to be no escape from the fratricidal destiny of Rome. We do not have to imagine Vergil undergoing an Augustinian conversion from Epicureanism to Stoicism to understand that he might have found Epicurean withdrawal inadequate to explain the world in which he lived.[14] As for Aeneas, part of his struggle (*labor*) in the *Aeneid* is to learn to make decisions in a world like Vergil's and to learn that, in the end, he makes them alone and at a cost.

Leaving Troy

"The Greek high command, broken by war and driven back by destiny"—that is what Aeneas and all the Trojans believe when they wake up to see the plain before Troy empty and the Greek camp by the shore deserted (*Aen.* 2.13). But the Greeks are not gone; they have withdrawn only as far as the nearby island of Tenedos, and they have left behind a mysterious gift, a giant wooden horse. Aeneas' account of the last hours of Troy begins with a misapprehension and follows with a series of decisions and choices. Most of them are wrong, and Aeneas needs help to make the few that align him with his destiny.

The first and perhaps most critical choices are made collectively, by the Trojans, and as he describes them to Dido, Aeneas almost, but not quite, removes himself from the deliberations. "We," he says, "believed that the Greeks had gone away and made for Mycenae on the wind" (*Aen.* 2.25). Who exactly is that "we"? Latin can use "we" for "I," a first-person plural where English would expect a singular, as when Catullus says that his girlfriend was "loved by us as no one will be loved" (8.5) or asks a missing friend, "We beg you, if it isn't any trouble, where are your hiding places?" (54.1–2). Vergil has Aeneas employ an emphatic first-person plural pronoun, *nos*, in *Nos abiisse rati et vento petisse Mycenas*. Since it follows a string of first-person singulars—Aeneas tells Dido, "I saw [the fall of Troy]," "I was part [of it]," "I shall begin [my story]" (*vidi*, 2.5; *fui*, 2.6; *incipiam*, 2.13)—a reader can easily suppose that the shift from singular means no more than it does in Catullus. It is simply Aeneas, still telling what he saw and believed.[15]

As his story goes on, however, Aeneas subsumes his individual experience into the collective perceptions of the Trojans, and the *nos* in line 25 begins to look like a transition, not a continuation. The Trojans first debate what to do with the great wooden horse that the Greeks have left behind (*Aen.* 2.31–39).

Thymoetes argues that it should be taken inside the wall, while Capys maintains that it should either be destroyed or opened up to see what is inside. The eventual fates of those two minor characters may reflect their roles at this point in the poem; Thymoetes survives the fall of Troy only to be killed by Turnus in Italy (12.364), while Capys, who has already appeared as the captain of one of Aeneas' ships, earns eternal fame as the eponymous founder of Capua (10.145). Aeneas does not report to Dido his own view regarding the horse, but he retrospectively labels Capys' view as a "better opinion" (*melior sententia*, 2.35). Aeneas offers another regretful look back after he describes the dramatic appearance of the priest Laocoon and his warning to fear the Greeks, even those bearing gifts. If the Trojans had noticed the groan resonating from inside the wooden beast as Laocoon's spear quivered in its belly, Aeneas laments, "Troy now would be standing, and you, citadel of Priam, would yet remain" (2.56).

Laocoon's dramatic intervention is followed immediately by an equally compelling episode. Sinon, a spy left behind by the Greeks, has let himself be captured by Trojan shepherds so that he can spin an elaborate story, first for the Trojans and then for Priam himself, to persuade them to bring the wooden horse, and the Greeks inside it, into Troy. As Aeneas tells the story, he continues to identify himself with the collective choices and actions of the Trojans. When Sinon proclaims himself abandoned by hostile Greeks and surrounded by hostile Trojans, "we urge" him to tell his story (*Aen.* 2.74); when he feigns despair and stops his story just before its climax, "we burn to know" (2.105); finally, "we grant him his life and take pity on him" (2.145).

Laocoon then returns to the story. He is sacrificing a bull to Neptune when two gigantic serpents suddenly appear on the horizon. As the horrified Trojans watch, the snakes come on shore, entwine and devour Laocoon and his two sons, and slither off to the citadel of Troy, where they take shelter under the shield of the cult statue of Athena. Now all seems clear to the Trojans. They shout together (*conclamant, Aen.* 2.233) that the horse should be brought into the city and that prayers should be offered to the gods. Once again, Aeneas includes himself in their choices: "we part the walls and lay open the city's fortifications" (2.234); the horse sticks at the threshold (a bad omen) and a sound like rattling weapons comes from inside it, but "still we press on heedlessly" (2.244).

The Greeks are inside the walls, but the Trojans, Aeneas among them, sleep their first carefree sleep after ten years of war. Up to this point in his tale for

Dido, Aeneas has made no distinction between the Trojan collective will and his own. Their choices have been his; Troy is his home, and his individuality is hardly distinguishable from Troy itself. Now, he is about to be plunged into a different world, in which he will be alone and he will be Troy.[16] The ignorance, pity, and *pietas* that the Trojans have revealed in their response to the horse, to Sinon, and to the portent of the serpents will remain part of Aeneas as he makes critical decisions during Troy's final night.

As Aeneas sleeps, his dead cousin Hector appears to him. It is a nightmarish vision, not Hector armed and glorious, but a walking corpse, pierced with wounds, covered with blood and dust, beard and hair caked with blood, and ankles showing gruesome piercings between heel and tendon, where Achilles had threaded oxhide thongs to drag the body around the walls of Troy (*Aen.* 2.270–279; see *Iliad* 22.396–398). Aeneas tries to engage the specter in conversation—Where has he been? Why has he come—but Hector will have none of it. He groans and utters an ominous command.

> Flee, o son of Venus! Snatch yourself from the flames.
> The enemy has the walls; Troy is tumbling down
> from its high peak. Our country's time, Priam's time, is over.
> If our citadel could have been defended by any hand,
> it would have been defended by this one, mine.
>
> *Aen.* 2.289–292

The vision then gives Aeneas his first direction toward the road that fate has laid out for him.

> "To you Troy now entrusts her religion and her gods;
> take them as companions of your fate, with them seek
> great city walls you will build, after you traverse the sea."
> Those were his words. Then with his hands he brought forth
> powerful Vesta, wreathed, and her fire from the inner shrine.
>
> *Aen.* 2.293–297

Aeneas wakes to the sound of combat, the screams of terrified Trojans, and the crackle of flames. He now faces the first decision that he might make on his own, as a man marked out by destiny. Does he obey Hector's command and leave the doomed city or not?

Without thinking, Aeneas stays and fights. As he looks back from his lofty couch in Dido's banqueting hall, he recognizes that his decision did not make sense. He was not in his right mind (*amens*, *Aen.* 2.314), and rage and anger (*furor iraque*, 2.316), not reason, were driving his intentions. The most important parts of Hector's authoritative message have no meaning for Aeneas. The critical information that he will travel across the sea to found a city and the offer of Troy's household gods play no role in the choice Aeneas makes. Vergil's portrait of Aeneas in the first 250 lines of book 2, as someone whose individual decisions dissolve into the collective actions of the Trojans, lays the groundwork for his first, undeliberated decision and, with it, his failure to follow the fated path that has been announced for him from the first eleven lines of the poem. Mindlessly, irrationally, seized by rage and anger, Aeneas wants only to gather a band of warriors and rush to defend Troy's citadel with his comrades (*cum sociis*, 2.316). That detail, emphatically placed at the beginning of a line, reveals an important part of his thinking at that moment. Servius got it right in his commentary on line 314: Aeneas "wants to show that his first thought was for his homeland but that taking up arms made no sense for him when his homeland was ablaze; for how would he defend a city on fire?" Vergil presents Aeneas' decision as an individual act, but Aeneas is still as much a part of Troy as when he merged his choices into those of his fellow citizens.

Aeneas makes it clear to Dido that while he fought valiantly as Troy fell, he knew, as Servius recognized, that doing so was futile. Like many survivors of combat, Aeneas wonders why he survived and swears that he did nothing to avoid the chances of battle (*Aen.* 2.431–434). He gathers a band of fighters—Panthus, the priest of Apollo; old Iphitus and Pelias; Rhipeus, Epytus, Dymas, and Coroebus, all doomed, all eager to fight—and exhorts them in words that do not conceal the grim reality of their situation: the gods have abandoned Troy, and their little squad is rushing to help a city in flames; if they want to follow a man bold enough to march into his certain end, he tells them, "Let us rush into battle and die—a conquered people's only deliverance is to hope for no deliverance" (2.353–354).[17] The band's desperation finds its predicted outcome: all his named comrades perish along with their city.

Aeneas presents his first actions after his vision of Hector as his and his alone, in a series of first-person singular verbs that parallels the three earlier in the book at lines 5–13: "I rouse myself" (*excutior*, 2.302), "I climb" (*supero*, 2.303), and "I stand" (*asto*, 2.303). As he describes the subsequent fighting, though, Aeneas again merges his will and action with the will of the Trojans, but now his little band of warriors becomes a synecdoche for Troy itself. We do not learn what Greeks Aeneas killed or what, apart from his short, desperate speech to his companions, he said or thought. As he did when he described the questioning of Sinon or the cheering of the fatal horse's entry, he identifies himself with Troy: a Greek, Androgeos, encounters "us" (2.371); "we charge" and "we surround" (*inruimus, circumfundimur*, 2.383) and "we lay them low" (*sternimus*, 2.385). Finally "we"—Aeneas and two survivors of his little squad, one an old man and the other wounded—are separated from the others (*divellimur*, 2.434). They make their way to the royal palace, where the fighting is concentrated. There, Aeneas says, "we see" (*cernimus*, 2.441) the palace gate assaulted by a "tortoise"—a formation of interlocking shields from Roman siegecraft, anachronistic here, but a reminder that the wars of the *Aeneid* are at once the wars of the heroic age and the civil wars of Rome. Aeneas and his comrades join in the defense and "we," help other Trojans topple a tower onto the Greeks (*convellimus*, 2.464; *impulimus*, 2.465).

Then suddenly Aeneas is alone. I do not think that we should imagine him as physically isolated from the remaining Trojans until line 564, where he looks around him to assess his forces and tells Dido, "All have fallen away, either hurled their bodies / to the ground below or, sick with despair, handed them over to the flames" (*Aen.* 2.565–566). Instead, a change in focalization takes us inside Aeneas' mind, as when the camera zooms in on a motion picture character, the motion slows, and ambient sound is replaced by music.[18] He now knows that he is alone. Vergil signals that change with a pair of similes, one comparing Achilles' son Pyrrhus to a snake (2.471–475), the other comparing the onrush of the Greeks to a wave of water overrunning fields when a levee breaks (2.494–499). The second simile introduces a pair of emphatic first-person verbs, marking another change in focus, to Aeneas as individual witness: "I saw" (*vidi*) Pyrrhus raging, he says, Agamemnon and Menelaus, Hecuba and her hundred daughters-in-law, and Priam bleeding out his life on an altar (2.499–502).

At the beginning of book 2, Aeneas had emphasized his two roles in the fall of Troy, as witness to atrocities (*quaeque ipse miserrima vidi*, 2.5) and as major participant (*et quorum pars magna fui*, 2.6). With the anaphoric repetition of "I saw" (*vidi*) five hundred lines later, Aeneas' role as witness becomes foremost, and Vergil's narrative, interrupted by the "Helen episode" (if it belongs in the text), turns to a pair of descriptive episodes: the death of Priam and the epiphany of Venus. Helen is a distraction from the main line of the narrative at this point. From a vantage point overlooking a courtyard in the royal palace, Aeneas witnesses the brutal killing of King Priam (*Aen.* 2.506–558); the sight of the old man breathing his last makes Aeneas think of his father, wife, and son (2.559–563); he looks around and sees that he is all alone (2.564–566). The natural thing for him to do is to make his way home, and that is what he does fifty-seven lines later (2.624–633). In between occur the textually puzzling Helen episode and the epiphany of Venus (discussed in chapter 1 above). No one has ever wanted to deny that the grand vision of the gods dismantling Troy is Vergil's work, but I cannot shake the feeling that it is imperfectly integrated into the text as we have it.[19] Without the Helen episode, Venus' questions to her son at lines 594–595 ("What great pain stirs your uncontrolled anger? Why are you in a rage?") seem unmotivated, since we have just seen him thinking of his family and deliberately assessing his situation, and her mention of Helen at line 601 is hard to explain. Venus may be necessary to help Aeneas make his way home through hostile Greeks, but as commentators note, his statement that he passed through the flames and enemies *ducente deo* ("with a god leading me," not, as we might expect, "a goddess," *dea*) needs explanation.[20]

Venus' presence reinforces Vergil's depiction of Aeneas at the fall of Troy as a man whose agency and decision-making depend on his identity as a member of society—as a Trojan. Through the first 250 lines of book 2, his decisions merge with those of his fellow Trojans; once the Greeks enter Troy, his resistance depends on the presence of a group of *socii* (comrades). When Hector's ghost forces him to choose between leaving Troy and staying to fight, Aeneas chooses mindlessly, as he tells Dido, to stay with Troy. When his last comrades are killed or fall away, he becomes a witness, able only to observe, not act. After Venus shows Aeneas the gods destroying Troy, he remains in witness mode: "All Troy," he says, "seemed to me to be settling into the flames." As before, a simile signals a change in Aeneas' psychological state: Troy is like an ancient ash tree, slowly felled by farmers and slowly collapsing. Venus guides him through the flames to his home and family. Now he must act, and the narrative shifts to first-person singular verbs.[21] From that point on, Aeneas separates himself, his choices, and his actions from those of the surviving Trojans in general and of his followers and family in particular. He uses first-person singular verbs not to position himself as actor or witness but to claim responsibility, as an agent, for what he does; instead of "we part the walls" or "we lay them low," Vergil has him say "I wanted" (*optabam*, 2.636; compare *opto*, 2.655) and "I take myself [to battle]" (*feror*, 2.655).[22]

Aeneas has now received two supernatural instructions to leave Troy, first from Hector and then from Venus, whose speech opens and closes with echoes of Hector's. Both Venus' first word at *Aen.* 2.594, "Son" (*nate*), and her final instruction at 2.619, "Take flight, son" (*eripe, nate, fugam*), recall Hector's first words to Aeneas, "Flee, son of Venus, and snatch yourself from the flames" (*Heu fuge, nate dea, teque . . . eripe flammis*, 2.299). As we have seen, Aeneas ignored Hector's instruction, but he obeys Venus and makes his way to his family's palace. Even so, it will take a third divine intervention to bring him to the point of deciding, finally, to leave his homeland. When he does, one specific order that he gives (and for which he takes responsibility) will cost him his wife.

Even though he is notionally a character from the Bronze Age, living through events that readers in Vergil's lifetime might have imagined as happening ten or eleven centuries before,[23] Aeneas thinks and acts in many ways like a Roman of the first century BC, and Vergil's contemporaries would have understood the difficult situation that Aeneas faces when he returns to his family's palace. In theory (an important qualification), the oldest adult male in a Roman family had absolute power over all other members of his household, including his adult sons. That *patria potestas*, or legally defined paternal power, was unparalleled in other ancient Mediterranean societies, and the Romans traced it back to laws established by their founder Romulus. Dionysius of Halicarnassus, a slightly younger Greek contemporary of Vergil, explained the custom to his Greek readers.

> But the lawgiver of the Romans gave virtually full power to the father over his son, even during his whole life, whether he thought proper to imprison him, to scourge him, to put him in chains and keep him at work in the fields, or to put him to death, and this even though the son were already engaged in public affairs, though he were numbered among the highest magistrates, and though he were celebrated for his zeal for the commonwealth.
>
> *Roman Antiquities* 2.26

Scholars debate the extent to which that primitive harshness was actually practiced,[24] and it seems likely that both legal and cultural measures mitigated the effects of *patria potestas* on adult male sons. For Romans, however, that power remained an ideal and a point of pride. In the second century AD, legal scholar Gaius wrote, "Practically no other men have over their offspring a power such as we have over ours" (*Institutiones* 1.55).

Thus, even when Aeneas returns to his family palace in the face of two supernatural instructions, he is inhibited from making his own decision to leave; before he can, his father, Anchises, must authorize the decision. Aeneas' inhibition is a matter of his defining quality, *pietas*—of, as I have said, accurately appraising social and familial bonds and responding appropriately to them. Anchises does not want to leave. He is old and crippled by the lightning strike Jupiter sent to punish him when he broke his promise to Aeneas' mother not to divulge their dalliance on Mt. Ida. The others can go, Anchises decides, but he will stay and take his own life; Roman readers might have thought of their senators during the Gallic invasion of 390 BC, who refused to leave their palazzos and sat in their halls, dressed in their robes of state and holding their insignia of office, waiting for the invaders to kill them (Livy 5.41).

Faced by his father's intransigence, Aeneas reproaches both his parents; his first word, *mene*, and the infinitives that follow, *efferre* and *posse*, recall Juno's outburst of rage at the beginning of the poem, *mene incepto desistere victim nec posse Italia Teucrorum avertere regem!* (*Aen.* 1.37–38). Desperate and angry, Aeneas can think of nothing else but to go on fighting until the end.

> Do you expect, father, that I can set foot outside this house
> and leave you behind? Has so shameful a word fallen
> from my begetter's mouth? If the gods want nothing left
> of this great city, and you get some pleasure from adding
> yourself and your family to Troy's destruction, a door lies open
> to that death: soon Achilles' son will arrive, drenched
> in Priam's blood, the man who butchered the son
> before the father's face, butchered the father at an altar.
> Was this why, dear mother, you rescued me from spears
> and fire? To see the enemy trampling our household shrines,
> my son, my father, my wife, slaughtered in each other's blood?
> To arms, men! To arms! Troy's last dawn summons the conquered.
> Let me at the Greeks; let me go back and renew the battle—
> Today none of us will die without taking revenge.
>
> *Aen.* 2.657–670

Aeneas invites his father to picture himself as the aged patriarch Priam, butchered along with the last of his family. He does not need to spell out what may be in his mind, perhaps below the level of conscious thought: that with Priam and all his sons dead, Anchises, Aeneas, and Aeneas' son, Iulus/Ascanius, are the only remaining male descendants of Dardanus, Ericthonius, and Tros, the royal stock of Troy. Anchises is now king of Troy, and Aeneas' responsibility to his family is also responsibility for his homeland.

Just as Aeneas is buckling on his sword and slipping his arm into the strap of his shield for what he believes will be his final battle, the gods intervene to confirm his family's royal destiny. As Creusa implores him to stay and defend her, their son, and Anchises, a miraculous flame begins to flicker from little Iulus' hair. That omen, like the flame that flickered in the hair of the sleeping Servius Tullius (Livy 1.39), marks Iulus as a future king. Anchises, though, remains unconvinced and prays to Jupiter: if the god answers prayers, if the house of Anchises has done anything in its *pietas* to deserve a response, let the lord of the sky confirm the omen. One can almost sense Jupiter's exasperation at the old man's stubbornness. Thunder crashes on the left (a good omen), and a meteor streaks across the sky; to rule out all ambiguity, it crashes into Mount Ida, making it clear not only that they should leave but in which direction.

In telling Dido the story of Troy's fall, Aeneas has thus far presented himself as someone whose individual decision-making merges with Trojan collective action, as someone who ignores compelling instructions from a dead kinsman in a dream, as an efficient but oddly detached fighter, as a spectator to horrifying events, and as a man guided to his home by his divine mother and, once there, inhibited from action by the authority of his father. At the banquet in Carthage, Aeneas knows that he and the other Trojans fell into the Greeks' trap because of ignorance, that he was deluded by rage when he forgot or ignored Hector's instructions, that fighting at Troy was a doomed cause, and that the events there could not have happened otherwise; deciding to override Anchises' wish to die in the sack of Troy was simply not possible in the moral universe within which Aeneas' operates. Aeneas makes it clear to Dido that, in hindsight, he regrets the decisions not made or made incorrectly because of ignorance or anger.

As his story continues, Aeneas is at last free to deliberate, decide, and act on his decisions. He gives a crisp series of orders (*Aen.* 2.707–720): he will carry Anchises on his shoulders and lead little Iulus by the hand, while Creusa follows *longe*, "at a distance." As we shall see, the word *longe* bears a heavy burden of interpretation in the light of what happens as they leave the city. Aeneas instructs his household to rendezvous outside the city walls at an abandoned temple of Ceres, marked by an ancient cypress tree. Anchises must carry their household gods, since Aeneas cannot touch them, because he is ritually unclean from the blood that still spatters him after his night of combat. Since, after Priam's death, Anchises is now in effect king of Troy, his household gods are now also the gods of Troy. The little family group begins to make its way through the burning city and the mopping-up operations of the Greeks.

Aeneas is (as he later admits to Dido) terrified by the responsibility he has for his family and for Troy. He could face Greek spears and battle lines undaunted; now, every gust of air frightens him (*Aen.* 2.726–729). Then Anchises thinks he sees Greeks approaching; the old man panics, and for the third time, Aeneas hears the words "Flee, son" (*fuge, nate*). He runs into an unfamiliar part of town, through winding streets that he has never seen, until he somehow reaches the rendezvous that he had arranged with his household. Only then does he notice that Creusa is not with him.

No fellow Trojan advised Aeneas to order Creusa to follow "at a distance"; no dream instructed him; no god took his hand. He alone gave the order that seems to have led directly to his wife's loss. When she disappears, does he not bear at least some share of responsibility for the consequences of his decision? The ghost of Creusa tells him, "This did not happen without the will of the gods; it is not right for you to convey Creusa from here, and the ruler of lofty Olympus does not allow it." But is that enough to save Aeneas' *pietas*? There has been no shortage of critics ready to blame him for the loss or to imagine that it complicates a simple understanding of his key quality. Perhaps the first to blame him was Ovid, who imagines Dido writing to accuse him of serial abandonment.

> You're a total liar, your tongue didn't begin its deceit
> with me, and I am not the first to be abused.
> If you ask where pretty Iulus' mother is, well,
> she died—abandoned by her harsh husband.
>
> *Heroides* 7.81–84

Nearer our own time, Christine Perkell looks at Aeneas' treatment of both Creusa and Dido and concludes, "This collocation of departure, female casualty, denied responsibility, and *pietas* is intended to reflect an incomplete humanity in Aeneas and in the *pietas* which he exemplifies" (1981, 370). Other critics have been more willing to sympathize with Aeneas but agree that his decision, its consequences, and his response complicate the picture of his central virtue.[25]

Understanding Aeneas as a moral agent and evaluating his choices—liking or disliking him, praising or blaming—require a close look at how he and Vergil think about and assign responsibility for the consequences of Aeneas' first deliberate, individual decision.

When Aeneas describes Creusa's loss to Dido, the first thing he says is that some unfriendly divine power (*male numen amicum*) had muddled his thinking (*Aen.* 2.725–736). He then suggests that the cause is uncertain. Was she carried off by some unlucky fate? Did she get lost? Simply slip down by the side of the road (2.738–739)? Whatever the reason, he says, he never saw her again (*nec post oculis est reddita nostris*, 2.740). That claim seems at odds with what he says only thirty lines later: that Creusa's ghost appeared to him and told him that what had happened accorded with the will of the gods. But when he describes that apparition, Aeneas is careful to qualify it, in three ways, as seeming not quite Creusa herself: it is a *simulacrum*, a "likeness"; an *umbra*, a "ghost" or "shade"; and an *imago*, an "image" (2.772–773). Here as when he woke from sleep and ignored Hector's advice to flee the city, Aeneas seems not to remember or understand what he hears from a supernatural vision. Creusa or her ghost tells him that after traversing a vast expanse of sea, he will come to a land called Hesperia, watered by the river Thybris (Tiber).[26] But in the first stages of his exile, he seems unaware of his destination and unsuccessfully attempts to restart Troy in Thrace, Delos, and Crete. Finally, just before he makes landfall in Italy, the prophet Helenus echoes Creusa's words and repeats the name of the river.[27]

Before Creusa's ghost appears to him, Aeneas' immediate reaction is to look for some external agent, either human or divine, who can be blamed for her disappearance: "What man, what god did I not accuse in my madness?" (*Aen.* 2.745). For the second time, he acknowledges to Dido that he acted irrationally, that he was out of his mind (*amens*), just as he had been when he woke after Hector appeared to him in his sleep (2.314). This time, though, he acts alone. He returns to the city and retraces his steps through streets and alleys now deserted. He makes his way to his ancestral mansion and finds it overrun with Greeks. He goes back to the royal palace, where he had witnessed the butchering of Priam; now Phoenix and Ulysses are overseeing the distribution of plunder, including lines of Trojan women and boys now looking at lives as Greek slaves. Finally, he makes Creusa's name echo through the deserted streets, in language that recalls Vergil's own account of Orpheus' loss of Eurydice at *Georgics* 4.486–527.[28] (In at least one earlier Roman version of the Aeneas legend, his wife was named

Eurydice.)[29] Aeneas' solitary search for his wife in the gloomy light of dying Troy becomes a literal anticipation of his later journey to the shadowy underworld of book 6.

It is possible, I suppose, to claim that because Creusa's loss was fated (because, as her ghost tells him at *Aen.* 2.783–784, he is destined to find a royal bride in the land watered by the Tiber), Aeneas bears no responsibility for it. But doing so means falling back on the discredited "Idle Argument" that Cicero condemned and Chrysippus tried to refute. Aeneas' own assessment of his responsibility reveals three things: first, even when Aeneas seems to choose and act without human advice or divine intervention, the complex view of distributed moral responsibility found in Pindar and throughout Greek and Roman thought still holds, and he retains his identity as *pius Aeneas*; second, in the world of the *Aeneid*, Aeneas chooses and acts belatedly, within a nexus of cause and effect created by a future that he cannot know (within, that is, the constraints of fate); and third, at this point in Vergil's narrative, Aeneas has not yet emerged as fully shaped by his heroic destiny.

In Troy, even when he chooses and acts without human advice or divine direction, Aeneas acts as a member of a society woven together by civic and familial threads. Those ties extend to the gods, both the great gods who are abandoning Troy and the household and civic gods that travel with him. Aeneas' distinguishing virtue, his *pietas*, grows out of that web of connection; as Pindar says, it "waxes as the vine growth in the young green tendrils, raised up among the men who are righteous and wise" (*Nemean* 8.40a–42, discussed earlier in this chapter). In such a world, a moral agent cannot bear sole responsibility for his or her actions. At Troy, Aeneas cannot be an autonomous, rational agent of the kind that Kant imagined. He presented his first decisions there as coextensive with those of the Trojans. His final decision is no less so. Even the orders that he gives to his family and household as they prepare to leave Troy belong to a world knit together from patriarchal families, shared civic institutions, and divine presences. Although he seems to give those fatal orders without input from his family, other Trojans, or the gods, his reaction when they go wrong reveals his belief in the collective nature of his own agency.

When he seeks to distribute responsibility for Creusa's disappearance—was it human accident, fate, or some malign divinity—Aeneas is not (as he easily can seem to be to a reader embedded in modern ideas of moral autonomy) attempting to deflect blame from himself. He is continuing to reason as he has since the Trojans looked out and saw the Greek camp empty and the great wooden horse on the shore. All his decisions at Troy are shaped not only by his own desires and reasoning but also by the desires, reasons, actions, status, or mere presence of other agents—chiefly his father and the gods, but also his wife, his son, and his fellow Trojans. Within Aeneas' world, there is no reason that he should look to himself as the sole cause of any decision he makes. That complex view of distributed moral responsibility remains Aeneas' default mode even after he and his band of exiles become all that remains of Troy; as we saw at the beginning of this chapter, his decision to continue on to Italy even after many of his ships have been burnt depends on the advice of a senior Trojan, a vision of his recently deceased father, and (Aeneas says) a command of Jupiter.

But now, as Aeneas tells his story to Dido in Carthage, seven summers have passed since Troy fell (*Aen.* 1.755–766), and Anchises is recently dead. Aeneas is looking back on his homeland's final night. He is no longer the man who awakened to find his city in flames, fought through the night, and carried his father into exile with his son at his side and his wife first following, then lost. Throughout his tale, Aeneas sounds a note of regret and incomplete understanding: if only we Trojans had been in our right minds, and fate not against us (2.54–56); if only we had not been blinded by mad excitement as the horse stumbled on the threshold of Troy's walls or noticed the clatter of weapons from its belly (2.240–245), Troy would still be standing. Even in Carthage and before he met Dido, Aeneas' eyes picked out from the paintings in Juno's temple scenes that recalled omens of Troy's fall, omens that the Trojans should have heeded.[30]

In Carthage, Aeneas looks back on the last night of Troy and knows what to regret. He can see that at several points he was in the grip of a kind of madness—*amens*, out of his mind, or moved by powerful emotions, rage (*furor*) or anger (*ira*).[31] In his seven years of exile, he has learned to see the fall of Troy as an event implicated in a larger structure of events that he only partially understands. He has received guidance, as he tells Dido in book 3, from Anchises, who interprets (not always correctly) the meaning of a series of apparitions, visions, and prophecies. After the ghost of Priam's murdered son Polydorus warns him not to settle in Thrace, where Aeneas makes his first landfall, Apollo's oracle on Delos offers the cryptic advice to "seek your ancient mother" (*Aen.* 3.96). Anchises interprets this saying to mean Crete, but when attempts to found a new Troy there have failed, Apollo, acting through the Trojan Penates (the family gods that Aeneas had transported from Troy), explains that the Trojans' goal must be Italy, the land the Greeks call Hesperia, ancestral home of one branch of the Trojan race (3.147–178). Finally, in northwestern Greece, another Trojan exile, the seer Helenus, confirms Aeneas' destination but predicts that the hero will reach his final landfall only after a roundabout series of detours and a visit to the Cumaean Sibyl, from whom he will receive further information (3.374–461).

When he looks back on the loss of Creusa and recalls how he reacted to it, Aeneas has to remember not only the events of that night but the lost framework of duties, obligations, and loyalties within and with which he made his choices. As he will in the underworld, he undertakes a difficult journey into his past. In words whose spondaic rhythm makes them seem almost dragged from him, he tells Dido that the pain she invites him to renew is unspeakable.[32] But speak it he does, because what has happened to him since the fall of Troy has showed him that the events of that night, including the loss of his wife, are part of a world in which his life seems to make sense, in which it tends toward a goal. As far as he knows at this point in his exile, that goal is Hesperia, or Italy, where he will rebuild Troy in all its glory. Readers of the *Aeneid*, though, with the prologue and Jupiter's speech (*Aen.* 1.257–296) behind them, understand that Aeneas' knowledge is incomplete, that he will never apprehend the sense that his life makes. Its larger structure must remain meaningless to him. He will not, in Lacan's phrasing, get better because he remembers, because the events that give meaning to his past are in a future that he will never know.

To exercise moral choice in a world shaped by fate and altered forever by the destruction of Troy, not only must Aeneas enact his defining quality of *pietas* by making choices that affirm his membership in a society where civic and familial threads have been frayed or broken, but he must also align his choices with an inevitable future that he cannot know. As he tells his story to Dido, his realization that the guidance he is given is and will remain incomplete or open to misinterpretation accounts for the note of regret that sounds again and again when he looks back to Troy. One by one, the elements to which *pietas* responds have fallen away: Troy is gone, his wife and father are dead, and he will soon leave a good part of his band of exiles in Sicily. He must now construct a new *pietas*, which will consist in understanding as best he can the road that fate has charted for him and making his way along it. Critics are right to point out that, as one puts it, by including "elements of forgetfulness, resentment, frustration and disappointment in Aeneas' account of the loss of Creusa, Virgil prevents a completely straightforward understanding of his *pietas*" (Grillo 2010, 65). But the incomplete, tortured understanding is not entirely ironic, a matter of the reader seeing something that a character in the narrative fails to recognize. Vergil presents his hero as responsible for and aware of the problem of what his *pietas* means. The fall of Troy is not all that Aeneas finds unspeakable. He struggles to know what it could mean to preserve a virtue when the world that gave it meaning has vanished, or to practice *pietas* between the end of one world and the beginning of another.

At this point, it is useful to turn again to the Lacanian idea of "perversion," which I used in chapter 1 as a way to think about what many readers regard as Aeneas' lack of a will or subject position of his own. Lacan used the term *perversion* as a clinical term for cases in which someone conflates his or her own desires with those of some other entity, or as Lacanians would say, with those of the Other. To many readers, including James Porter (2004, 138), Aeneas has seemed to be just such a Lacanian pervert, blindly following the instructions of fate and the gods without exercising any will or choice of his own. But if I am right to suggest that Aeneas' regret for lost Troy is also a regret for the divine and human society that made his *pietas* possible, Aeneas gains agency by struggling to preserve and redefine his signal virtue—his identity—in a world that he barely understands and whose meaning he can never know. His ironic self-introduction at *Aen.* 1.378, *sum pius Aeneas,* gives a glimpse of that struggle, which is often waged in silence, just beneath the surface of the narrative. When it does come to the surface, as it does in Vergil's framing of Aeneas' responses to Mercury's commands that he leave Carthage and to Dido's reproaches (*Aen.* 4.279–295, 393–396; discussed in chapter 1 above), it is often obscured by the overarching authority of the *Aeneid*'s plan and the tragedies of characters who, like Dido, have no place in it. But Aeneas is far from conflating his own desires with those entailed by that plan. He knows the difference. As he travels the road dimly charted for him by fate, moral agency consists in separating those desires from his choices. The struggle to do so is what *pietas* means, now that Troy is gone.

CHAPTER 4

The Silences of Aeneas

Ite meae, felix quondam pecus, ite capellae.
Non ego vos posthac viridi proiectus in antro
Dumosa pendere procul de rupe videbo;
Carmina nulla canam.

Go on your way, once happy flock, go now, my goats.
From my green and shady cave I will watch you no more
hanging in the distance on a brushy crag.
I will sing no more songs.

Vergil, *Bucolics* 1.74–77

Sometime after 42 BC and about a decade before he began writing the *Aeneid*, Vergil wrote the *Bucolics*, a group of poems full of silences, memory, and forgetting.[1] Those silences shed light on Aeneas' silent struggle to preserve and redefine his *pietas*. Into the *Bucolics* intrude civil wars and the civic collapse that they brought. One of those poems, *Bucolics* 9, imagines an encounter between two rustic characters, Lycidas and Moeris. (A Lycidas appears in the seventh *Idyll* of Vergil's Hellenistic Greek model, Theocritus, and the names of Vergil's pair embed them in the literary tradition of pastoral poetry.) Moeris is trudging down a road somewhere near Mantua, carrying a wooden crate with kids destined for market. Lycidas gives him a cheery greeting, but Moeris' reply takes us from the imaginary setting of pastoral poetry to the Roman reality of the land confiscations that followed the battle of Philippi.

> Oh Lycidas, to think we've lived to come to this—that an outlander squatting on our little holding (something we've never worried about) would say, "This is my land now! *Former* tenants, find somewhere else!"

Now beaten, sad, seeing that Fortune has overthrown everything,
we're sending these kids to market for *him*—may he get no joy from it.
Buc. 9.2–6

Lycidas is surprised—he had heard that a famous singer, Menalcas, had somehow used his poems to get Moeris' land restored to him. Not only is that rumor false, says Moeris, but both he and Menalcas were at risk of losing their lives during the confiscations.

In the idealized and idyllic countryside of pastoral poetry, shepherds forever woo nymphs and engage in song contests, green shade entices goatherds to contemplation while their flocks graze in the middle distance, and the stink and hard work of real country life are kept just out of sight, though never entirely out of mind.[2] Songs and poetry knit that world together and make things happen in it; thus it is not at all unreasonable for Lycidas to believe the rumor that Menalcas used a song to restore Moeris' land. When Lycidas hears that Menalcas himself had been in danger, Lycidas wonders who would make the turf burst into bloom or bring shade to the springs if Menalcas is gone, as though Menalcas' song could create the things that it celebrates (*Buc.* 9.19–20).

Memory plays a crucial part in this world created out of song. The shepherds of Arcadia do not always improvise but sometimes remember songs, their own or someone else's. The first *Idyll* of Theocritus begins with a request for a memorized song: a goatherd asks a shepherd, Thyrsis, to sing one of his past hits, "The Griefs of Daphnis" (Theocritus 1.19). Vergil picks up this theme in *Bucolics* 5, where Mopsus and Menalcas trade songs on the death of Daphnis; Mopsus, who is an instrumentalist as well as a singer, has written down his song to set it to music (5.13–15), but Menalcas offers a song from memory, one that he composed long ago (5.55).

In *Bucolics* 9, that world of memory and exchanged song threatens to fall apart and grow silent, as contemporary events put pressure on the pastoral idyll.[3] Lycidas and Moeris try to recall some of the songs of Menalcas. First, Lycidas remembers three lines from a song that Menalcas sang for someone called Amaryllis as Lycidas quietly eavesdropped (*sublegi tacitus*, *Buc.* 9.21). Then Moeris suggests another song, one that Menalcas once sang for Varus. Thus Publius Alfenus Varus, one of the commissioners in charge of appropriating and assigning land for the triumvirs' veterans in the aftermath of the battle of Philippi, crashes into the pastoral idyll. Once again, the broken world of proscriptions and confiscations intrudes on Arcadia. Moeris can remember these lines:

> Varus, singing swans will bear your name aloft to the stars,
> if only Mantua survives for us, poor Mantua,
> all too near to Cremona.
>
> *Buc.* 9.27–29

Lycidas wants Moeris, who is clearly grieving for the loss of his little farm, to try to remember a different song (30–36), and Moeris struggles to comply: "That's what I'm doing, Lycidas, and I've been pondering silently [*tacitus*], to see if I can remember" (38–39). He manages to bring out five lines of a standard pastoral song, based on Theocritus' *Idyll* 11, about the sea nymph Galatea. But he breaks off because he remembers the meter but cannot retain the words (*Buc.* 9.45).[4] Lycidas responds with another quotation from Menalcas, one that also makes reference to contemporary events but puts a hopeful spin on them.

> Daphnis, why do you gaze up at old constellations rising?
> Look—the star of Caesar, descendant of Dione, has come out,
> a star to make fields of wheat rejoice in their yield,
> to bring color to the grapes on sunny terraces.
> Graft your pears, Daphnis—your grandchildren will pick your fruit.
>
> *Buc.* 9.46–50

The star is the *sidus Iulium*, the "Julian star," a comet that appeared in the northern sky for a week in July of 44 BC, four months after Caesar's assassination and at the moment when Caesar's heir, Octavian, was presiding over a festival that his adoptive father had instituted two years earlier.[5] Vergil has his optimistic shepherd interpret the Julian star as a sign of returning prosperity, perhaps even a foreshadowing of the returning Golden Age of *Bucolics* 4.

The good times will not return for Moeris. The disruption of civil war, the confiscation of his little farm, and the destruction of the way of life that he thought would go on forever ("something we never worried about," *Buc.* 9.3) have made the music vanish from his world.

> Time carries everything away, and memory with it. Often as a boy,
> I remember, I used to set the suns to rest with singing.
> Now I've forgotten so many songs, language itself
> now flees from Moeris: the wolves have taken Moeris' tongue.
>
> *Buc.* 9.51–54[6]

For Vergil's broken shepherd, civil war, proscriptions, and land confiscation have not merely disrupted the social and political order. They have intruded into the world of pastoral song and obliterated it. Memory creates that song world, and forgetting silences it.

Memory and forgetting also helped to shape the turbulent political sea into which Vergil launched the *Bucolics*. The aristocrats who competed to dominate senate and provinces in the Roman Republic had always framed their rivalries as struggles over memory and advertised their importance to the commonwealth with monumental tombs, buildings, and dedications to the gods. In this arena as in so many other things, the civil wars of the eighties BC between Sulla and his rivals changed the rules. Sulla's proscription of his political enemies after he recaptured Rome from the partisans of Cinna in November of 82 BC marked what one historian has called a "caesura in Roman memory" (Flower 2006, 90). Sulla no longer sought, as his grandfathers might have, to overshadow his political rivals' reputations and to be favored above them in memory.[7] Instead, he set out to obliterate them. Those who were proscribed lost their wealth and thus their ability to create monuments to their memory, and their descendants were prohibited from holding public office for two generations. Sulla reserved special memory sanctions for his greatest rival, Marius, who had engaged in his own memory war against the dictator. Sulla ordered the ashes of his dead rival to be dug up and scattered in the Anio River.[8] Marius' relatives, such as his unfortunate nephew Marcus Marius Gratidianus, found themselves at the top of the proscription lists. At Rome, portrait statues of Marius and the trophies commemorating his victories were destroyed, and Sulla recalled and overstruck coins issued by Marius (Varner 2004, 18).

Julius Caesar remembered Sulla and pondered his example. Early in his career, Caesar played the same game of shaping and sanctioning memory but from the other side of the board; he set out to reverse Sulla's attempt to obliterate Marius from the public record.[9] At the public funeral of his aunt Julia, Marius' widow, Caesar displayed the *imagines* of Marius and his relatives. Such portraits of distinguished ancestors were a customary part of Roman aristocratic funerals, and bringing Marius back into the Forum earned Caesar criticism but also popular favor; as Plutarch says (*Life of Caesar* 5), the people "received Caesar with applause and admired him for bringing back, as it were from Hades, the honors of Marius into the city." Four years later, as aedile (the official in charge of public works at Rome), Caesar restored the statues and trophies of Marius that Sulla had removed (Plutarch, *Life of Caesar* 6). As civil war with

Pompey loomed in the early forties BC, however, Caesar developed a policy of *clementia* (mercy or forgiveness) that he intentionally opposed to Sulla's example.[10] Once secure in power, Octavian followed his adoptive father's trajectory from Sullan contestation of memory to measured clemency. After the defeat of Brutus and the other assassins (or liberators) at the battle of Philippi in 42 BC, Octavian vowed to build a temple to Mars the Avenger; he also sent Brutus' head to Rome to be thrown down at the feet of Caesar's statue (Suetonius, *Augustus* 13). The temple was not dedicated until 2 BC, but by then Octavian had metamorphosed into Augustus and his proofs of clemency were, his ancient biographer says, too numerous to count (Suetonius, *Augustus* 51).

During the civil wars that followed Julius Caesar's assassination and into the creation of the Augustan principate—during, that is, Vergil's creative life—the questions of who to remember, how to remember, and whether to speak or keep silence acquired new urgency and complexity. Julius Caesar's legacy was a two-edged sword: on one hand, Octavian's claim to power depended on his legacy from the dictator; on the other, the example of a politician whose unprecedented, absolute power led to his assassination was uncomfortable to contemplate. As Ronald Syme explained, "Seeking to establish continuity with a legitimate government, Caesar's heir forswore the memory of Caesar: in the official conception, the Dictatorship and the Triumvirate were blotted from the record" (1939, 317). Perhaps the best course was to declare Julius Caesar a divinity, as duly happened. Some commemorated the cabal of senators who had killed him as liberators, whose example, tucked safely away in the works of historians like Livy or Asinius Pollio, could guide principled opposition to any autocrat who forgot the fiction that the *princeps* was merely first among his senatorial peers; others remembered them as assassins, no better than the warlords whose rivalries had brought down the republic and led to proscriptions, confiscations, and the breakdown of moral and civic order (Flower 2006, 108–109). Knowing what to say and whether to say it posed a challenge not only for political actors but for anyone within range of the powerful. As Horace advised Asinius Pollio in 23 BC, reaching back to recover memories of the recent past could easily become a work fraught with hazard (*periculosae plenum opus aleae, Odes* 2.1.6).

Vergil's two shepherds map these anxieties about silence and memory onto the delicate landscape of pastoral poetry. The hard realities of civil war have taken Moeris' little farm and, with it, the songs and human relationships that gave meaning to his life. *Aetas*, he says, carries everything away, even memory (*Buc.* 9.51). The word *aetas*, which I translated as "time" above, can also mean "the time(s)"; with one word, Moeris acknowledges that he is growing older and that he lives in a time when silence is one outcome of trying to remember. Lycidas takes a more optimistic view.

> By pleading you move my desire into the distance.
> Now all the sea grows quiet, and look, all the murmuring
> breaths of wind have died. Here is the middle of our road,
> for the tomb of Bianor comes into view. Here, where
> farmers are pruning their orchards, here let us sing.
> Put the kids down here; we'll get to the city all the same.
> Or, if we worry that night may bring in rain,
> we may go singing on our way—the road will bother us less.
> So that we may go singing, I'll carry the crate for you.
>
> *Buc.* 9.56–65

Lycidas believes that he can sing his way through a world that is growing silent. For him, the times demand not songs about the old constellations, but something like Menalcas' verses on the new star of Caesar (9.46–50). Yet Lycidas and Moeris are only halfway along their journey, and that midpoint is marked by a visible, built evocation of memory, the tomb of Bianor. In the closing lines of the poem, Moeris demurs, "Stop, boy—no more. Let us do the job at hand; / we will sing our songs better when the master comes" (9.66–67). *Bucolics* 9—with its unresolved tension between the songs of Lycidas and Menalcas, its silences first of Moeris and then of the world around, and the offstage presence of civil war and its consequences—presents the breakdown of society as a silencing and a forgetting, and it cautiously offers poetry as a way through to an unseen future. It is a good place from which to begin thinking about what Aeneas' silences mean.

What Aeneas Doesn't Say

At the midpoint of his journey to Rome, Moeris responds to the loss of his home by falling silent and by forgetting the songs that knit his life together. Aeneas also responds to loss and exile with silence and failures of speech, and at the midpoint of his journey, a wall of silence begins to divide him from his inmost thoughts. His silences and failures emerge from his complex relationship not only to the trauma of his past but also to the hope of his unknowable future. Aeneas' silence exists in dialogue with memory and forgetting as he moves from Troy to Italy and from past to barely understood future. For Vergil, silence and song, forgetting and memory, opened up one possible path through the precarious stability of the early Augustan principate, toward a future that remained in the distance when he died in 19 BC. That path led him to imagine a hero who, like Moeris, falls silent and forgets.

Epic depends on speech and dialogue to advance its narrative; there are nearly seven hundred speeches in the *Iliad* and a similar number in the *Odyssey*. An epic hero cannot be mute, but Aeneas is comparatively reticent and grows more so as the poem advances. Gilbert Highet counts 333 speeches in the *Aeneid*. Aeneas speaks 69 times, for a total of 527 lines, excluding his first-person narrative in books 2 and 3. He speaks 345 lines over 44 speeches in books 1–6, but only 182 lines over 25 speeches in books 7–12.[11] Dido, in contrast, who speaks only in books 1 and 4, speaks 13 times, for 231 lines—more in two books than Aeneas in the entire second half of the epic. Other characters in the *Aeneid* also tend to eschew debate, conversation, and dialogue; they speak at each other, not to each other (Feeney 1983, 210–219). Aeneas speaks once to his son (*Aen.* 12.435–440), and Ascanius never speaks to his father.

The Journey to Italy: Speech Frustrated

Silence comes in many forms, and being sparing of utterance is only one of them. Especially in the first half of the *Aeneid*, Aeneas often wants to speak or continue speaking, but something prevents him. Sometimes a supernatural event renders him speechless: the specter of Creusa (*Aen.* 2.774), the subterranean ghost of Polydorus (3.48), or the epiphany of Mercury at Carthage (4.279–280). After the messenger god's appearance, Aeneas issues terse sailing orders to his captains and then retreats into desperate, silent isolation, as he tries to work out how to approach Dido; in the end, she anticipates his announcement, as rumor confirms her latent suspicions (4.296–299).[12] The Vergilian formula that describes those silences after supernatural events, *vox faucibus haesit* ("his voice stuck in his throat"), appears only once in the second half of the *Aeneid* (12.868), where it describes Turnus as he recognizes the demon that Juno has sent as a portent of his death.

Interrupting or shutting off speech is also a form of silencing. Aeneas is often frustrated when he tries to speak with those about whom he cares; again, these occasions concentrate in the first half of the *Aeneid*. The first of them appears early in the poem and is the third occasion on which Aeneas speaks.

Shortly after the Trojans land at Carthage, Aeneas encounters his mother, Venus, disguised as a huntress (*Aen.* 1.305–410). He suspects that she is a goddess, but she stays in character and, in the best epic fashion, asks him who he is, where he comes from, and where he is bound.[13] Venus thus foreshadows Dido's later request for the story of Aeneas' wanderings (1.754–756), and her request contributes to an identification of Aeneas' mother with his lover, which lurks (as we saw in chapter 1) below the level of the text's consciousness. Aeneas finds it difficult to answer Venus' questions, just as he will find it difficult to speak his unspeakable grief (*infandum dolorem*, 2.3) to Dido.

> To Venus' questions the hero replied,
> sighing, dragging his voice from the depths of his heart,
> "O goddess, if I go back to the beginning of my story,
> and you have time to hear the history of our toils,
> evening will lay the day to sleep and shutter Olympus."
>
> *Aen.* 1.370–374

He goes on, though, to begin an answer: he is Aeneas, a Trojan, cast away on Libyan shores, carrying the Trojan Penates and on his way to Italy. Then in five and one-half lines (1.381–385), he begins to catalog his toils: twenty ships left Troy, barely seven survive; he is a stranger in need, driven from Europe and Asia and wandering in an African wasteland. Perhaps, unlike Dido, his mother does not have patience for a story that will take all day. She interrupts him mid-complaint (*medio sic interfata dolore est*, 1.386) and dismisses his introduction: "Whoever you are, I believe, you breathe this life-giving air and are not hated by the gods above" (1.387–388). She gives him curt instructions—keep going, get yourself to the queen's doorstep—and follows up with an elaborate and partially accurate interpretation of a bird omen that conveniently appears overhead.[14] Then she drops her disguise (and possibly her clothing, as discussed in chapter 1) and vanishes. It is no wonder that Aeneas is hurt yet again.

> When he recognized his mother
> as she ran away, he followed her with these words:
> "Cruel like the rest! Why do you play tricks on your son
> so many times? Why am I not allowed to join my hand
> to yours, to hear and answer honest words?"
>
> *Aen.* 1.405–409

Aeneas' first speech in the *Aeneid* (1.94–101) reveals one aspect of his condition as the narrative begins: his longing for Troy and his despairing sense that heroic death there might have given his life some meaning. His second speech, to his men after the landing at Carthage (1.198–207), established another essential aspect of his character: the difference between his public utterance and his private thoughts. His encounter with Venus at Carthage, the third occasion on which he speaks, establishes a pattern that will recur in his interactions with others: attempts to connect or communicate, followed by frustration. In book 2, astonished at the nocturnal vision of his dead cousin Hector, Aeneas blurts out a series of questions. The apparition answers none of them, and Aeneas himself acknowledges that the questions were useless (2.287). Later in book 2, the apparition of his wife, Creusa, fades from him as he weeps, leaving many things unsaid; he tries three times to put his arms around her and finds nothing but empty air each time (2.790–794). Three identical lines describe his attempt to embrace the shade of his father in the underworld;[15] earlier in the same book, the Sibyl frustrates Aeneas' attempt to continue a conversation with his dead comrade Deiphobus. In book 5, before the visit to the underworld, the dead Anchises appears to Aeneas by night and fades away as Venus did at Carthage, leaving Aeneas frustrated.

> He finished speaking and fled like smoke into thin air.
> "Where are you hurrying?" says Aeneas, "Where rushing?
> Who are you fleeing? Who keeps you from my embrace?"
>
> *Aen.* 5.740–742

His penultimate question to Anchises echoes in the underworld, when Dido refuses to speak or look at him and stalks away to join her husband, Sychaeus (6.450–476). Not all such encounters are with divinities or the dead; even his discreditable performance in the great triptych of speeches at the center of book 4 culminates in frustration, as he leaves his deepest feelings for Dido unsaid.

Aeneas' most revealing silences, however, fall in the gap between his inner life, which readers only occasionally glimpse, and his expressed thoughts. Vergil makes it clear that Aeneas is a man whose thoughts cannot always be known from his words or demeanor. His second speech in the poem (*Aen.* 1.198–209), in which he encouraged his men with a hopeful expression but repressed his own deep sorrow, is not unique. After the Trojans land in Italy, Aeneas and

Achates discover the body of their trumpeter, Misenus, who has been missing—he foolishly challenged a sea god to a musical contest and was drowned for his presumption. The Trojans begin to cut down trees for a funeral pyre, and Aeneas, again showing the kind of leadership that makes his men want to follow him, puts on work clothes and toils alongside them (6.183–184). Even as he does this, though, he is once again gripped by sadness, communing with his gloomy heart: *atque haec ipse suo tristi cum corde volutat* (6.185).

In Italy: Speech Inaccessible

When he encourages his men by his words during the landing at Carthage and by his actions in Italy, Aeneas conceals thoughts of which he is aware. He knows that his sadness and worry might have an adverse effect on morale at critical times. In the first stages of his exile, his father, Anchises, guides him. Even after Anchises' death, Aeneas consults friends and counselors at moments of perplexity, as he does in Sicily after the loss of part of his fleet (*Aen.* 5.700–718). Once he reaches Italy, though, his thoughts and feelings, his perplexities and fears, remain behind a wall of silence that even he sometimes cannot penetrate. He becomes increasingly isolated and faces critical situations alone and in silence. In the second half of the poem, Vergil allows readers to see behind the veil of Aeneas' silence through the words of divine interlocutors who appear to Aeneas during his moments of silent perturbation. Two drivers of his approach to his immediate situation, fear and anxiety for the future, disappear from his awareness but not from his psyche.

The second half of *Aeneid* 7 describes Juno's interference in the initially peaceful encounter between the Trojans and the inhabitants of Latium, the beginnings of war, and the gathering of Italian allies under the leadership of Turnus. At the beginning of book 8, Vergil summarizes the situation and introduces Aeneas alone on the bank of the Tiber, troubled by the grim war that, as the Cumaean Sibyl had foretold, is now inevitable. His thoughts surge from one problem to another, in a billowing wave of worry (*magno curarum fluctuat aestu, Aen.* 8.19); Vergil compares these thoughts to light darting over a coffered ceiling as it is reflected from a mirror or a disturbed bowl of water (8.22–25). At last Aeneas tries to rest, and in his sleep, the god of the Tiber appears to him. The river god assures him of his destiny as guardian of the memory of Troy and founder of a new Trojan homeland in Italy (8.36–39); tells him to look for a confirming omen, a white sow with thirty piglets (8.42–48); and gives him a plan: to seek an alliance with King Evander, the Greek who has settled upriver on what will become the site of Rome (8.49–65).[16] Aeneas wakes at daybreak, prays to the local gods, and detaches ships from his remaining fleet for the voyage up the Tiber.

Vergil's description of Aeneas' thoughts emphasizes their liquid, turbulent incoherence, but the river god's first words stabilize the currents (as the Tiber himself will do for Aeneas' voyage upriver) and reveal the nature of the great wave of worry (*cura*) that has washed over Aeneas.

> O seed of the gods' stock, who carry the Trojan city
> back to us and guard its eternal citadel,
> o one awaited by Laurentian land and Latin fields,
> here is your home assured, here assured your household gods.
> Don't shrink back, don't be frightened by threats of war:
> all the swelling anger of the gods has given way.
>
> *Aen.* 8.36–41

The Tiber's god, like some damp, blue-green therapist, articulates what Aeneas has been feeling, by telling him not to feel it—not to shrink back (*ne absiste*, 8.39) and not to be afraid (*neu terrere*, 8.40). Aeneas acknowledges fear on several occasions; in his narrative in books 2 and 3, for example, he admits to Dido that he was fearful for little Ascanius and for Anchises as they left Troy (2.729)[17] and that when he returned to look for Creusa, he found the silence of the devastated city terrifying (2.755). At his first stop after leaving Troy, a horrible portent, followed by the words of a ghost, make his hair stand on end and leave him unable to speak for fear (3.47–48). But after book 6, as Agnes Michels notes, "he is not described as fearful."[18] That is not to say that he isn't. In the second half of the epic, Aeneas pushes his fear below the surface of articulate thought; it becomes part of the *infandum* (unspeakable) that he manages to speak only to Dido. After Carthage, he is silent. The privileged narrative voice of the poem can find only turbulent, inchoate thought behind the silence; only divine insight like that of the Tiber can give voice to what Aeneas cannot say.

Another epiphany near the beginning of book 10 similarly brings Aeneas' subconscious concerns to light. Aeneas is returning to his Trojan forces, who are besieged in their camp by Italian forces led by Turnus. Aeneas has been away—book 9 is the only one in which he does not appear—on a diplomatic mission to King Evander at the future site of Rome. He is sailing back along the coast with reinforcements, including a contingent led by Pallas, Evander's son.

> Here Aeneas sits, massive, and turns over in his thoughts
> the possible outcomes of war. Pallas, planted at his left,
> asks now about the stars, their path through dark night,
> now about what Aeneas had been through on land and sea.
>
> *Aen.* 10.159–162

The final words of that description, *passus terra marique*, evoke the opening lines of book 1, in which Vergil announces to the reader his poem and his hero, "much buffeted on land and sea . . . , having gone through much in war as well" (*multum ille et terris iactatus et alto . . . , multa quoque et bello passus*, 1.3–5). Pallas, eager to hear the story of Aeneas, becomes a kind of surrogate reader of the *Aeneid*. He, like Dido, wants to know about Priam and Hector, the weapons of Memnon, the horses of Diomedes, and how big Achilles was (1.750–753).[19] Unlike Dido, Pallas does not get to hear the tale of Troy and exile (or if he does, we readers do not get to eavesdrop on it). As Vergil makes clear, Aeneas has his mind on other things: the chancy outcomes of war (*eventus belli varios*, 10.160). As dawn breaks, he is alone at the helm of his flagship, apparently single-handedly managing the sails (*ipse sedens clavumque regit velisque ministrat*, 10.218). He has not been able to sleep; unspecified worry has kept him awake (*neque enim membris dat cura quietem*, 10.217).

Once again Aeneas receives divine guidance, this time in the form of sea nymphs who appear and swim around his ship. In his absence, the Italian forces led by Turnus have made an attack on the Trojans in their fortified camp and threatened to burn the ships drawn up on the shore; in response, the mother goddess Cybele has transformed the ships into nymphs. Aeneas does not know about any of those developments (he is called *ignarum*, "unaware," at 10.228), but one of the nymphs, Cymodocea, brings him up to speed. After she introduces herself and explains the metamorphosis of the ships, she, like the Tiber, moves immediately to voice the worry (*cura*) that has kept Aeneas from sleep: "Yet the boy Ascanius is safe behind wall and ditch / though hemmed in by weapons and Latins dreadful in war" (10.236–237). Cymodocea's speech goes to the heart of Aeneas' silent worry and touches something so deeply part of him that he almost never gives voice to it: his love for his son.

In the *Aeneid*, Ascanius is difficult to pin down. Even his name fluctuates between Ascanius and Iulus.[20] Readers often want to know how old he is. At one moment, he (or his doppelganger, Cupid) is small enough to snuggle on Dido's lap (*Aen.* 1.717–719); not much later, he is riding with a hunt, hoping to encounter a boar or lion (4.156–159). In book 9, he shoots and kills a man from the walls of the Trojan camp, but the god Apollo, disguised as Butes, a Trojan elder who seems to have been assigned to watch over the young prince, forbids him to take any further part in combat (9.590–663). Vergil is consistent, however, about two things: first, Ascanius/Iulus represents the hope of Aeneas' future and of Rome's, the beginning of a line of descent that will lead, as Jupiter proclaims, to the Julian family and thus to Caesar (1.288); second, Aeneas loves and cares for his son. With her final words, the ghost of Creusa urges Aeneas, "Keep safe the love of the son we share" (2.789).

The two ideas fuse when Jupiter sends Mercury to persuade Aeneas to leave Carthage. "If he is not heaping up these labors for his own glory," says Jupiter to his messenger, "does his father begrudge Ascanius Roman citadels?" (4.233–234). Mercury relays the message as a blunt command: "Look to Ascanius rising and the hopes of your heir, Iulus" (4.274–275). Like the Tiber's god and the nymph Cymodocea, though, Mercury may be giving voice to anxieties that Aeneas already feels but does not express. When Aeneas tries to justify his departure to Dido, he lists the divine messages, dreams, and concerns that have been troubling him: messages from Grynean Apollo and the oracle of Lycia, frightening dreams of his father, and, finally, "the boy Ascanius and the wrong I do his dear person, / whom I cheat of his Italian kingdom and destined land" (4.354–355). Only then does he mention Mercury, and it is reasonable to infer that Aeneas' concern for Ascanius, like the hero's dreams about his own father, preceded the god's epiphany.

Aeneas struggles to redefine *pietas* in a world that left him bereft of all the human connections from which that virtue was constituted, except for his son. That struggle entails a gradual separation of Aeneas' will and desires from the choices that align his actions with the overriding narrative of fate working through history. At the beginning of the *Aeneid*, Aeneas knows who he is: "I am Aeneas the good" (*sum pius Aeneas*), he tells his disguised mother (*Aen.* 1.378). He has a story and an identity. As he stabs Turnus to the heart at the end of the poem, he refuses that identity: "Pallas, yes Pallas, sacrifices you with this wound" (*Pallas te hoc vulnere, Pallas / immolat*, 12.947–948). In Carthage, he can tell the story he knows, and he can also keep silent to conceal thoughts that might compromise his ability to lead his Trojans, who represent the surviving ground of his *pietas*. As the narrative moves forward, his speech is checked time and again, and silence grows around him. The silence finally extends to his soul, to his deepest fears for the future and love for his son, his only surviving family. Only the gods know who Aeneas is. When his thoughts reach out to embrace him—once, twice, three times—there is no one there.

Silence, Memory, and Forgetting

Memory and its necessary concomitant, forgetting, frame Aeneas' silences, just as they helped to structure Romans' understandings of their place in time and history.[21] At the beginning and middle of the *Aeneid*, Vergil brings memory to the foreground. Thinking about his attention to memory can shed light on the silence that shrouds the *Aeneid*'s central character.

Memory: The Beginning of the Journey

Twice in the first thirty-three lines of the *Aeneid* Juno, Aeneas' divine adversary, is linked to the adjective *memor* ("mindful" or "remembering"), and memory shapes her implacable hostility toward Aeneas and the Trojans. Aeneas is tossed about on land and sea "on account of the mindful anger of Juno" (*Aen.* 1.4), and Juno herself is "mindful of the ancient war that she had taken the lead in waging for her dear Greeks at Troy" (1.23–24). Vergil then itemizes additional causes of Juno's anger, which are lodged in the depths of her memory (*alta mente repostum*, 1.26): the Judgment of Paris, in which she came off second-best to Aeneas' mother, Venus (1.27); the fact that the Trojan race traced its origin to the offspring of her spouse, Jupiter, and a nymph (*genus invisum*, 1.28); and the honors that the king of the gods heaped on the Trojan prince Ganymede, who, according to Servius, had displaced Juno's daughter Hebe as Jupiter's cupbearer and was yet another sexual rival to Juno (*rapti Ganymedis honores*, 1.28). Juno is the goddess who neither forgives nor forgets. Memory also shapes Vergil's introduction of Aeneas, the victim of Juno's relentless persecution. His first two speeches in the poem are acts of memory. He speaks his first words in the midst of a violent storm sent by Juno. Sure that death is at hand, he recalls his Greek counterpart Diomedes, his cousin Hector, and the Trojans' ally Sarpedon.

O three and four times happy,
you whose lot it was to meet death at Troy,
under those lofty walls, before your fathers' eyes!
O Diomedes, bravest of the Greeks! Why could I
not have fallen by your hand on the Trojan plain,
poured out my blood where Hector lies, and huge
Sarpedon, where the Simois tumbles so many shields of heroes,
their helmets and strong bodies, under its waves!

Aen. 1.94–101

The entire *Aeneid* is an act of memory, a massive recollection of Homer's two epics, and Vergil hoped that his readers would join him in remembering a similar episode from the *Odyssey*.[22] Odysseus is almost within sight of Phaeacia when Poseidon sends a storm to shatter the raft he has built with Calypso's help so that he can leave her island and make his way homeward, to Ithaca and his wife, Penelope.

Ah, wretch that I am, what's my ultimate fate to be?
All that the goddess told me, I fear, is true—
she said that out on the deep, before I reached my homeland
I'd get my fill of trouble, and now it's all happening!
Look at the clouds with which Zeus is obscuring the wide
heavens, the way he's roiled up the sea, how the blasts
of all the winds drive at me! Now my sheer destruction's
for certain! Three and four times blessed those Danaäns
who perished in Troy's broad land, bringing aid to Atreus' sons:
How I wish I too had died then, had met my fate that day
when a mass of Trojans pelted me with their bronze-tipped spears,
battling around the dead son of Peleus! Then
I'd have had proper burial, and from the Achaians renown:
whereas now I'm doomed to suffer a most piteous death.

Odyssey 5.299–312, trans. Green

The differences between Vergil and his model highlight the importance of memory for Aeneas' character. Odysseus begins his speech with a clear-eyed look at his situation and only then wishes that he had died at Troy; then, he says, he would have had a hero's funeral instead of an unmarked death at sea. Aeneas says nothing about the storm around him and does not imagine any heroic funeral. His speech begins at the halfway point of Odysseus' and concentrates on the past, on death at home in front of the witnesses and with the comrades that give death meaning and create the context for *pietas*. Vergil describes, and Aeneas sees, "weapons of heroes" (*arma virum*, 1.119) tossed on the waves, but for him, the flotsam before his eyes fuses with the "shields of heroes" (*scuta virum*, 1.101) tumbling in the waves of a Trojan river years before. Odysseus looks around him; Aeneas remembers.

After the landing at Carthage (*Aen.* 1.198–207, discussed briefly in chapter 1), Aeneas tries to inspire his men with an optimism that he does not feel. His speech begins by asking the weary Trojans to remember their past and draw strength from it. They have survived worse trials—sailing past Scylla and Charybdis, evading the Cyclops—and some god will surely bring this one to an end too. Once again, looking at Vergil's Homeric model clarifies the extent to which Aeneas is a hero driven by memory. Vergil has patterned Aeneas' second speech on the one that Odysseus gives to rally his men as they are about to row the perilous strait between the monster Scylla and the whirlpool Charybdis.

> My friends,
> we've not hitherto gone short on experience of trouble!
> This danger we face now is no greater than when the Kyklops
> by brute force and strength shut us up in his hollow cave—
> even then, my courage, invention, and presence of mind
> freed us: this peril too, I think, we'll live to recall!
> So now, please all do exactly as I command: you must
> stay seated there at the rowlocks and with your oars
> strike the deep surf of the sea, so that maybe Zeus
> will grant that we escape, steer clear of this evil fate.
> And to you, steersman, I give this command: store it well
> in your memory—you control the hollow ship's helm!
> Keep the ship well away from all this smoke and surf:
> stay close to the headland, don't let her veer unnoticed
> across to the other side, or you'll destroy us all.
>
> *Odyssey* 12.208–221, trans. Green

This time, Vergil follows the main lines of his Homeric model. Both Odysseus and Aeneas begin with a general statement about their men's past experience of danger; in fact, Vergil's *O socii (neque enim ignari sumus ante malorum)*, "O comrades (we are not, you know, ignorant of evils before this one)" *Aen.* 1.198), is an almost word-for-word translation of Homer's ὦ φίλοι, οὐ γάρ πώ τι κακῶν ἀδαήμονές εἰμεν (*Odyssey* 12.208).[23] Reminding their men of specific dangers, both leaders mention the Cyclops, but Aeneas first invokes Scylla and Charybdis as a kind of footnote to the corresponding Homeric episode.[24] Both leaders point their men toward the future: Aeneas reminds his men of their goal, recreating Troy in Italy, and Odysseus gives instructions for his oarsmen and helmsman to follow in the next crucial minutes.

These structural similarities make the differences between Homeric model and Vergilian reworking all the more evident and important. Odysseus' whole purpose is to inspire his men in the present moment, and he puts himself firmly in that moment; if his men have escaped danger in the past, it is because of his leadership—his skill and brains and strategy. In contrast, Aeneas erases himself from his men's past; a god, he says, will surely grant an end to these present troubles (*dabit deus his quoque finem*, *Aen.* 1.199), just as he has ended their troubles in the past. Homer's αἴ κέ ποθι Ζεὺς / δώῃ ("in the hope that Zeus may grant us") also expresses a wish for the present, not a hopeful statement about the future. Unlike Odysseus, Aeneas does not mention himself or his own leadership; if he did, he might have to get too close to the sadness that he is hiding deep in his heart. Odysseus' speech focuses on the present. Past danger and future hopes serve only to highlight the need for present action. Aeneas wants to inspire hope, not action. He encourages his men to look past the present by remembering past dangers and by thinking of their destined future. In Vergil's significant modification of his Homeric model, he has Aeneas frame even that future as an act of memory. "Perhaps," the hero says, "someday it will be a pleasure to remember even these things" (1.203).

Memory and Silence: The Middle of the Journey

From the beginning of the *Aeneid*, Aeneas is a creature of memory, not only a hero marked out by fate, but a man who is constituted by his memories and who uses memory as part of his leadership. As he journeys through the underworld at the midpoint of the poem, he meets characters who take him back through his past, from the sack of Troy to the arrival in Italy, and forward through the future, to the present of the *Aeneid*, the Rome of the Augustan principate. Both memory and forgetting transform Aeneas on that journey. Memory, forgetting, and silence play a role in that transformation and help to determine how it unfolds in the second half of the *Aeneid*.

Midpoints matter to Vergil; as we have seen, Moeris and Lycidas conclude their conversation midway between Moeris' home and the town where he will market his master's lambs, and Aeneas' significant self-introduction, *sum pius Aeneas*, appears exactly halfway through *Aeneid* 1. To notice that emphasis, modern readers have to count lines (an ancient reader might have found it easier to notice the halfway point of a scroll as the rolled and unrolled portions became equal in size), but Vergil marks the midpoint of Aeneas' underworld journey in a way that is impossible to miss. Aeneas' allotted time in the underworld begins 264 lines into book 6, when Vergil asks the gods who command souls, the silent spirits of the dead, and Chaos and Phlegethon to allow him to reveal the secrets of the dead world. The strongly marked midpoint of his journey occurs nearly halfway between that invocation and the end of the book.

Aeneas has just encountered the horribly disfigured ghost of his Trojan friend Deiphobus, who had married Helen after the death of Paris. Aeneas asks Deiphobus about his death and mutilation, and Deiphobus tells his story—how he was betrayed by Helen during the sack of Troy and killed in their bedroom by Menelaus and Odysseus. Aeneas is about to respond with his own story when, yet again, he is interrupted and prevented from speaking.

> During this conversation Dawn with rosy chariot
> had already crossed the meridian on her celestial route;
> they might have used all the allotted time in such talk,
> but the guide, the Sibyl, briefly spoke in warning:
> "Night rushes on, Aeneas; we are drawing out hours in weeping.
> This is the place where the road divides in two:
> the right fork runs under the walls of Pluto's palace—
> that is our way to Elysium—but the left track
> takes sinners to punishment and leads to Tartarus."
>
> *Aen.* 6.535–543

At this midpoint of his underworld journey, time and Aeneas' road both split apart; as Aurora, the dawn goddess, reaches the zenith of her journey across the sky in the upper world, the road in front of Aeneas likewise divides. One path leads to Tartarus, where the wicked receive eternal punishment; the other leads to the Elysian Fields, where the virtuous spend the afterlife in pleasant fields and groves. On this journey, Aeneas has already compared himself and been compared to Hercules (6.123, 392–394). Now, as Hercules did, Aeneas faces the road of vice, on the one hand, and the road of virtue, on the other.[25] Unlike

Hercules, Aeneas is not given a choice about which road to take. The Sibyl directs him, and he says nothing.

That central point, with its passive, silent protagonist, reinforces the sixth book's role as the pivot where Aeneas turns away from the despairing hero he has been, who remembered Troy as he faced death in a storm, and turns toward the victor he will be, who identifies himself with the dead Pallas as he kills Turnus and who takes on characteristics of his adversaries, the Greeks and Juno. Like the *Aeneid* itself, Aeneas' underworld journey in book 6 divides into two halves. In the first, Aeneas revisits and revises his past through encounters with dead comrades and, crucially, with Dido; in the second, he encounters a future that he cannot share—even though it is, as Anchises tells him, "your destiny" (*tua fata*, 6.759). The first half depends on memory and the revision of the past; the second, on forgetting and the creation of the future.

Before the Sibyl tells him that half his allotted time in the underworld has gone by, Aeneas encounters several figures from his past, some recently dead and others casualties of the Trojan War. Among the unburied on the near bank of the River Styx, he notices Leucaspis and Orontes, captains who were lost with their ships in the tempest sent by Juno at the beginning of the poem (*Aen.* 6.333–336; see 1.113–117). Farther along, in the region occupied by those who were famous in war, he sees a group of those killed at Troy, both Greeks and Romans (6.477–494). Between and after these sightings, Aeneas speaks with (or to) three figures: Palinurus, Dido, and Deiphobus. With each encounter, he plunges deeper into his past: Palinurus is recently dead and waiting with the unburied, hoping to cross the Styx; Dido's death occurred some weeks earlier (book 5 covers a stormy crossing from Carthage to Sicily, a nine-day interval before Anchises' funeral games, and time needed to reconfigure the fleet for the voyage to Italy); and Deiphobus was killed in the sack of Troy. In each case, Aeneas is forced to confront his memories—what he thought he knew about his past—and responds with silence. For readers of the *Aeneid*, these encounters raise questions about memory and compel reconsideration of Aeneas' relationship to his past and of his story about it.

Palinurus

First comes Palinurus, the helmsman (*gubernator*) who piloted Aeneas' flagship from Troy to Italy.[26] On the final night of their voyage, with Italy almost in sight, the god Sleep visited Palinurus, who was alone on deck. The god, disguised as a Trojan named Phorbas, first tried to persuade Palinurus to take a break: "The sea itself carries the fleet, / the breezes blow fair, it is time for rest, / put down your head, steal your weary eyes away from work" (*Aen.* 5.843–845). Palinurus resisted, but Sleep took out a branch dipped in the water of the Lethe, the underworld's river of forgetfulness, and shook it over the helmsman's head. Palinurus tried not to doze off, but there is no resisting a god. He fell overboard, still clutching the steering oar, which carried away along with it the fittings securing it to the stern. Palinurus thus fulfilled a promise made by Neptune to Venus earlier in book 5: the final leg to Italy will cost one life (5.814–815), just as the passage to Carthage cost one ship.

Now Aeneas meets his steersman in the underworld. For readers, the immediate challenge is to reconcile the discrepancies between what Vergil has told us in book 5 and what Aeneas and Palinurus say to each other in book 6. In book 5, Neptune predicts the loss of Palinurus, the sea is calm, the sky is clear, and the stars are visible because the god Sleep has cleared away the clouds (*Aen.* 5.838–839). In book 6, Aeneas refers to a prophecy of Apollo suggesting that Palinurus would not be lost at sea (6.343–346), and Palinurus tells Aeneas that no god pitched him into the sea (*nec me deus aequore mersit*, 6.348); rather, he fell overboard while he was attempting to steer the ship amid rough seas (*maria aspera*, 6.351) and rising waves (*surgentibus undis*, 6.354). In some ways, the easiest solution for the reader is to appeal to ancient reports that Vergil left the *Aeneid* unfinished at his death; inconsistencies like this, then, are simply absentminded anomalies that Vergil would have harmonized if he had lived longer. But as Christine Perkell observes in discussing this passage, "One man's anomaly is another's brilliant innovation" (2004, 136), and the explanation from incompleteness remains, for me, an unsatisfying last resort. Some scholars see Palinurus as a figure like Dido or Turnus, one of the sacrifices that are part of Aeneas' founding of Rome, and read the contradictions as signs of unreconciled tensions in the values of empire.[27] Following Cyril Connolly's "case study" in *The Unquiet Grave* (which Connolly wrote under the pseudonym "Palinurus"), Perkell imagines a Palinurus whose motives are unclear (who may have abandoned ship and mission deliberately and offers apologia and justification on the other side of the grave) and an Aeneas who says nothing in response to his speech, so that we wonder what his silence means.

> Could Virgil's close readers sense dismay or anger in Aeneas' silence? Where really was the fault? Was Palinurus' death the sacrifice of an "innocent"? an ac-

> cident? desertion? As it stands, Virgil's text implicitly poses these haunting questions, but refrains from answering them. (Perkell 2004, 140)

I want to build on Perkell's insights and read the Palinurus episode as part of the revision of Aeneas' memory that takes place during his underworld visit. Perkell's haunting questions are not for only Vergil's readers; they are also for his hero, and Aeneas has no answer for them.

Book 5 ends with Aeneas' tearful words as he takes over the helm vacated by Palinurus.[28] This first response to the loss of Palinurus forms the basis of the memories that Aeneas will take into the underworld: "O Palinurus, too trusting of calm weather and sea, / naked you will lie on an unknown shore" (*Aen.* 5.870–871). Aeneas' perception at this point coincides with that of the poem's narrative voice; forty lines earlier, Vergil describes the fleet proceeding under sail in light breezes as the sailors trim the sails to take advantage of the shifting winds, and the last words of that description, "favorable gusts carry the fleet along" (*ferunt sua flamina classem*, 5.832), are echoed in Sleep's first words to Palinurus, "favorable currents carry the fleet along" (*ferunt ipsa aequora classem*, 5.843).[29] When he sees Palinurus in the underworld, Aeneas greets him with a question: "What god, Palinurus, / snatched you from us and drowned you in the middle of the sea?" He goes on to wonder about a prophecy (so far unmentioned in the narrative) from Apollo—the god who had never misled him (*fallax haud ante repertus, Aen.* 6.343)—that Palinurus would reach "Ausonian territory" (that is, Italy) safe and sound.

Palinurus challenges and contradicts not only what Aeneas has just said but also the understanding that both he and the Vergilian narrator expressed at the end of book 5. According to Palinurus, no god precipitated him into the sea. Apollo did not lie, since Palinurus touched Italy, though only with his fingertips (*Aen.* 6.360). The sea was not calm, and he does not lie unburied on an unknown shore; rather, his body tosses in the surf, rolled by the wind (6.362). The dead helmsman then makes a request: will Aeneas give him at least a pro forma burial (*mihi terram / inice*, 6.365–366) or even take him by the hand and lead his unquiet spirit over the Styx to rest?

The Sibyl gives Aeneas no chance to respond, as she reprimands Palinurus.

> Palinurus, where did you get this abominable desire?
> Will you, unburied, look upon the Styx's waters,
> the Furies' gloomy stream, and go unbidden to its bank?

Stop hoping to bend the god's decree by praying,
but take these words to heart, solace for your misfortune.

Aen. 6.373–377

The Sibyl then tells Palinurus that the natives of the place where he was cast ashore, prompted by omens in the sky, will perform funeral rites for him; that place, she says, will forever be called by his name. (It is known to this day as Capo Palinuro.) She calls him to think on—to remember (*cape dicta memor*, 6.377)—the future as the only comfort for his present, fated distress. Aeneas also has only a vague future to console him for the loss of Troy and all that it meant. He also has had to learn that the gods' decree cannot be evaded or deflected. Here as elsewhere, he can look on another and recognize himself or see an analogue for his own situation.[30] Here too, his reaction to inward reflection is silence, whether voluntary or forced by the Sibyl's peremptory response. Aeneas' agency, like his thoughts, remains concealed behind a veil of silence.

Dido

Once they have crossed the Styx, Aeneas and his guide pass through various regions occupied by the unfortunate dead—infants (*Aen.* 6.426–429), those falsely accused of capital crimes (430–433), and those who have taken their own lives (434–439). The hero and the Sibyl then come to the Mournful Fields (*Lugentes Campi*), where those who have died because of love wander, still feeling the pain that they felt in life. There are the heroines of mythology: Phaedra, Procris, Eriphyle, Evadne, Pasiphae, Laodamia, and the transgendered Caeneus. There finally, at the exact midpoint of book 6, is Dido. Aeneas recognizes her, like the newly risen moon seen or glimpsed through scudding clouds (6.453–454). He weeps as he addresses her.

Ill-fated Dido! Was the news that came then true
that you were dead, had sought your final breath
with steel? Was I the cause of death for you?
I swear by stars, by gods above and by whatever trust
is here below—I left your shores against my will.
And yet the gods' command, which drives me now
through these shades, through regions overgrown
with gloom and night, has brought me here. How could

I know that taking leave would bring such grief?
Wait! Don't go away—let me see you!
Who are you fleeing? These are the final words
that fate will let me speak to you.

Aen. 6.456–466

Dido says nothing and refuses to look at Aeneas. Then she moves off through the gloom to join her husband and first love, Sychaeus. Aeneas, still in tears, tries to follow her, but in vain; struck, Vergil says, by her unfair destiny, he pities her as she goes.

In this meeting with Dido's spirit, Aeneas replays two earlier encounters, his exchange with Dido at the center of book 4 and his meeting with Palinurus earlier in book 6. He and Dido reenact their last dialogue in the world of the living, but their roles are reversed. In Carthage, Dido gave voice to her emotions in a pair of passionate speeches and, by her own account, wept while Aeneas held his gaze away from her (*Aen.* 4.369); in the underworld, Aeneas weeps and tries to express the conflict between his feeling for Dido and his unwelcome destiny, while Dido turns away with downcast eyes and expressionless face (6.469–470). In Carthage, Dido asked Aeneas whether he was running from her (*mene fugis*, 4.314); in the underworld, Aeneas asks Dido why she is running from him (*quem fugis*, 6.464), and his question echoes not only Dido's words but their place at the beginning of a line. It also repeats verbatim his words to his father's shade as Anchises faded from his grasp in Sicily (5.742). In Carthage, where Vergil compared Aeneas to an ancient oak, battered by the storms of Dido's words and tears but firmly rooted and unmoving, Dido's tears and perhaps Aeneas' as well had no effect (4.438–449); in the underworld, Dido is like flint or marble (6.471), and Aeneas tries in vain to rouse her tears (6.468).[31] In Africa, he was unmoved but still a living thing; in hell, Dido is equally unmoved but lifeless.

The last confrontation with Dido echoes the thematic notes of the earlier meeting with Palinurus. In both cases, Aeneas learns something that challenges or revises his beliefs about the death of that person: Palinurus may have been swept overboard in heavy weather, rather than being tricked by a god into falling asleep at the helm; Dido killed herself, as Aeneas had heard but chose not to believe. The encounters with Palinurus and Dido also prompt Aeneas to question or at least wonder about part of the foundation of his signal virtue, his *pietas*. Trust or reliability, *fides*, between gods and men is entangled with the dutifulness or loyalty, *pietas*, that men owe to gods and each other. Nowhere is that connection clearer than in a poet whom Vergil read with care, his older contemporary Catullus.

> If a person has any pleasure in recalling previous good deeds, / when he reflects that he is *pius*, / has not done violence to holy *fides*, nor in any agreement / abused the gods' divine power to cheat human beings, / many joys remain for you, Catullus, in a long life, / from this thankless love.
>
> Catullus 76.1–6

When he sees Palinurus in the land of the dead, Aeneas is shaken to recall the prophecy of Apollo that Palinurus would make it all the way to Italy. "Well!" he exclaims (*Aen.* 6.346), "Is this the trustworthiness [*fides*] that was promised?" In Palinurus, Aeneas recognizes a sign not only that what he thought he knew about the past may be unreliable but that the moral underpinnings of that understanding, *fides* and *pietas*, may be unstable. His response to this hint of existential crisis is silence. When he assures Dido's ghost that he left her shore unwillingly—as as he does so, nearly quotes a line of Catullus that seems to many readers bizarrely out of place—he swears by the stars and the gods above but then wonders whether there is any *fides* in the place where he now finds himself (6.459).[32]

Both the meeting with Palinurus and the confrontation with Dido end with Aeneas brought to silence by a woman. The Sibyl reduced Aeneas to literal silence by reprimanding Palinurus for wishing to cross the Styx in contravention of fate's decree for the unburied. Dido's adamantine silence does not render Aeneas literally speechless; in fact, the eleven lines that he speaks to her are his longest utterance in the underworld.[33] When Dido stalks away to rejoin Sychaeus, Aeneas "follows her with tears at a distance" (*prosequitur lacrimis longe*, *Aen.* 6.476), and Vergil's uses of *prosequitur* elsewhere imply that the tears were accompanied by words.[34] Rather than compel speechlessness, Dido silences Aeneas by refusing to allow his words to have effect. She joins the group—including his mother, Venus, in book 1; his wife, Creusa, in book 2; and his father, Anchises, in book 5—of those he loves who leave him trying to say things unsaid.

Deiphobus

The meetings with Palinurus and Dido set a pattern, and it is not surprising to find its basic elements in the encounter with Deiphobus (*Aen.* 6.494–547).

Once again, Aeneas learns that his beliefs about the past are mistaken. He had heard that Deiphobus had died heroically atop a heap of enemy dead on Troy's last night (6.502–504); now he learns that Deiphobus had been betrayed by his wife, Helen, and killed when she let Menelaus and Ulysses into their bedroom (6.520–529). There may be a second revision of memory as well, if the "Helen episode" of book 2 belongs in the poem (see the discussion in chapter 1 above). Just as Palinurus' story seemed to contradict the narrative of book 5, so Deiphobus' story that Helen played an active role in bringing the Greeks into Troy on the city's last night and plotted with Menelaus, whom Deiphobus describes as her "lover" (*amanti*, 6.526), seems in conflict with the Helen who, as Aeneas told it, cowered in a temple doorway for fear of the Greeks and Menelaus, the husband she had deserted (2.567–573). Once again, also, Aeneas confronts a challenge to *fides* (trust) and to *pietas*. With bitter irony, Deiphobus explains how his "distinguished spouse" (*egregia coniunx*, 6.523) removed all the weapons from their bedroom and the sword from beside his head as he was sleeping. "May the gods," he says to Aeneas, "pay back the Greeks in kind, if I am demanding their punishment with a *pius* mouth" (*pio si poenas ore reposco*, 6.530). The irony continues; as Vergil explained (using and repeating the same word for mouth), Menelaus and Ulysses had mutilated Deiphobus' features, *ora* (6.495–496). And once again, as we have seen, a woman, the Sibyl, silences Aeneas.

When Aeneas enters the underworld, he enters what Alan Itkin has called a "space of memory" that "both represents and actually produces an act of remembrance" as he travels through it (Itkin 2017, 27). As he does so, he repeatedly travels deeper into his past and confronts figures—Palinurus, Dido, Deiphobus—who force him to revise what he thought he knew about it. Not only the events that he remembers but also the ethical foundations of his identity come into question. On each occasion, Aeneas falls silent, and neither the narrator nor any other character gives us a clue to his thoughts or purchase on the meaning of that silence. This mystery of silence at the heart of the *Aeneid* points to an opening void in the heart of its central character. For Aeneas to become the figure announced in the first eleven lines of the *Aeneid*, the founder of Rome, he must empty his Trojan identity and reconfigure it as essentially Roman. He cannot become Roman, because Rome is still in the distant future, and he cannot cease to be Trojan Aeneas, the son of Anchises. But he can acquire a new basis for his thoughts and actions and a new grounding of his signal virtue, his *pietas*. His tragedy is both that he can never be conscious of what that new grounding is and that the new grounding entails an ineradicable flaw. In the second half of the *Aeneid*, Aeneas must remain a man alienated from the existential ground of his character.

I have argued that Aeneas' *pietas* grows out of the web of human and divine connections that constituted his Trojan identity. The hellish final night of Troy, culminating with the loss of Creusa, shook that foundation to its core and anticipated the questioning of *pietas* that Aeneas encounters in the literal hell of the underworld.[35] In the first half of the *Aeneid*, Aeneas' moral agency is complicated by his struggle to know how *pietas* can exist for him in a world where the human nodes of its net of obligations—his wife, father, and city—have all vanished. His steadfast attention to the will of the gods, which seemed very close to Lacanian "perversion," begins to seem more like the act of a desperate man clinging to all that was left of his life's meaning.

Yet, in the epic's first half, Aeneas knows who he has been and what his past was. He remembers. He tells his story to Dido, recognizes himself in the scenes on Juno's temple, and offers to tell the tale to his mother. To commemorate his father's death, his Trojans perform the funeral games of their city, as they had for his cousin Hector. Even the regrets that Aeneas expresses to Dido are regrets for incomplete understanding, not admissions of ignorance. When he saw the gods destroying Troy and experienced the visions and omens directing him to lead his Trojans into exile, he concluded that if Troy was to exist, it would have to exist somewhere else, in a place to which the gods would guide him. In the underworld, the meaning of Troy and Aeneas himself must be reinvented. During that process, his final response to figures from his past can only be silence.

Anchises

At this point it is worth asking what the Sibyl is doing there in the first place. In the underworld, she guides Aeneas, answers his questions, and, as we have seen, moves him along his way and cuts short his conversations with figures from his past. Aeneas seems to surrender his agency to her; she even carries the magical Golden Bough—the essential talisman that Aeneas had plucked for travel through the underworld (*Aen.* 6.136–141)—and takes it from beneath her cloak when it is needed to persuade Charon to ferry Aeneas across the Styx (6.405–407). The Sibyl seems to be thoroughly familiar with the underworld up to the point at which the road forks between Tartarus and Elysium; as she tells Aeneas, when the grim goddess of the underworld, Hecate, had put her in charge of the cult at Lake Avernus, the goddess had given her a tour of Tartarus and explained the punishments of the damned (*Aen.* 6.564–565). But once on the road to Elysium, she has to stop and ask the legendary bard Musaeus for directions (6.666–671), and although she remains with Aeneas until the end (6.897), she does not say anything more to him, or he to her. For the second, Elysian half of his journey, Aeneas needs a fourth figure from his past as guide and informant, the person he has come to find, his father.

In Elysium, Aeneas speaks only three times: once to greet Anchises and beg to embrace him (6.695–698); once to ask about the crowd of souls waiting to cross Lethe, the river of forgetfulness (6.719–721); and once to ask the identity of a soul waiting for incarnation (6.863–866). For the rest of his time there, he is silent. Aeneas' passivity once he is in the underworld contrasts with his actions immediately before he enters—seeking out the Sibyl, helping his men build a funeral pyre for Misenus, finding and plucking the Golden Bough—and especially with two speeches that he makes to the Sibyl before they enter the underworld. The first (*Aen.* 6.56–76) is a heartfelt prayer to Phoebus Apollo and the other gods who have protected the Trojans on their journey to Italy, asking them to put an end to the "Trojan fortune," the bad luck that has dogged the Trojans' way so far, and to the Sibyl asking her for guidance. The second (6.103–123) follows the structure of a Roman formal speech, with *exordium* (103–105), *propositio* (setting forth) of his request to visit his father with the Sibyl as guide (106–109), *probatio* making the case for his *pietas* toward his father (110–116), and *peroratio* asking the Sibyl to take pity on father and son and affirming Aeneas' right to descend to the underworld—he too, like Theseus or Hercules, is the son of a god (116–123).[36] Before he enters the underworld, Aeneas is a man of action and confident speech; in the land of the dead, he is an onlooker asking questions and falling silent again and again.

It is easy enough to say that Aeneas needs the Sibyl and Anchises because the underworld is a strange place in which he does not know the way, but other heroes, including those Aeneas himself cites as precedents for his journey (6.116–123), do not need the same kind of help. Orpheus and Pollux enter, negotiate with the lords of the dead, and leave on their own; Theseus enters accompanied by his friend Pirithous, and in some versions, returns alone to rescue his comrade, though Vergil suggests that Pirithous remains imprisoned forever in Tartarus (6.617–620); according to the *Odyssey*, Herakles harrows hell with the aid of Athena and Hermes, but their exact role is unspecified (*Odyssey* 11.613–626).[37] Unlike those figures, who enter the underworld as explorers to recover a lost wife or brother or on a raid, Aeneas enters following a guide along a known path. As the Sibyl explains to Charon, Aeneas has come not to carry off Cerberus, as Hercules did, or to kidnap Persephone, like Theseus and Pirithous, but in search of his father; he is a man marked out not only by heroic feats of arms but also by *pietas* (6.399–404). As Anchises says to him, *pietas* overcame the hardships of the journey to the world beyond (*vicit iter durum pietas*, 6.688)—but when Aeneas tries to embrace the figure around whom he had constructed his *pietas* in the aftermath of Troy's destruction, he grasps only empty air or something very like a dream (6.702). In the underworld, Aeneas finds something far more difficult to recognize or understand than a lost relative or a prophet's prediction: a past that he can no longer be sure about and a future that is beyond his understanding. While the Sibyl led Aeneas through encounters with his past that forced him to challenge and revise his memories, Anchises guides him into the future—not Aeneas' future, but the future of Rome. On that journey, there can be no memory to revise. In a temporal paradox at the heart of the *Aeneid*, the key to reaching Rome's future lies both in memory and in forgetting.

Aeneas' first meeting with his father follows a pattern that has become familiar to readers of the first half of the *Aeneid*: like Venus, like Creusa, like the nocturnal image of Anchises in Sicily, Anchises in the underworld eludes Aeneas' embrace and fades into insubstantial air. This time, however, the wraith continues to speak and guide his son, but Aeneas' long-sought connection with his father now has something strange about it. First, Aeneas looks away from his father to see, in the distance, a valley full of activity, with the River Lethe flowing through it. There, countless nations and peoples flit about, reminding Aeneas of bees in a summer meadow,

> . . . just as in meadows on a calm summer day
> bees settle on flowers of all kinds; shining lilies
> spread around them, and the whole field buzzes.
>
> *Aen.* 6.707–709

An unthreatening pastoral scene, it seems, and so Aeneas' reaction is distinctly odd: he shudders at the unexpected sight (*horrescit visu subito*, 6.710) and asks Anchises to identify the streams in the distance and the men in that great array. Something a little uncanny about those bee-like souls of the underworld operates, to use Ellen Oliensis' phrase, in the unconscious of the poem or of Aeneas. The lilies will resurface in Anchises' lament for young, dead Marcellus at the end of his grand review of Roman heroes, and the bees themselves are not, as they are elsewhere in Vergil, engaged in the kind of activity that made them a useful microcosm of human political life.[38] Bees have other associations, though; they can be a way of thinking about the winged human soul or about the inspiration of poets who produce such sweetness from so much work. A swarm of bees can also endorse the founding of a new city, as they do in the very next book of the *Aeneid* (7.64–70).[39] All those associations—death and sorrow, society and labor, human souls, the founding of a city—are alive in Aeneas' mind as he gazes down on the throng of souls, and they make him uneasy. His unease surfaces in his follow-up question to Anchises and in yet another significant silence that punctuates his tour of Rome's future.

After Anchises explains that the river is Lethe, the river of forgetfulness, and that the crowd of souls is waiting to drink so that they can be reincarnated (*Aen.* 6.713–718), Aeneas continues his question, this time in direct discourse; that is, Vergil quotes the hero's exact words.

> O father, must we think that some souls go
> aloft from here and return to heavy bodies?
> What lust for light afflicts these wretched souls?
>
> *Aen.* 6.719–721

Aeneas finds it impossible to imagine that anyone would prefer the world above to afterlife in Elysium. His question marks a point of existential crisis for the *Aeneid*'s central character, and we need to take it seriously.[40] After Vergil's description of life in Elysium (6.637–676)—beautiful, green country lit by its own sun and stars, where the residents spend their days in sports or art, Musaeus and Orpheus provide the music, there is no war, and no one owns a fixed abode—Aeneas looks back to life in the world from which he has just come and wonders why any soul would wish to return to a mortal body. In that upper world, he has been stripped of everything that gave meaning to his life. His ancestral city, his home, his wife, and the father who guided him on his quest to rebuild Troy have all been taken away. His life since the fall of Troy has been a wasteland of wandering, struggle, and false starts, with only fitful glimpses of a destined home that remains elusive. Palinurus, Dido, and Deiphobus have just forced him to question his very memories of that struggle, and memory, for a man whose *pietas* is grounded in a lost city and dead relatives and comrades, is very nearly all he has to anchor his being. Here in Elysium, he can speak with his father and see before him his Trojan ancestors (6.648–650). Where else, then, will his existence have meaning, and why should he return to the upper world? The Sibyl had told him that the way down to the underworld was easy but that the real work and toil (*opus* and *labor*) was to return. Now Aeneas knows what she meant. Just as he had done in Sicily (5.700–703), he hesitates. Should he continue on the road that fate has mapped out for him, or should he forget his destiny and stay where he is?

Anchises must now answer both his son's actual question and the existential despair that lies underneath it.[41] He does so in two ways, and like Jupiter's answer to Venus when she asked about the fate of her son, neither of them has much to do with the living, suffering man at the center of the *Aeneid*. First, Anchises explains the mechanism of reincarnation (*Aen.* 6.724–751). His account blends elements of Platonic, Orphic or Pythagorean, and Stoic thought: human souls participate in the divine soul of the world; after death, they retain some elements of the corporeal, earthly taint that has imprisoned them in this world; they must undergo a long process of purification before God summons them to drink the water of the river of forgetfulness, Lethe; then, because they have no more awareness of their previous life, they begin to want to return to new bodies (*incipiant in corpora velle reverti*, 6.751).[42] That explanation answers Aeneas' question but does not address the emotion behind it; it can be only slight comfort to know that the only way to want to enter the world of the living is to know nothing about it.

Second, Anchises shows Aeneas the long series of his Roman progeny.

> Now the glory that hereafter follows Troy's offspring,
> descendants from Italian race who await,
> glorious souls about to enter our name,
> those I will expound as I tell your destiny.
>
> *Aen.* 6.756–759

Aeneas could reasonably interpret these words as announcing a catalog of his own descendants, as Anchises had promised in the nocturnal vision on Sicily (5.737). The first third of the long parade of souls consists of figures who might, on a generous interpretation, be thought of as descendants of Aeneas: Silvius, the son of his old age by the Italian princess Lavinia, then the kings of Alba Longa following in his line, and then Romulus, who (through his mother, Ilia) can claim to be descended from Aeneas' great-grandfather, Assaracus (6.777–

779; compare *Iliad* 20.215–241). Romulus is followed by "Caesar and all the descendants of Iulus" (6.76–770), the gens Iulia who claimed descent from Venus through her grandson, Ascanius/Iulus, one of whose names conveniently resembled theirs.

The emphasis, though, is on "Caesar," that is, Augustus. He will bring back the golden age.

> Here is the man, this one, promised you too often,
> Augustus Caesar, scion of a god, who will found
> a Golden Age again in Latium, fields where Saturn
> once ruled, who will carry empire beyond Indians
> and Garamantians, to land beyond the stars,
> beyond the zodiac, where Atlas Sky-bearer
> on his shoulders spins the star-studded axis of heaven.
>
> *Aen*, 6.791–797

Anchises goes on to announce that even now the lands around the Caspian Sea, Lake Maeotis (the Sea of Azov), and the Nile tremble at the prospect of the future Augustus' conquests. Vergil thus brings into Anchises' prophecy the conquest of Egypt after Actium and perhaps an allusion to the recovery in 20 BC of the legionary eagles lost at Carrhae a quarter of a century earlier; the allusion, if it is there, is necessarily delicate, since Augustus liked to present that successful diplomatic negotiation in language more appropriate to a military victory.[43] Augustus, Anchises continues, will surpass Hercules and Bacchus, the hero and god who extended their influence over the known world.

After the drums and trumpets of that encomium, Anchises asks his son, "Do we still hesitate to advance our virtue by deeds? Does anxious fear keep us from taking our stand on Italian soil?" (*Aen.* 6.806–807). Aeneas does not reply. In a book full of silence and silencings, this one is perhaps the most revealing. As he hesitates—for surely Anchises' question, like the exhortations of Tiber or Cymodocea in the second half of the *Aeneid*, opens a window into Aeneas' state of mind—Aeneas stands poised between his past and his future and between memory and forgetting. His underworld journey has taken him deep into his past, and Anchises has just shown him a vision of his future descendants, culminating in the glories of Augustus. Aeneas and his father are standing on a mound (*tumulus*, 6.754) in a plain studded with groves of trees, with open areas for athletic and cultural exercise and a river winding through it. To Vergil's first readers, that landscape might have suggested the northern Campus Martius (Field of Mars), the level area between the urban center of Rome and the Tiber. In the twenties BC, that area was not yet built over, and the only considerable structure north of the original Pantheon was the Mausoleum of Augustus, a mound-like structure begun as early as 28 BC.[44] Aeneas thus hesitates not only in his own present but also in the present of his Augustan readers. When Vergil died in 19 BC and left the *Aeneid* unfinished, the glories that Anchises describes—empire without end, the conquest of the Parthians, a "Golden Age again in Latium" (6.793)—lay in an unrealized and perhaps unrealizable future. In that moment, perhaps the only authentic response to an exhortation like that of Anchises was silence.

When the glorious prospect of descendants and Augustus fail to elicit a response from Aeneas, Anchises tries another tack. "Who is that off in the distance," he asks, "marked by olive branches and carrying sacred objects?" (6.808–809). Numa Pompilius, the second king of Rome, begins a group of Romans-to-be who are unrelated to Aeneas, with one exception. Halfway through the group appear two unnamed souls. Anchises' description makes it clear that they are Julius Caesar and his rival Pompey.

> Those you discern who gleam in equal armor
> spirits harmonious now, while in this gloom,
> what war, what battle and slaughter they will stir up
> between them, if they reach the light of life—
> father-in-law descending from the Alps and Gaul,
> son-in-law drawn up with armies of the dawn.
> Don't, lads, don't get your spirits used to such war,
> Don't turn your mighty strength against your country's vitals!
> And you, you who trace your descent to Olympus,
> be first to throw down your weapons, blood of mine!
>
> *Aen.* 6.826–835

By emphasizing the relationship of the two men by marriage (even though Pompey's wife Julia had been dead almost five years when her father descended from Gaul and crossed the Rubicon in 49 BC), Vergil configures the Roman civil war of the early forties as a breakdown of family relations—of *pietas*, in fact.[45]

Recognizing that emphasis changes the valence of two immediately preceding examples of Roman greatness. The "spot-lit figure of Brutus," as R. D. Williams calls it (1972, 505), casts deep shadows with almost every word. The founder of the Roman Republic (and ancestor of the Brutus who led the assassination of Caesar) has a "proud spirit" (*animam superbam*, *Aen.* 6.817) and thus assumes the characteristic quality of Tarquin the Proud, the hated king whom he deposed; he is an "avenger" and the first to hold consular imperium and the "cruel axes" that were bound up in a bundle of rods to form the fasces, the symbol of a consul's power to flog and behead. The first Brutus used that power. He ordered his own sons executed when they joined with Tarquin to restore the monarchy and crush the nascent republic; as Anchises puts it, he "will call his sons to punishment on behalf of beautiful liberty" (*Aen.* 6.821; see also Livy 2.5). In reading this passage, we need to put as much emphasis on the shadows as on the bright lights, as much on the "cruel axes" and "punishment" as on "beautiful liberty" (*pulchra libertas*). Vergil, like his contemporary Livy, sketches Brutus as a tragic figure torn between public duty and private affection. Brutus is also a reminder of the ways that civic conflicts disrupt and destroy family ties, as Anchises highlights in his presentation of Caesar and Pompey.

Reading back from Caesar and Pompey through Brutus, we come to Romulus (*Aen.* 6.777–787). Like Augustus, who immediately follows him in Anchises' presentation of Rome's future, Romulus will expand Rome's dominion until it is coextensive with the earth (*imperium terris . . . aequabit*, 6.782). By immediately moving from a reference to Romulus' wall around the seven hills to a simile (6.784–787) comparing him to the tower-crowned mother of the gods, whose immortal progeny dominate heaven and earth,[46] Vergil distracts readers' attention from the awkward fact that Romulus founded Rome but did not notably extend Roman territory. Anchises' description of Romulus contains another authorial sleight of hand. Aeneas' father begins by zooming in on the twin crests (*geminae cristae*, 6.769) of Romulus' helmet and ends by telling Aeneas to direct his twin glance (*geminas acies*, 6.788) to "this race and your Romans." Mention of twins anywhere near Romulus inevitably recalls a well-known story about the second founder of Rome: his murder of his twin brother, Remus (Livy 1.7.2–3). Vergil simultaneously suppresses and calls attention to the archetypal act of fratricide that accompanied the founding of Rome. Remus is not mentioned in Anchises' presentation, but he is there all the same. Vergil remembers and forgets him at the same time; Remus is like the ghostly letters that remain when the name of some inconvenient person has been chiseled out of an inscription.

Read in this way, the explicit invocation of civil war in Anchises' description of Pompey and Caesar casts a shadow, back through Brutus and the beginning of the republic, to Romulus and the founding of Rome. Once we recognize the ambivalence in Vergil's simultaneous introduction and suppression of fratricide and civil war, other features of the parade of future Romans jump into high relief. Ancus Marcius, the fourth king of Rome, is "too boastful" (*iactantior*, *Aen.* 6.815) and rejoices too much in the breezes of popular favor. A two-line list of eminent Romans includes Manlius Torquatus, "cruel with his axe"—a reminder that, like Brutus, Torquatus ordered his own son executed for violating military discipline (Livy 8.7). Anchises' pageant of heroes encodes a deeply ambivalent, difficult truth about Rome: its imperial glories and personal virtues are inextricable from the primal flaw that makes brother kill brother, fathers kill sons, and son-in-law and father-in-law stir their fellow citizens to war against each other. That essential flaw persists in those Roman souls despite the thousand-year purification that Anchises described (6.735–751). As Vergil wrote in *Bucolics* 4, "a few traces of our ancestral deceit will remain" in the golden age, whether Saturn or Augustus presides over it, and it will not escape the return of war: "there will be wars again / and a second time will great Achilles be sent to Troy" (*Buc.* 4.31–36). Aeneas is bringing that second Trojan War to Italy, as the Sibyl had hinted (6.86–90), and he, with all his flaws, heroism, and *pietas*, is the ancestor of those Romans. His silence in the face of Anchises' forecast of Augustan glory responds as much to that revelation's shadows as to its light.

For Aeneas and for Vergil's readers early in the reign of Augustus, the path to the future lies through forgetting and remembering in the right way. In the underworld, Aeneas exists in a complicated relationship to what Anchises shows him. From the beginning of the *Aeneid*, its hero's destiny—his fate—has been to set in motion the sequence from Silvius to Augustus; the Romans are his people and his future, and in that future lies the meaning of his life and struggle after Troy. When he looks at the pageant of Roman heroes, he is looking at himself; his journey through the future continues the journey through his past that occupied the first half of his time in the underworld. To return to the world into which the Roman souls will eventually pass, Aeneas must follow their path across Lethe, the river of forgetfulness. Like them, he will emerge with his memory purged; in the second half of the *Aeneid*, he shows no sign that he consciously remembers any person or event from the underworld.[47] Aeneas will, however, emerge with surviving traces of the ingrained, fratricidal impulse that he shares with the souls of Caesar and Pompey, Brutus, Romulus, and other Romans. That flaw will lead him to the necessary conclusion of the

Aeneid, when he loses contact with his past identity as he kills a foe who has in many ways become his twin, at the end of a conflict that Vergil has presented as a kind of civil war.[48]

Because he is that Roman future, Aeneas will carry another trace of it. He will not be entirely freed from his Trojan past, and he will not remember future events and persons that he can never know, but along with the ingrained flaw, he can retain an impression of his descendants' virtues; in fact, Anchises instructs him to do so. The second third of Anchises' parade of Roman heroes concludes with a list of midrepublican soldiers and statesmen (*Aen.* 6.841–846), ending with the Fabian clan and its most prominent member, Quintus Fabius Maximus, called Cunctator, "the Delayer,"[49] for the tactics with which he forced Hannibal to leave Italy. Anchises then punctuates his review with an exhortation.

> Others, I do believe, will more delicately
> beat bronze into statues almost breathing
> and draw from marble life-like expressions.
> They will plead cases better, better describe
> the heavens' motion and name the rising stars.
> You, Roman, remember: rule peoples with command
> imperial, add civilization to peace—for you
> these will be art—spare the conquered, subdue the proud.
>
> *Aen.* 6.847–853[50]

Along with Jupiter's prophecy in book 1, the encomium of Augustus at the end of the first third of Anchises' review of heroes, and the description of Aeneas' shield in book 8, Anchises' panegyric of Rome has been read as a programmatic announcement of the political intent of the *Aeneid*, to be weighed against Aeneas' actions at the end of the poem.[51] My concern here, however, is with its effect on Aeneas in its immediate context.

Anchises addresses Aeneas as "Roman" (*Romane*, 6.851). Commentators are right to suggest that Anchises' vocative includes Vergil's Roman readers, but at this point, as I have argued, Aeneas' own identity has merged with the Roman future. That vocative is the only time he is addressed as "Roman," but he has heard the word twice before, once just before the soul of Augustus appeared, when Anchises directed his attention to "your Romans" (6.789), and once in Carthage, when Mercury commanded him to think of Ascanius, "to whom the kingdom of

Italy and the Roman land is owed" (4.275–276). As the potential Roman that he will be when he leaves the underworld he will obey Anchises' command to "remember" or "be mindful of" (*memento*, 6.851) the peculiar virtues of Rome. The way to Aeneas' future involves both forgetting the past and being mindful of its lessons. In the temporal paradox that is book 6, it also involves forgetting the future while holding on to a belief in its continuity with past and present.

In the aftermath of nearly a century of intermittent civil war, when the Augustan settlement seemed as precarious as walking on newly crusted lava (Horace, *Odes* 2.1.7–8), Vergil's first readers faced the same tension between memory and forgetting. During his journey through his past in the underworld, Aeneas encounters the horrors that they had experienced: on the threshold of hell sit avenging Care, Hunger, War, and Discord with her snaky locks (*Aen.* 6.273–281); as he and the Sibyl walk past Tartarus, she describes the sinners punished there, among whom are brothers who have hated each other, sons who have done violence to their father, and those who took part in the wars that destroyed *pietas* (*arma secuti / impia*, 6.612–613). Coping with those memories and revising them, as Aeneas revised his memories of his past, became urgent tasks in the uncertain years of the early Augustan principate. Vergil suggests a way forward—not a sure or definite path, but a road that can be seen leading into the distance, like the road that Moeris and Lycidas find themselves halfway along at the end of *Bucolics* 9. Like Aeneas, who must "forget the past in order to remember his future" (Most 2001, 162), Vergil's first readers—and perhaps especially his principal reader—faced the task of rebuilding their memory of the Roman past to heal the wounds that it had caused. Lacan observed, "One does not get better because one remembers. One remembers because one gets better" (2006, 521). While acknowledging that the Romans have begun to get better, Vergil is creating the difficult memory that will serve as token of their recovery.

Marcellus

At the end of *Bucolics* 9, the optimistic Lycidas proposed to sing his way through a fractured world. Moeris, broken and silent, demurred. His world wanted not new songs but a new master of song. For Vergil, "getting better" did not mean the new song of Menalcas or the triumphant notes of *excudent alii* (*Aen.* 6.847, quoted above). Some things either must be remembered or cannot be forgotten. So we come, at the end of Anchises' parade of heroes, to Marcellus.

After Anchises' injunction to remember the Roman arts of sparing the conquered and warring down the proud, Vergil inserts a line in his own narrative voice to mark off the last third of the parade: "Thus speaks father Anchises and adds this for his marveling audience" (*Aen.* 6.854). The next and penultimate future Roman is Marcus Claudius Marcellus (ca. 268–208 BC). This Marcellus earned the *spolia opima*, a rare and high honor for a Roman general, by killing the Gallic chieftain Viridomarus at the battle of Clastidium in 222 BC, and Anchises focuses on that episode from his distinguished career. Other aspects of his career are perhaps less in harmony with Rome's mission as Anchises has just outlined it (Freudenburg 2017), but Aeneas' attention does not fall on the future consul and commander. He notices someone with him and speaks for the last time in book 6.

> Father, who is that who accompanies the hero as he goes?
> His son? Or someone from a great line of descendants?
> What cheers from the circling crowd! How great he looks himself!
> Yet dark night flits round his head with mournful shadow.
>
> *Aen.* 6.863–866

The companion is another Marcus Claudius Marcellus, the namesake of the victor at Clastidium. Marcellus the Younger, as he is sometimes known, was the son of Augustus' sister Octavia and Gaius Claudius Marcellus, the undistinguished consul of 50 BC. Lacking male heirs of his own, Augustus arranged for his nephew to become his son-in-law by marrying the emperor's daughter (Marcellus' first cousin) Julia; according to Plutarch, Augustus also adopted Marcellus as his son.[52] With this move, Augustus secured a male heir and the prospect that his grandchildren would inherit the empire he was building. All this dynastic chess came to nothing; in 23 BC, Marcellus fell ill and died. His burial was the first in the new Mausoleum of Augustus.

In eighteen lines—the same number that he gave to Augustus at the climax of the first third of the parade of heroes—Anchises laments the fate of Marcellus the Younger. Romans knew how to memorialize noble youths who died young, and Anchises evokes the pomp and sorrow of Marcellus' funeral, which would have been fresh in the memories of Vergil's first readers: the mourning crowd, the procession to the newly built mausoleum (*tumulum recentem*, *Aen.* 6.874), the Tiber flowing by, and then the funeral speech, which Augustus himself may have delivered (Dio 53.30). Vergil's version, like others before it in similar circumstances,[53] praises the dead young man for what he might have done and been.

> No one would have met him in battle with impunity,
> whether he was marching on foot against the foe
> or digging his spurs into the flank of his foaming steed.
> Oh, lad, you deserve our pity; if you break Fate's bonds,
> you will be Marcellus.
>
> *Aen.* 6.879–883

According to an ancient report, these lines caused Octavia to swoon with grief when Vergil read them to the imperial family shortly after her son's death.

Anchises' description of Marcellus can still move readers, but some features of it betray the anxiety that must have figured at the young prince's funeral in 23 BC, when Augustus' health was in question (he had been treated for the same disease as Marcellus, and by the same physician) and when the durability of the Augustan settlement was very much in doubt. Vergil plants that context squarely in the reader's mind: Anchises is speaking from a mound on a plain, with a crowd of figures filing by and a river alongside, and his evocation of Marcellus' funeral (*Aen.* 6.872–874) mirrors that topography (Pandey 2014). Underneath his mournful eulogy runs a current of doubt and melancholy pessimism that breaks to the surface on two occasions. Halfway through, Anchises utters an exclamation that seems to be part of his lament for Marcellus' unrealized virtues: "Oh *pietas*, oh old-style trust [*fides*] and right hands unvanquished in war!" (6.878–879). As we have seen, *pietas* and *fides* are precisely the qualities that Aeneas' underworld encounters with Palinurus, Dido, and Deiphobus have forced him to question. The premature death of Marcellus raises questions about them again. At the beginning of his eulogy, Anchises speculated that the gods might have deemed the Romans too powerful if Marcellus' potential had been realized (6.870–871). Not human disloyalty or lies but simply the destined death of a young man may make it impossible for Rome to recover the *pietas*, *fides*, and martial valor that Anchises has tried to show through his parade of Roman heroes. Side by side with the stain of fratricide, the sadness of unrealized and unrecovered virtue will persist.

Anchises' final words in the *Aeneid* confirm this undercurrent of melancholy. A Roman aristocratic funeral embodied *pietas* and memory in ceremony. Like the nobility's weddings, a funeral was as much about family and state as about the principal figure of the ceremony. Images of the dead ancestors accompanied the corpse on its last journey, and speeches, often given in the Forum or other public place, praised the dead person and fixed his (and sometimes her) place in a line of forbears. Funerals often meant more than they said; as pointed out earlier in this chapter, Julius Caesar used the funeral of his aunt Julia to make a statement about the place of Marius in public memory. Anchises has just shown Aeneas the grandest possible procession of descendants and given Vergil's readers a procession of ancestors in the world of the dead and a representation and reenactment of Marcellus' funeral. With his last words to his son, Anchises empties all that pomp of meaning. "Fill your hands with lilies," he says, (the same flowers around which the uncanny and disturbing bee-like souls buzzed when Aeneas noticed them), "I shall sprinkle scarlet flowers and heap the soul of my descendant with these gifts, at least, and perform the empty ceremony" (*Aen.* 6.883–886). *Pietas* and *fides*, unrealized in Marcellus, become unrealizable even in the solemn pageant of the Roman state at his funeral. A question inevitably arises: Are they unrealizable also in the pageant of Roman history leading to Augustus?

In the face of this challenge to what his father has shown him and to his future, Aeneas is silent. He had seen (as perhaps his father had not) the shadows gathered around Marcellus' head, and he had asked his father to give attention to the elder Marcellus' young companion. Nothing is left but for Aeneas to leave, or be led, through the Gate of False Dreams into an upper world full of other dead young men: Nisus, Lausus, Pallas, and, finally, Turnus.

CHAPTER 5

The Tears of Aeneas

Zwischen Mensch und Fatum liegt ein Meer von Tränen.

Between Man and Fate lies a sea of tears.

Theodor Haecker, *Vergil: Vater des Abendlandes*

Aeneas smiles once in the *Aeneid*, but he weeps many times. The unique smile is enigmatic and not entirely pleasant, and the difficulty of reading it guides us to the greater difficulty of interpreting his many tears. In the funeral games held for Anchises in Sicily a year after his death, the leading runner, Nisus, slips on a place where the grass has been left slick by the blood (and, no doubt, other bodily products) of recently sacrificed animals (*Aen.* 5.228–230). Nisus then deliberately trips the second-place runner, so that Nisus' young friend and lover, Euryalus, who had been running third, can win the race. As sponsor and referee of the games, Aeneas decides to award a consolation prize to Salius, the runner who was tripped. Nisus complains—surely he also deserves a prize, since he would have finished in first place if hostile fortune had not treated him as it had Salius (5.353–356). He delivers his eloquent, mendacious appeal through a face covered in mud, blood, and dung (*fimo*, 5.358; see *Georgics* 1.80). Aeneas smiles and gives him a prize, too.[1]

Does Aeneas smile because he sees through Nisus' claim that Salius tripped because of bad luck, because Nisus' appearance is ridiculous, or because he rejoices in an opportunity to fulfill his promise that no one would go away from the footrace without a prize (*Aen.* 5.305)? Does his smile betray bemused tolerance, mockery, or good cheer? Does Vergil show him smiling here to connect him to Achilles, whose only smile in the *Iliad* comes at a similar moment during the funeral games of Patroclus (*Iliad* 23.555–556)? Or does the poet mean to point up similarities between Aeneas, "father supreme" of the Trojans (*pater optimus*, 5.358), and Jupiter, father of gods and men, who smiles at Venus at the beginning of the *Aeneid* (1.254) and at Juno at the end (12.829)? Each goddess is designated by an unusual, archaic pronoun, *olli*, that also points to Nisus at 5.358. Whose smile occurs in the Nisus episode, Aeneas' or Vergil's?

If Aeneas' only smile raises complex problems of interpretation, his many tears are even harder to read. In this chapter, I focus on one aspect of his weeping: its entanglement with his Trojan identity and with *pietas*, the signal virtue grounded in that identity. Aeneas weeps at first for lost Troy and for the *pietas* that Troy had created in him. As he makes the transition from Troy to Italy, from refugee to founder of Rome, and from broken man to problematic hero, his tears dry. When they well up again, near the climax of the *Aeneid*, they are as hard to decipher as that lone, enigmatic smile.

Tears in Carthage

Perhaps the most famous tears in the *Aeneid* occur when Aeneas and Achates, veiled in a cloud of invisibility by Venus, investigate the new city of Carthage. They come upon a temple of Juno established by Dido to commemorate the discovery of a buried horse's head, which was taken as an omen that the city would be great in war. As they marvel at the splendid workmanship of the temple, Aeneas sees "the battles at Troy in order, and the war now famous throughout the world" (*Aen.* 1.456–457). Vergil does not reveal how Aeneas sees those battles until eight lines later, when we learn that they are pictures (1.464). At least in the first instant of reading, they might be flashbacks to the lost world of Aeneas' Troy; for those few lines, they are his reality, not—as Vergil will reveal them to be—empty images.

> He stopped and wept. "Achates," he said, "what place,
> what region of earth is not full of our toil?
> Look—Priam. Here too are rewards for glory,
> tears for things, and mortal matters touch the mind.
> Let go your fear. This fame will bring you safety."
>
> *Aen.* 1.459–463

Alessandro Barchiesi calls line 462, *sunt lacrimae rerum et mentem mortalia tangunt*, "a line written to be cited, destined from the beginning to lose its context" (1999, 332). It is easy to detach the syntactically independent line from its surroundings; between them, the genitive *rerum*, "things," and the neuter plural *mortalia*—literally, "mortal (things)"—carry a full charge of indeterminacy. An English-speaking interpreter feels compelled to choose between a universalizing reading of *rerum* and a specific one, between an objective and a subjective genitive. Is Aeneas saying, "here too there are tears for human happenings" (R. Williams 1972, 196), "the universe has sympathy for us" (Stewart 1971, 119), "they [the heroes in the panel] are weeping over sorrows" (Alexander 1954, 400), or something else altogether? Vergil's language does not impose a choice. The line is, as one critic says, "semantically incomplete or 'underdetermined'" (Wharton 2008, 267).

Just at the moment when Aeneas is looking at pictures of the Trojan War in which he himself is mirrored (*Aen.* 1.398), Vergil creates this indeterminacy between particular and universal. He does so to highlight something important about Aeneas at this early point in the epic: the way in which Aeneas both participates in the particular events of the narrative and constitutes, in his person, the universal meaning of them.[2] Aeneas is the picture and the interpretation of it. He is the man who flees Troy and finds his way to Italy; he is also the founder of Rome and the line that leads to Augustus, and that belated outcome, as Jupiter explained earlier in book 1 (lines 257–296), gives meaning to Aeneas' life and suffering. Vergil leaves the meaning of Aeneas' words undetermined in order to point to the central tragedy of Aeneas. Trojan Aeneas, as we have seen, can never know the meaning of his life, because it lies in a Roman future beyond his horizon. His tears, like every other part of his life, are bound by their context in the narrative, but their meaning extends beyond it, and he says more than he knows, just as he is more than he will ever understand.

When Aeneas in Juno's sanctuary interprets pictures of himself and of events in which, as he will tell Dido, he played no small part (*Aen.* 2.6), he has to get things wrong, because his information about the meaning of events is always necessarily incomplete. Vergil's description of the scenes makes clear that they are a celebration of Trojan defeat and humiliation, adorning Juno's temple as a reminder of her triumph over the people and city that she hates (*genus invisum*, 1.28). The slaughter of the Trojans' ally Rhesus by Diomedes (and Odysseus, whom Vergil does not mention), the killing of Priam's son Troilus by Achilles, the futile attempts of Trojan women to win over the goddess Athena (who averts her gaze from their gifts), Achilles dragging Hector's body around the walls of Troy and then ransoming it for Priam's gold, and Achilles' further victims Memnon and Penthesilea—the message could not be clearer. Aeneas, however, looks at these depictions and sees something else: an indication that he, his Trojans, and their suffering are known throughout the world. Thus he finds grounds for hope, thinking that if the people of Carthage reward glory and recognize suffering, surely they will show kindness to Aeneas and his band of refugees.

Aeneas is mistaken about the general intent of the paintings; he may also be wrong about specific interpretations. He not only embodies both the action of the *Aeneid* and its meaning but is also the lens through which Vergil focuses readers' knowledge of the pictures on Juno's temple. There is something wrong with his account of the picture of Troilus. In the usual version of the myth, Troilus, one of Priam's sons, went off to water his horses and was ambushed by Achilles.

> In another picture Troilus flees, his weapons lost,
> unlucky boy, unequal match for Achilles.
> His horses drag him, on his back he clings to the empty chariot
> still holding the reins; neck and hair are dragged
> through the dirt; the dust is marked by his trailing spear.
>
> *Aen.* 1.474–478

If Troilus has lost his weapons, how can he have a spear? Its presence seems to have troubled Servius, who comments on the word *hasta*, "*Spear:* the enemy's, of course." Other commentators have suggested that *armis*, "weapons," in the phrase *amissis armis*, "with his weapons lost," means everything but the spear.[3] It is also troubling that Greek and Roman depictions of the death of Troilus show the boy riding or leading horses, not in a chariot. Peter Heslin suggests that Aeneas has mistakenly taken a painting of Hector dragged behind Achilles' chariot for a picture of Troilus, and that this is one of a series of misinterpretations. "Aeneas' failure to understand the Trojan paintings in Carthage," Heslin concludes, shows that he has not fully understood the events of that war and that he cannot foresee how he will repeat the tragedy of Achilles."[4]

The tears flowing from these misinterpretations stream down Aeneas' face as he speaks to Achates (*largoque umectat flumine vultum*, *Aen.* 1.465) and connect him to his Trojan identity; at and in this moment, his tears are for Troy. A short while earlier, he described himself to his mother, Venus, as an exile from Troy, unknown, in need, driven from two continents and lost in the third

(1.384–385). As he introduced himself to the disguised goddess, Aeneas emphasized two aspects of his identity: Troy and the *pietas* that is part of it. Yet what he said to Venus revealed that he finds it difficult to hold on to his belief in Troy's renown.

> From old Troy—if by chance Troy's name
> has reached your ears—we have sailed the seas;
> now a storm in its caprice has driven us to Africa.
> I am *pius* Aeneas, famous over the earth;
> I carry Troy's gods snatched from the enemy;
> my quest is Italy and a home; I descend from Jove.
>
> *Aen.* 1.375–380

Aeneas has no doubt about Troy's reputation or his own, but he cannot be sure how far that story has spread or that his unknown interlocutor has heard it. When he sees pictures of Troy in Juno's temple a short while later, his first response is to interpret them as a sign that his uncertainty was mistaken: here, too, people have heard of Troy and even of *pius* Aeneas. He and his Trojans can hope, and his *pietas*—he believes—still has meaning.

It matters that Aeneas has an audience in Juno's temple. Vergil makes clear that Aeneas addresses his interpretation to Achates: "This fame will bring you [*tibi*] some kind of safety" (*feret haec aliquam tibi fama salutem*, *Aen.* 1.463). The presence of Achates as Aeneas' audience emphasizes Aeneas' role as interpreter of the pictures and confirms that Aeneas remains the leader who addressed his castaway followers with feigned hope on the beach at Carthage (1.198–209). Achates' role invites readers to measure, once again, the distance between Aeneas' words and his inner state. This time, Aeneas' words to Achates agree with his thoughts as reported by Vergil: the sight of the pictures makes him dare to hope for safety in Carthage (*sperare salutem / ausus*, 1.451–452), and so he tells Achates. In this passage, there seems to be no conflict between inner thought and outer word.

Yet those words to Achates sound a dissonance between the message heard by Achates in the narrative and a meaning known to Vergil's readers. When Aeneas interprets his tears and the pictures that prompt them, Vergil gives him words freighted with indeterminacy; his words to Achates, *sunt lacrimae rerum*, constitute both a particular interpretation of the pictures, grounded in Aeneas' response to them, and a generalizable statement that goes far beyond Aeneas, weeping there in Carthage. The conflict is not between Aeneas' words and his feelings but between his present situation and his destined future, which forms the meaning of his existence even though he cannot know what that future is. The necessary condition of that meaning, the virtue without which he will not be able to move toward it, is his *pietas*, and *pietas* makes him weep here. At this moment, however, he is beginning to be mistaken about that *pietas*, just as he is mistaken in his interpretation of the paintings' meaning. Aeneas thinks that *pietas* means recovering Troy. In the pictures before him, he sees a reminder of his lost city, to which he remains dutifully loyal, and of its fame, but as he declares the centrality of Troy and his past for his life, his words escape him and disappear into an indeterminate future inhabited by Vergil's readers, where Augustus' reign may give meaning to Aeneas' tears. In the present moment of the poem, there in Carthage, his tears are the by-product of a misinterpretation, part of a scheme of illusion that implicates Aeneas himself in the greatest danger that he will face on his way to Italy.

Empty Tears and Carthaginian Theatrics

At the close of Aeneas' words to Achates, Vergil adds a transitional comment before continuing with a description of the pictures as Aeneas sees them: "Thus he spoke, feeds his thoughts on the empty picture [*animum pictura pascit inani*] / with many groans, and moistens his countenance with a stream of tears" (*Aen.* 1.464–465). Even when Vergil uses *inanis* (empty) to refer to a container missing its usual contents, like Troilus' chariot in the pictures in front of Aeneas (1.475) or Ascanius' helmet when he tosses it on the ground (5.673), the word often retains connotations of "useless," like the "empty service" (*inani munere*) that Anchises performs for the doomed spirit of Marcellus (6.885), or "meaningless," like the "empty words" (*inania verba*) of the uncanny phantom Aeneas that Juno produces to deceive Turnus (10.639). The pictures whose meaning Aeneas misunderstands are empty because they cannot provide any real nourishment for his thoughts, which are bound to an illusion about *pietas*, Troy, and his immediate future; in fact, Vergil's characterization of the picture as "empty" is perhaps his strongest affirmation of the peculiar nature of Carthage in the *Aeneid*. Aeneas has come ashore in a land where deception and illusion reign. There he is, as he told Venus, not only "unknown" (*ignotus*, 1.384) but also "unknowing" (*ignarus*, 1.332) and "wandering" (*errans*, 1.333). His last epithet in that description, *errans*, can also mean "mistaken."

The Trojans' first sight of this country of illusions reveals a landscape that takes on the character of a stage set. Vergil describes a secluded cove with a wooded backdrop (*Aen.* 1.157–169). The harbor is at once sheltering and ominous; as the Trojan ships glide in, it broods over them. On either side, twin cliffs "threaten" (*minantur*); a forest brandishes its limbs (*silvis coruscis*), and a grove dark with quivering or bristling shadow (*horrenti umbra*) overhangs the scene. Yet Vergil chooses a word from the theater, *scaena* (1.164), to sum up the scene. E. W. Leach describes the effect of that choice.

> It is not a descriptive word here, but a substitute for a description that provokes a chain of wandering associations. By evoking the theater, it may well seem to tame the ominous chiaroscuro of the wilderness into an orderly structure, yet a dressed stage provokes expectations of action, while at the moment neither Aeneas nor the reader knows what future event to expect. (Leach 1988, 35)

Vergil's Carthage itself is theatrical fiction.[5] As Aeneas and Achates look down on the city from a nearby hill (*Aen.* 1.418–429), they see all the features of a city under construction: gates, streets, walls, and harbors. Vergil gives the theater under construction two and one-half lines (more than any other feature) and an emphatic place at the end of the catalog. Vergil's characterization of Dido draws on heroines of tragedy like Antigone, Medea, and Phaedra and compares Dido's dreams to the hallucinations of figures from tragedy (4.469–473).[6] In the Carthaginian plotline, in fact, drama nearly displaces epic as the literary ground of the narrative.

This theatrical motif and the chain of indeterminacies, uncertainties, and delusions that it sets in motion echo throughout the winter in Carthage. "Why," Aeneas asks his mother as she drops her disguise and glides away, "do you mock your son with deceptive images?" (*falsis imaginibus*, *Aen.* 1.407–408). Those purple buskins, a tragedian's footgear, that she was wearing before she revealed herself may connect her to tragedy; in effect, she is the divine prologue to the tragedy that will unfold in Carthage.[7] In that drama, the principal figures act out their parts in the grip of illusion, ignorance, and mutual incomprehension. From the beginning, as Jupiter sends Mercury to Carthage to make sure that she welcomes the Trojan refugees, Dido is ignorant of (her) fate (*fati nescia*, 1.299). Vergil later compares her to a doe wounded by an arrow that a shepherd practicing with his weapons has shot in ignorance (*nescius*, emphasized by enjambment, 4.72); Aeneas, *ignarus* and *errans*, is that shepherd.[8] Dido believes that her relationship with Aeneas is a form of marriage; he denies that he entered into any such thing. In Carthage, Dido and Aeneas are players in a drama whose significance neither of them understands.

That drama ends for one of its players when the Lacanian Real bursts onto the stage that is Carthage, just as the Real loomed out of the flames and smoke at Troy in Aeneas' inset tale, like a messenger speech, that forms part of the Carthaginian tragedy (*Aen.* 2.608–623, discussed in chapter 1). Prompted by a prayer from one of Dido's rejected African suitors, Jupiter sends Mercury to command Aeneas to remember *pietas*, leave Dido, and get on with his journey to Italy (*Aen.* 4.219–278). The god finds Aeneas dressed like a king from the stage, in a jeweled sword and purple cloak (4.261–262). Aeneas, as he later tells Dido (4.358), recognizes that this epiphany is no dream or hallucination; the god himself stands in front of him in the clear North African sunlight.

Aeneas heeds the god's command, although, once again, his interpretation of it suggests that he fails to understand the meaning of what he has seen. When he reports the epiphany to Dido and attempts to justify his decision to leave for Italy, he appeals to traditional anchors of *pietas*: his father, who has been haunting his dreams (*Aen.* 4.351–353); and Ascanius, his son whom he is cheating of his destined kingdom by lingering in Carthage (4.354–355). If fate allowed Aeneas free choice, he tells Dido, he would reestablish Troy on its original site with its few surviving citizens; as is, a fate he does not understand commands him to go to Italy and settle his Trojans there, as Dido has settled her Phoenicians at Carthage (4.339–350). Jupiter made it clear to Mercury that Aeneas' entire life, including his survival in the Trojan War, has a single purpose: "to rule an Italy pregnant with empire and growling with wars, to bring forth a race from the high blood of Teucer, and to send the whole world under its laws" (4.229–231)—that is, to set in motion the founding of Rome. Mercury reports the gist of Jupiter's order and even mentions the "Roman land" that is owed to Ascanius (4.275), but Aeneas does not seem to take in the unfamiliar name, just as he failed to recognize the iconographic program of the murals on Juno's temple. There can be no mistaking, though, what Jupiter wants him to do. From this point onward, he and Dido are actors performing in two different plays, and at the center of book 4 (lines 305–392), Dido's passionate arias bracketing Aeneas' lawyerly, controlled brief reveal the lovers' distance from each other. Jupiter's decision resolves the conflict between Aeneas' present situation and his destined future, which opened up when he wept in Juno's temple, but the resolution comes with more tears, more emptiness, and at the cost of Dido's life.

While Aeneas makes preparations for departure, the god Love (Amor), drives Dido to resort once more to tears and supplications. She uses her sister, Anna, as a go-between to convey a message: the queen no longer begrudges Aeneas his Italy; all she wants is a little time. Can he not wait just until spring, for favorable winds? "I ask an empty time," she says, "rest and breathing room for this madness" (*tempus inane peto, requiem spatiumque furori*, 4.433). The empty time Dido asks for must also be a meaningless time, like the empty pictures in Juno's temple that lost their meaning when Aeneas misinterpreted them. Just as Aeneas' tears have meaning on two levels, the particular and the universal, Dido's *tempus inane* threatens to be meaningless on two levels: it will only delay, not prevent, Aeneas' departure for Italy; and it will not advance the grand narrative of the Aeneid, Aeneas' journey toward Rome and Augustus. Dido asks, in fact, for what Aeneas has had with her. From the point of view of Jupiter in the narrative or of the *Aeneid*'s drive toward Italy, Aeneas' time in Carthage has been meaningless. It is time to get on with the story. In the underworld, Anchises acknowledges the threat that Carthage, with its illusions and vacancies, posed to his son's destiny (6.694).

Dido's requests leave Aeneas unmoved.

> Thus Dido kept begging, thus her sister carried her sobs
> back and forth. But Aeneas is not moved by sobs,
> he does not change for any words nor hear them;
> Fate is in the way. God has stoppered the man's ears.
> And just as north winds from the Alps compete
> to topple an ancient oak with blasts from here
> and then from there—they rise to a roar; branches
> from high up the shaken trunk strew the ground;
> the tree clings to its crag; as high as its crown
> extends to heaven, so far its root to hell.
> Thus the hero is battered by a storm of words
> on every side and feels the cares in his great heart;
> his mind remains unmoved, and tears roll down, empty.
>
> *Aen.* 4.437–449

"Some critics," Servius says, "take these 'empty tears' as Aeneas', or Dido's, or Anna's, or everyone's."[9] Modern criticism has not been able to remove the indeterminacy.[10] Like Aeneas' tears before the pictures in Juno's temple, these tears and the words that describe them (*lacrimae volvuntur inanes*) are indeterminate, detachable from their context, and generalizable. At the end of his time in Carthage, as at its beginning, tears flow from the central enigma of Aeneas' identity. Here, too, he is both the actor in the drama and the meaning of it. Just as he was both the content of the pictures on Juno's temple and the interpreter of them, he is here the lover with burdened heart and the hero on whom, like the great tree that spans heaven and Tartarus, the future pivots. Tears—empty, useless, meaningless, universal—are the sea between him and the destiny toward which he sails.

Interlude: Tears on Olympus

A hero is "a man who wants to be himself."[11] Aeneas' destiny is to be both his story and the meaning of it, and his tragedy is never to be able to bridge the gap between participant and interpreter—never to be himself and never to understand the meaning of his story. At the end of book 8, Venus gives Aeneas armor forged by Vulcan, as Thetis had given her son, Achilles, armor forged by Hephaestus (*Iliad* 18.368–617). Like the shield of Achilles, that of Aeneas has images on it: it depicts Rome's future, culminating in Augustus and including some figures (Romulus, Augustus, Cato) whom Aeneas has already seen in the underworld. Aeneas admires the pictures; they are "wars in the order of their fighting" (*pugnataque in ordine bella, Aen.* 8.629), like the "fights and wars in order" (*ex ordine pugnas / bellaque*, 1.446–447) that he had admired on the walls of Juno's temple in Carthage. Yet Aeneas does not recognize or understand anything that he sees on his new shield; at the close of the book, as he hoists the shield onto his shoulder, "he marvels and, not understanding the subject matter, rejoices in the images" (8.730).

Unknowing Aeneas goes toward Italy in ignorance and through passion, suffering, and labor, bound to his ignorance by time and history. As he goes, he is shadowed by two figures, one from the future that he cannot know and one from the legendary generation that preceded his own. The future figure is Augustus, who appears at three critical points in the *Aeneid*: at the beginning, in Jupiter's prophecy (*Aeneid* 1.285–290); in the center, as a second founder immediately following Romulus in Anchises' parade of heroes (6.790–800); and at the center of the shield made by Vulcan, where Augustus appears at the celebration of his triple triumph in 29 BC (8.714–728). The figure from the immediate past is Hercules. Because he is a figure from Aeneas' past, Hercules can serve as model and foil not only for Aeneas' present but also for his future, as represented by Augustus.

Hercules is mentioned many times in the *Aeneid*, but his importance in relation to both Aeneas and Augustus becomes clearest in book 6.[12] In the twelfth of his famous labors, Hercules went down to the underworld to retrieve the three-headed dog, Cerberus; in the *Aeneid*, Hercules appears as a pattern for Aeneas on the same journey. Aeneas claims Hercules and Theseus as exemplars for his descent in search of his father (*Aen.* 6.123), and Charon cites the same two examples in an attempt to explain why he should not ferry a living hero across the Styx this third time (6.392–394). Hercules, the hero known for his labors, is an obvious analogue for Aeneas, whose own word for his sufferings and those of Troy is *labor* (2.11, 284, 362) and who uses the same word to characterize his archetypal act of *pietas* as he lifts his crippled father onto his shoulders to carry him from Troy (2.708). As he does so, Aeneas drapes himself in a lion's skin, the costume of Hercules (2.722–723).

In the procession of future Romans that closes book 6, Hercules appears again, this time linked with Augustus. After a catalog of Aeneas' immediate descendants, Anchises points to Romulus, the founder under whose *auspicia* Rome will extend its dominion until it is coextensive with the earth and match its courage with the Olympian gods (*Aen.* 6.781–782). *Auspicia* are bird omens that Roman magistrates consulted at the beginning of an enterprise, to determine whether or not the gods favored their undertaking; as founder, Romulus inaugurates the rise of Rome and confirms the favor of the gods toward her. Many readers will think, though, of the contest of augury in which Romulus and his brother vied to be named founder, as well as the fratricide that followed it in one version; here, as so often in the *Aeneid*, we glimpse a shape in the distances of the text—Remus, just out of reach but not quite forgotten.[13] Immediately after Romulus and out of chronological sequence, Anchises points out the second founder of Rome.

> Here is the man, this one, promised you too often,
> Augustus Caesar, scion of a god, who will found
> a Golden Age again in Latium, fields where Saturn
> once ruled, who will carry empire beyond Indians
> and Garamantians, to land beyond the stars,
> beyond the zodiac, where Atlas Sky-bearer

on his shoulders spins the star-studded axis of heaven.
Already kings of Caucasus consult the omens
and shudder at his coming; the Sea of Azov
quakes, the seven mouths of Nile roil in alarm.
Yes, not Hercules traversed so much of Earth,
although he shot the bronze-hoofed deer, brought peace
to Erymanthus' woods, put his arrow into the Hydra.
Nor did the one who yokes his triumphal car
with vines, Bacchus driving his tigers from Nysa.
Do we still shrink from advancing valor with deeds?
Does fear still keep us from taking a stand in Italy?

Aen. 6.791–807

The sighting of Augustus prompts a crucial moment in the *Aeneid.* As we saw in chapter 4, Anchises' questions catalyze Aeneas' reluctant, only partially successful pivot from Trojan past to Roman future. The hero hears the questions and goes forward, but he says nothing in response. In his silent advance, he embodies and struggles with a central question of the *Aeneid*: How much does a glorious destiny cost?

At this moment, Augustus, the promised imperial future, is likened to two divinities known for their globe-spanning travels, Dionysus and Hercules. Aeneas has already compared his underworld journey to that of Hercules; now Hercules appears as a model for the culmination of Aeneas' future in Augustus. The comparison between Hercules and Augustus is not as straightforward as it seems, though, and here too a rival appears in the distances of the text. Mark Antony, the last warlord defeated by Octavian on his way to becoming Augustus, claimed descent from Anton, a son of Hercules, and was also compared to Dionysus.[14] The two gods here highlight the geographical scope of Augustus' future conquests, but they also hint that those conquests entailed defeat of those gods' earthly descendant and avatar in a bloody civil war. As with Romulus and the shadowy Remus, Rome's glory under Augustus is entwined with a vanquished rival and internecine strife.

Reading Hercules in the *Aeneid*, then, can be a model for reading both Aeneas' present and his future. As an immortal, Hercules stands, like Jupiter, in a place where Aeneas' future can be known and understood. As a mortal hero (who becomes a god, as Aeneas will), Hercules can be an actor in the narrative's immediate past, as he is in book 8. He thus bridges Vergil's Augustan present, which is Aeneas' future, and Aeneas' narrative present, which is Rome's remote past. In a way, Hercules offers a solution to Aeneas' inevitable failure to know and understand the meaning of his story. When he, like Aeneas, weeps, his tears may shed light on those of Aeneas.

In book 10 of the *Aeneid*, the war for Italy is in full spate. Aeneas returns from his visit to King Evander with reinforcements, including the king's son, Pallas; when Aeneas lands, the Trojans break out of the fortified camp in which they have been besieged, and combat between the Trojans and the Italian forces, led by Turnus, becomes general. Vergil develops and compresses motifs from the climax of the *Iliad*: the *aristeia* of Patroclus, his death, and Achilles' revenge. In books 15 through 22 of the *Iliad*, a series of duels and deaths leads up to a climactic combat between the epic's hero and his foe: Patroclus kills Sarpedon, Hector kills Patroclus, and finally, Achilles kills Hector. Vergil's Iliadic grounding of the text sets up an expectation that a similar series will culminate in a duel between Turnus and Aeneas. Pallas corresponds to Patroclus, Turnus to Hector, and Aeneas to Achilles.[15]

Fate, in a way, is a story with a necessary ending, and Pallas is doomed to recapitulate Patroclus' history, encounter Turnus, and be killed. As the young man squares off against the Italian champion, he prays. His prayer appeals to the recently deified Hercules; as Evander told Aeneas (*Aen.* 8.184–272), Hercules had visited Evander's kingdom and rid it of an ogre-like monster called Cacus.

> "By my father's hospitable table at which you sat,
> I pray, O Hercules: attend my great attempt.
> May Turnus' dying eyes behold me snatch
> his weapons from him and carry them away."
> The god heard, suppressed a mighty groan
> beneath his heart, and poured out empty tears.
> The Father of All then uttered kindly words:
> "For each his day stands waiting, for everyone
> brief life is irrecoverable. But to draw out fame
> by deeds, this is manhood's work. At Troy
> fell so many sons of gods, and with them died
> my own Sarpedon, my son. His own fate now
> calls Turnus; he has reached life's finish line."
>
> *Aen.* 10.460–472

Hercules responds to the doomed youth's prayer because Pallas' appeal to *hospitium et mensas*, the hospitable table that Hercules shared as Evander's guest, establishes a bond between the god and Evander's son. That bond deserves examination.

Hospitium, the tie created by guest-friendship, motivates the important relationship between Aeneas and Pallas in the second, Iliadic half of the *Aeneid*, especially Aeneas' reaction to Pallas' death. Much has been made of homoerotic elements in that relationship,[16] and I do not deny their valence, but they remain (as Eros so often does in encounters with other people) latent in the dialectic of the text. *Hospitium* is on the surface, proclaimed by author and characters. In book 8, Aeneas reenacts Hercules' visit to Evander. Aeneas arrives at Evander's settlement on the day of the festival commemorating Hercules' visit; when Evander welcomes him to his humble palace, the king reminds him that Hercules had also crossed its threshold and invites Aeneas to conduct himself as his earlier guest had (*Aen.* 8.362–365). When Evander entrusts his son to Aeneas, he makes clear that Aeneas is to guide and protect the young man, teach him the war god's work, and serve as an example and guide (8.514–517). The tie of *hospitium* between Evander and Aeneas, for which Hercules served as pattern, creates the bond between Aeneas and Pallas.

In praying to Hercules, Pallas prays to the divinity who serves as example for his relationship with Aeneas, and Hercules' response prefigures Aeneas' tears as he gazes down on Pallas' body at *Aeneid* 11.41. Hercules attempts to stifle a groan (*sub imo / corde premit gemitum*) and pours out "empty" tears (*lacrimas effundit inanis*, 10.463–464). Like Aeneas, Hercules struggles with his emotional response to events, and Vergil signals the resemblance by echoing language used for Aeneas in Carthage. (With *sub imo / corde premit*, compare *curam sub corde premebat* at 4.332 and *premit altum corde dolorem* at 1.209.) Like the empty tears that rolled down from Aeneas, Dido, or everyone (*lacrimae volvuntur inanes*, 4.449) or the tears that Aeneas shed as he also looks at scenes of warfare with which he has a connection (1.459–462), Hercules' tears are "tears for things," not only for Pallas, but for all the young men whose fathers have been unable to protect them in the war god's work. Hercules, like Aeneas, is both participant and interpreter of events; the bond of *hospitium* connects him to Pallas, but his divine status gives him a perspective outside those events. Hercules' stifled groan and empty tears show the same tension between participation and understanding that marks Aeneas, but for Hercules, Jupiter's speech resolves the tension. Unlike Aeneas, Hercules can learn from

Jupiter the connection between events and fate; he can understand the meaning of the story through which he moves.

Tears in Italy

Pallas' unequal contest with Turnus followed a Homeric pattern: Pallas threw his spear but only grazed Turnus' body; Turnus' spear rammed through Pallas' shield (past layers of bull's hide, bronze, and iron), before drilling through Pallas' corselet and into his chest. When Pallas pulled out the point, his life came with it (*Aen.* 10.474–487). As dawn breaks on the next day, Aeneas faces a crowd of worries: the Trojans are in possession of the field, but dispositions have to be made to carry the fight to the enemy's city, and a truce must be arranged to bury the dead. Nevertheless, Aeneas does not neglect the obligations of *pietas*: he offers up prayers to the gods and erects a trophy—the trunk of an oak draped with the armor and weapons of Mezentius, an exiled Etruscan king whom Aeneas had killed on the previous day. Like Aeneas' prayers, the trophy is an act of *pietas*, not merely proclaiming victory, but consecrating it and warding off evil from the victorious army.[17] Only then does Aeneas give orders to his commanders and arrange for the burial of the previous day's dead. Finally, shedding tears (*inlacrimans*, 11.29), he sets in motion the process of returning Pallas' body to his father, Evander.

Surrounded by a lamenting crowd of Trojan men and women, Aeneas stands in front of the tent where Pallas has been laid out and gazes down at the pale body with the gaping wound in its chest. Through welling tears (*lacrimis . . . obortis*, *Aen.* 11.41; *deflevit*, 11.59), he speaks.

> "Poor boy" he said, "when Luck came smiling
> was she jealous of me, that you'd behold
> my kingdom rise and return in victory
> to your father's house? This is not
> the promise I gave Evander when I left,
> as he sent me off from his embrace
> to fight for empire and anxiously warned
> that our foe are keen, our fight with a hard race.
> And now perhaps, seized by empty hope,
> he is making vows and piling his altars with gifts,

while we mourners escort with useless tribute
his lifeless son, who owes no more to heaven.
Unlucky man, you'll see your son's funeral!
Is this the return and triumph that we hoped for?
Is this my mighty promise? At least, Evander,
you won't behold a son struck down by shameful wounds,
you won't desire grim death because your son survived.
O Italy, and you, Iulus—you mourn a defender."

Aen. 11.42–58

The *Aeneid* is full of dead young men, some nearly anonymous, like Acron, the young bridegroom killed by Mezentius (*Aen.* 10.719–720), others more fully realized. Two of these, like Pallas, receive extended commemorations in which Aeneas takes part: Augustus' nephew Marcellus the Younger, the last figure in Anchises' parade of future Romans (6.854–886); and Lausus, Mezentius' son, who dies at Aeneas' hands while defending his father (10.789–832). Aeneas' first words over the body of young Pallas recall Anchises' earlier lament for Marcellus and look ahead to his own lament for Lausus, and they implicate both in Hercules' empty tears for his doomed guest-friend and the prayer from Pallas that prompted them.

When Turnus kills Pallas, Aeneas is on another part of the battlefield. As soon as word reaches him that Pallas is dead, his forces near defeat, Aeneas erupts into an exalted frenzy of killing, the kind of *aristeia* that elevates Diomedes, Achilles, and the other heroes of the *Iliad*. With the image of Pallas, Evander, and their hospitality before his eyes (*Aen.* 10.515–517), Aeneas seems to slip free of the *pietas* that has otherwise never left him; he reserves prisoners for human sacrifice (10.517–520), does not spare suppliants even when they appeal to his feelings for his own son (10.521–536), kills a priest (10.537–542), and leaves a trail of victims in his wake, raging like a flash flood or tornado (*torrentis aquae vel turbinis atri / more furens*, 10.603–604). At the end of that rampage, he encounters Mezentius. The exiled Etruscan king has been on his own killing spree, and the two champions meet in a duel that prefigures Aeneas' climactic meeting with Turnus.[18] Mezentius throws a spear, which misses Aeneas but kills another warrior, and Aeneas throws his, which pierces Mezentius' shield and wounds him in the thigh (10.762–788). Aeneas draws his sword and moves in for the kill.

At that point, young Lausus brings *pietas* back before Aeneas' eyes. He steps between his father and Aeneas, parries the thrust, and covers the wounded Mezentius, who retreats, hampered by Aeneas' spear hanging from his shield. A barrage of missiles delays Aeneas, but he finally shakes them off and goes after Mezentius. Lausus again stands in the way, ready to save his father by fighting a battle-hardened killer twice his age.[19] Aeneas recognizes the discrepancy; he also recognizes Lausus' motivation and its deceptive power: "Where are you charging, you on the point of death?" he asks. "Your *pietas* is deluding you in this heedless act" (*Aen.* 10.811–812). Then he kills him, quickly and efficiently.

> But when Anchises' son looked on the face
> of the dying boy, saw death's amazing pallor,
> he groaned deep in pity, stretched out his right hand
> and in his mind welled up the face of fatherly *pietas.*
> "What now, poor boy, what will *pius* Aeneas
> give you in return for such a noble act?
> Keep your armor—it made you happy. But you
> I release to your fathers' ghost-gods, if that concerns you.
> Still, be consoled by this in your misfortune:
> you died at the hand of Aeneas the Great."
>
> *Aen.* 10.821–830

Vergil makes sure that readers see Lausus as more than another item in Aeneas' catalog of victims. The poet inserts his own voice into the poem by addressing Lausus directly: "If the antiquity of a story brings any credibility to such a great deed, I certainly shall not stay silent about the hard death that befell you, your glorious deeds, or you, o youth worthy of commemoration" (10.791–793). The same figure of speech (known to grammarians as *apostrophe*) heightens the pathos around the deaths of two other young men, Nisus and Euryalus in the previous book (9.446–449). Like Euryalus (9.473–502), Lausus has a mother whose presence in the narrative creates sympathy for his youth and premature death; Lausus' mother had sent him off to war with a tunic made of material spun with gold thread, which Aeneas' sword rips through and leaves soaked in blood (10.818–820).

Nisus and Euryalus, however, die while Aeneas is away at Evander's city, and although I will return to the gold thread, I want to focus on the connections among three commemorations at which Aeneas is present, those for Pallas, Marcellus, and Lausus. Vergil chooses language that connects Aeneas' speech over Lausus in book 10 to Pallas at the beginning of book 11 and Marcellus at the end of book 6. The same vocative phrase, *miserande puer*, "boy who must be pitied," links the two speeches over Lausus and Pallas and Anchises' eulogy for Marcellus in the underworld (*Aen.* 6.882, 10.825, 11.42); further, Vergil's epithet for Aeneas, *Anchisiades*, "son of Anchises" (10.822), emphasizes Aeneas' relation to his father and evokes not only their last meeting, when Anchises showed him Marcellus at the climax of the series of future Romans, but also the quasi-filial relationship that exists between Aeneas and Pallas. Finally, all three passages contain the same hint that the ritual gestures of *pietas* may be empty. Anchises honors Marcellus' spirit with an empty service (*inani munere*, 6.885–886). Faced with Pallas' corpse, Aeneas asks, "Is this the return and triumph that we hoped for? / Is this my mighty promise?" (11.54–55). When he says to the dying Lausus, "You I release to your fathers' ghost-gods, if that concerns you," the phrase *si qua est ea cura* suggests a deeper skepticism about the obligations of *pietas* than my translation conveys. The words might equally well be translated, "if that concern [*cura*] amounts to anything." Whose *cura* is it, and to whom does it matter? Does Aeneas say to Lausus, "I'll return your body, if that matters at all to you," or does he say, "I'll return your body, if that act of mine means anything at all"? Like the empty tears that roll down in book 4 or the enigmatic smile of book 5, this *cura*, which might have given us a window into Aeneas' mental and emotional state, slips from our grasp.

Now, Marcellus. Both Aeneas' lament over Pallas and Anchises' lament over Marcellus are introduced by "welling tears" (*lacrimis obortis*, *Aen.* 6.867 ≈ 11.41), and both address the dead with a key phrase that links Marcellus, Lausus, and Pallas: *miserande puer*. Those signposts point to other connections. Both Anchises contemplating Marcellus and Aeneas speaking over Pallas emphasize the promise of a youthful life cut short; it is a conventional topic, as we have seen in chapter 4. Both speeches also invite reflection on Aeneas' cardinal virtue, *pietas*, and on promises of another kind. Anchises laments Marcellus' unrealized virtues: "Oh *pietas*, oh old-style honor [*prisca fides*] and right hands unvanquished in war!" (6.878–879). Underworld encounters with Palinurus, Dido, and Deiphobus forced Aeneas to question his understanding of *pietas* and *fides*, and the appearance of young Marcellus, the last person introduced in book 6, sends Aeneas through the ivory gates with an unresolved question: If Marcellus represents the culmination of Roman virtue, what does his fated, premature death say about the relation between those virtues and the history, culminating in Augustus, that Aeneas will set in motion? Anchises heaps up flowers to honor Marcellus' spirit, but it is an empty service (*inani / munere*, 6.885–886). Are the tears shed over Pallas equally empty? Pallas' corpse, lying on a hurdle woven of oak and arbutus, looks like a flower cut by a maiden's fingernail, a violet or hyacinth with freshness still visible on it but life gone (11.64–71). Those metaphorical flowers hint that the rites for Pallas are a service as empty as Anchises' handfuls of underworld lilies.

Aeneas also touches on Pallas' unfulfilled promise: with his death, Italy lost a champion, and Iulus lost a protector (*Aen.* 11.57–58). Most of Aeneas' tribute, however, focuses on another kind of broken promise: the vow that he made to Evander to guide Pallas in military service, show him the war god's work, and be an example to him (8.514–519). When Evander entrusts Pallas to him with ringing words and a commitment of four hundred cavalry, Aeneas responds with one of his silences; he and Achates, who know what the war god's work is like, stand with downcast gaze and ponder its hard realities (8.520–522). A sign from heaven interrupts their silence: lightning, thunder, a blare of trumpets, and a vision of armor glowing red and sounding from the blow of hammers.[20] Aeneas rightly interprets this omen to mean that his mother, Venus, has arranged for her husband, Vulcan, to make armor for him. He announces his eagerness to fight (8.523–540), although his closing words suggest that the "many hard things" (*dura multa*) that he and Achates were pondering have not left his mind.

> Ah, what slaughter now presses the people of Laurentum!
> What penalties you'll pay me, Turnus! Under your waves, O Tiber,
> how many shields you'll tumble, men's helmets and strong bodies!
> Let them demand their battles and break our agreements!
>
> *Aen.* 8.537–540

These words can be read as a vaunting threat but also as a lament; the call to father Tiber (*quam multa sub undas / scuta virum galeasque et fortia corpora volves*, 8.538–539) echoes Aeneas' despondent closing of his first speech in the poem, when he remembered another river, the Simois at Troy, choked with armor and bodies (*ubi tot Simois correpta sub undis / scuta virum galeasque et fortia corpora volvit*, 1.100–101). His promise to Evander is implied rather than stated, but one word in the text suggests that he accepted the trust. The epithet *Anchisiades* (son of Anchises) appears here at his moment of silent thought (8.521) and foreshadows its appearance as he looks down on the dying Lausus.

By emphasizing Aeneas' connection to his father, Vergil hints that a quasi-filial relationship will obtain between Aeneas and Pallas. That relationship, summed up by the word *fides* (8.55) and superimposed on the bond of *hospitium* between Aeneas and Evander, is broken by Pallas' death. The bond among Aeneas, Evander, and Pallas is a bond of *pietas* and *fides*.

Now Pallas, like Marcellus, has died young. As he laments over Pallas' body, Aeneas is forced once again to question his understanding of his distinguishing virtue. "Is this," he asks, "my mighty promise?" (*haec mea magna fides*, 11.55). His question comes at the end of a line of thought that shows him reimagining Anchises' questioning of the relation between Roman virtue and history. Even though Aeneas does not remember his experience in the underworld (as his ignorance of the scenes from Roman history on his shield confirms), Anchises' words emerge to shape Aeneas' passage through Italy—or, to be more precise, to shape the language that Vergil gives Aeneas on that passage.[21] From Aeneas' limited perspective, the grand historical arc from founder to princeps and the shadowy ghosts of fratricide and civil war in the distances of the text remain invisible, but he can recognize the gap between his Trojan *pietas* and the new realities of war in Italy. Especially after his arrival in Italy, Aeneas is punctilious about the obligations of *pietas*; prayers and offerings to the gods are the first thing on his agenda, even when other, seemingly more pressing concerns are at hand.[22] By heeding these obligations, he declares that his actions have some meaning beyond their immediate context. Faced, however, with the mutilated corpse of Pallas, Aeneas struggles to reconcile interpretation with participation, the formal actions of *pietas* with the events in which he is an actor. He imagines Evander, unaware that his son has been killed, piling offerings onto his altars at Pallanteum, a prisoner of empty hope (*spe multum captus inani*, *Aen.* 11.49) Evander's empty hope as he heaps his altars with offerings (*cumulat altaria donis*, 11.50) echoes Anchises empty service (*inani / munere*, 6.885–886) as he loads the soul of his descendant Marcellus with offerings (*animamque nepotis . . . accumulem donis*, 6.884–885). What Aeneas experienced in the underworld remains with him, a ghost in the distances of his psyche, and Marcellus becomes part of his response to Pallas.

Aeneas never shakes off those ghosts of his past; they lurk just below the level of his consciousness. Just as the thought of the Tiber choked with bodies summoned past words he had used to describe the Simois running red, the corpse of Pallas called up Anchises' eulogy of Marcellus and the futile *pietas* of Lausus' attempt to defend his father on the previous day. Blended with these memories may be others, deep below his conscious mind, like the thoughts that he has so often pressed down. As his Trojans prepare Pallas' body to be escorted in state back to Evander, Aeneas brings out two garments to wrap the body. They are woven with gold thread, like the tunic that Lausus' mother had made for him. Dido had made them with her own hands, when she was happy, and "had picked out the warp with fine-spun gold" (*Aen.* 11.73–75). The same words, *tenui telas discreverat auro*, describe the cloak that Aeneas is wearing when Mercury finds him overseeing the building of Carthage and commands him to leave (4.264). He now shrouds Pallas in the same garment or its twin.

As Aeneas wraps Pallas' body in Dido's cloak, its gold threads point back to Carthage and invite readers of the *Aeneid* to interpret Aeneas' position at the beginning of book 11 in the light of all that has gone before. Dido represents an existential threat to the grand arc of the *Aeneid*'s narrative. Once Jupiter unrolls the scrolls of Fate (*Aen.* 1.262), the journey from Troy to Italy that leads toward Rome and Augustus has to happen—because, as readers know, it did happen. Aeneas cannot stay in Carthage. He obeys Jupiter's orders, Dido kills herself, and with her dying curse (4.622–629), she sets in motion another fated arc of history, one leading to the enmity between Rome and Carthage, the Punic Wars, and the destruction of Carthage. Yet Pallas and Dido, linked by the cloak that one made and the other takes as a shroud, are the only non-Trojans with whom Aeneas forms any emotional connection—the only ones for whom he can weep. What kind of promise and what kind of threat does Pallas represent?

Aeneas' words (*miserande puer*, *Aen.*10.825 = 6.882, 11.42) and his tears (*lacrimis obortis*, 11.41 ≈ 6.867) connect Pallas to another dead young man, Lausus, who was killed at the end of the previous day's battle; words and tears connect both those men to Marcellus the Younger, whose premature death Anchises foretold and mourned at the climax of the parade of Roman heroes in the underworld.[23] As he addresses the dying Lausus and mourns over the dead Pallas, Aeneas echoes his father's lament for Augustus' nephew, who embodied or would have embodied Roman *pietas*, *fides*, and military valor (6.879–881). Aeneas Anchisiades (10.822) assumes his father's role and assimilates the dead young men to Marcellus, the symbol of Augustan promise and the Roman future. But Aeneas also acknowledges that Lausus' *pietas* toward his father, Mezentius, deluded Lausus into a rash act of valor (10.812), and he questions his own *fides* when he ponders the useless prayers of Evander, back in Pallanteum and unaware that his son is dead. Aeneas has absorbed Anchises' lesson about the future of Rome, but he has also carried with him the implications of the very last words that Anchises says in the underworld: that the obligations of *pietas*—heaping flowers for Marcellus; returning Lausus, with his armor, to his people; protecting Pallas in the war god's work—may be empty gestures (*inania munera*, 6.885–886).

Pallas and Lausus, joined in their deaths to Marcellus, represent the future that Aeneas cannot know. They stand for the Italian and Roman future that will give meaning to Aeneas' exile and labors. That distant, Roman future is their promise, but it comes at a cost and poses a threat to Aeneas and his immediate, Trojan past. The two young men, one Etruscan and the other an Arcadian Greek ally, anticipate the fulfillment of Juno's settlement with Jupiter in book 12 (*Aen.* 12.808–842): the name of Troy and the Trojan language will disappear from the earth, and the Trojans will be absorbed into the Italian peoples, from which will come world-dominating Rome. Aeneas cannot know that outcome; what he saw and heard in the underworld remains part of him but not part of his memories, which are of Troy. His *pietas*, which defines his being, has always been grounded in his family, in the survivors of Troy whom he shepherds over the Mediterranean, and in Troy's gods whom he conveys to Italy. When Troy disappears, so will Aeneas' Trojan identity.

Aeneas is bound to the small-scale view of a single lifetime. To him, the grand movement from Troy through Italy to Rome looks like an exile's journey from Troy to Italy. When he looks down at Pallas' body and weeps for the last time in the *Aeneid*, Aeneas' tears constitute an interpretation of events grounded in ignorance, as they did when he wept before the pictures on the wall of Juno's temple at Carthage. As on that former occasion, his tears point to ways in which he misunderstands or incompletely understands the events in which he takes part. He sees Pallas, whom he promised to protect, dead before him. He imagines Evander heaping his altars with empty offerings. Aeneas does not see that Pallas is also Marcellus or see Rome standing on the site of Evander's city. He neither hears himself echoing Anchises' words about Marcellus nor imagines himself sharing the grand view of Rome's progression from Romulus to Augustus. He knows only the dead boy and the cost. He weeps for Pallas, as he wept for the memory of Troy at Carthage, but once again his tears are for the world.

CHAPTER 6

The Anger of Aeneas

Anger, Pietas, *and the Future of Rome*

"Wrath—sing, Muse, the wrath of Peleus' son Achilles." Western literature begins with the *Iliad*, and the *Iliad* begins with "wrath," *mênis*. Vergil begins his epic with a salute to Homer by echoing the first words of the *Iliad* and *Odyssey*, "wrath" and "a man," but by transforming *mênis* into *arma,* he turns individual wrath into collective war and hints at the driving importance of the Roman civil wars for his poetic project. Aeneas is not or not quite a Roman Achilles. Passionate, personal rage drives Homer's Achilles—rage at Agamemnon when the high king appropriates Achilles' war prize, rage at Hector for killing Achilles' comrade Patroclus, rage at any Trojan who crosses his path. Achilles is a hero because he is the son of a goddess and a supremely good killer, and until the very end of the *Iliad*, he operates in a world from which he is alienated and without strong connection to any collective or social entity. *Pietas,* in contrast, marks and drives Vergil's hero, and *pietas* is a web of connections to family, city, religion, and the gods. As we saw in chapter 3, Aeneas merges himself into the shared decision-making and combat of his fellow Trojans at the sack of Troy. So strongly does Aeneas feel his connections to Troy and his remnant Trojans, to his father and son, and to the destiny represented by Ascanius that he can seem to disappear in a web of affiliations, less a human hero than an abstract symbol of Rome's future, a Lacanian pervert in complete subservience to a dimly understood divine mission, or a pious cad. He is a warrior—in the *Iliad*, second only to Hector among the Trojans—but war is his job, not his joy, and he can describe fighting as "toil" (*labor*).[1] Yet anger, when it comes, links Aeneas to his past and present rivals, Achilles and Juno.

This opposition between *pietas* and *furor* drives the *Aeneid* to its conclusion. The epic's overture—book 1, lines 1–11—establishes that opposition and situates it in myth and history. One long sentence, lines 1–7, announces Juno as the engine of the epic's plot and sets her cruelty and her grudge-holding anger against Aeneas (*saevae memorem Iunonis ob iram, Aen.* 1.4); in Vergil's epic, anger belongs first to a divinity, not to its hero. Aeneas himself is passive—an exile by fate, tossed about on land and sea, and suffering much in war (*fato profugus . . . terris iactatus et alto . . . multa quoque bello passus*, 1.2, 3, 5). The first participial phrase, *iactatus et alto,* foreshadows the Odyssean first half of the *Aeneid*; the second, *multa quoque et bello passus,* elides the Iliadic battles of books 7–12 in favor of their ultimate goal: "until he founded a city / and brought its gods to Latium, whence the Latin race, / Alban fathers, and walls of lofty Rome." The poem's second sentence, in lines 8–11, invokes the Muse but keeps the focus on Juno and her wrath; Aeneas appears only as an object of her impelling anger.

> Muse, help me remember: what was the wound
> to her divinity, what the pain that led
> the queen of gods to drive a man marked out
> by *pietas* to tumble through so many
> mishaps, to undergo so many toils?

A final question, "Can heavenly minds contain such wrath?" (*tantaene animis caelestibus irae*, 1.11), repeats and emphasizes the Junonian anger, *ira*, of line 4. Aeneas figures only as the "man marked out by *pietas*" (*insignem pietate virum*, 1.10). *Virum* in line 10 picks up the second word of the poem and creates a chiastic reworking of the first words of the *Iliad* and *Odyssey*: ***Arma virum*** *que . . . insignem pietate* ***virum*** *. . .* ***irae***. The fury of war and the anger of the queen of the gods bracket and oppose an elusive hero whose only distinguishing characteristic is *pietas*.

Vergil thus establishes two oppositions from the beginning of the poem: Juno against Aeneas, *ira* against *pietas*. About a hundred lines later, he again opposes *pietas* and rage in a context of divine anger and human politics. The first act and the first speech in the poem belong to Juno as she rages against the Trojans (*Aen.* 1.37–49). The opening words of her speech, ***Men' in****ceptam*, may reach back to the first word of the *Iliad, mênin*; the anger of Achilles reappears as the *ira* of the queen of the gods.[2] Juno entices Aeolus, a minor deity who rules the winds, to release all his winds from their prison and stir up the storm that drives Aeneas and his fleet toward Carthage. Deep under the sea, Neptune senses a disturbance, lifts his head above the waves, and rebukes the winds; they can, he says, tell their master that imperium, the Roman power to command, belongs to him, not Aeolus. Neptune checks his anger, cutting off his words before he can discover a verb for what he wants to do to the winds: "You! I'll—but the task at hand is to settle the moving billows" (1.135).[3] Vergil elaborates the dynamics of this scene in a simile.

> Just as in a crowd unrest arises often
> and the low-born mob rages in passion,
> now torches fly and rocks, rage serves up weapons;
> if then by chance they see some man weighted
> with *pietas* and worth, they fall silent and listen;
> he guides their minds with words and soothes their hearts:
> so subsided the crashing of the sea.
>
> *Aen.* 1.148–154

With this simile, Vergil expands *ira* with a new word for anger, *furor*; builds on his reworking of Homeric *mênis* as Roman *arma*; and establishes a context within which the anger of his hero can be connected to the world of his first readers.

At least two things about the *Aeneid*'s first simile can surprise readers. First, Vergil inverts what, if we can believe Cicero, was a commonplace of political discourse in his time: comparing the Roman people to the sea—both naturally peaceful but capable of being aroused by wind or demagogue.[4] Second, Vergil reverses the tenor and vehicle of his Homeric model.

> The assembly was stirred into motion like the long sea rollers
> of the Ikarian deep, which winds from the east or south
> roil up, rushing on them from the clouds of Zeus, the Father.
>
> *Iliad* 2.144–146, trans. Green

In Homer, the assembly of the Achaeans before Troy is compared to a stormy sea; in Vergil, the waves of the sea are compared to a turbulent crowd. Epic similes usually connect the world of heroes and gods to the natural world; during his narrative in book 2, for example, Aeneas compares his desperate band of

Trojan fighters to wolves driven by hunger (*Aen.* 2.355–360), and in book 10, light glinting from Aeneas' armor is compared to the red glow of a comet or the baleful Dog Star (10.272–275). But in the first simile of the *Aeneid*, Vergil draws on contemporary Roman political reality to illuminate Juno's storm and Neptune's quelling of it. Instead of comparing human activities to natural phenomena, Vergil compares natural phenomena to human activities. Building on his transformation of Achilles' individual *mênis* into collective *arma*, he invites us to read the political imagery of the simile into the events of the narrative.[5]

Some readers accept that invitation and try to identify the "man weighted with *pietas* and worth" with an individual in Roman political life. Cato the Younger and Augustus have been popular choices, along with others, but no certainty emerges—or can.[6] I prefer to ask how the relationship between narrative and simile illuminates and complicates the opposition between *pietas* and *furor* that Vergil has established in the prologue. The mapping of narrative onto simile seems straightforward at first: the winds driving the turbulent sea are like an unruly mob armed by *furor*, and Neptune's calming of the waves is like the soothing of the stormy crowd by the "man weighted with *pietas* and worth." Neptune's authority over the winds derives from a very Roman nexus of personal obedience, loyalty to tradition, and legal power. The winds, he says, have betrayed the trust (*fiducia*, *Aen.* 1.132) that their ruler, Aeolus, owes to Neptune; they have violated the primal allotment of earth, sea, and underworld between Jupiter, Neptune, and Hades and confused the natural order (1.133–134, 138–139); and they have forgotten that Neptune has the power to command the sea and, like a Roman magistrate with lictors and fasces, holds the trident as symbol of that imperium (1.138). But Neptune is not (and being a god, cannot be) distinguished by *pietas*. That virtue belongs to the human magistrate of the simile. The "man weighted with *pietas* and worth" seems, like Aeneas, burdened with *pietas* but, curiously, without human passions. He speaks, he guides, he soothes; but what does he feel? Reading back from simile to narrative provides an answer.

Neptune feels anger but holds it back in midsentence (*Aen.* 1.135). There is a job to be done and order to be restored. It is not unreasonable to infer that Neptune's analog in the simile, the "man weighted with *pietas* and worth," also feels anger and represses it; again like Aeneas, the man's words do not reveal his inner state. Nothing is gained by abandoning the search for a real human being (a Cato or Augustus) behind the man in the simile, only to replace it with a facile equation of that man with Aeneas. But recognizing that Neptune's checked anger can be read onto the simile's "man weighted with *pietas*" complicates the opposition between anger and *pietas* that Vergil foregrounded at the beginning of the poem. Anger and *pietas* are opposed but not separate, with Juno representing one, Aeneas the other. Anger and *pietas* can be entangled and can coexist in the same person. The control of anger is necessary if *pietas* is to do its work: quelling an angry mob with speech and authority or bringing Troy's gods to Latium.

In a second variation on his opening theme, Vergil entangles anger with Aeneas' future, the Roman present of Vergil's lifetime. After Neptune calms the waves and the Trojans straggle ashore in Africa, Venus goes to Jupiter to complain. What has her son Aeneas done to deserve all these misfortunes? Jupiter had promised her that from Aeneas and his Trojans would arise a race called Romans who would rule the world; she wonders what has changed his mind. Jupiter smiles and reveals to her the course of destiny.

> There will be born a Trojan Caesar from beautiful family,
> one to bound his empire with Ocean, his fame with the stars,
> Julius, a name derived from Trojan Iulus.
> Someday, Venus, you will receive him into heaven
> laden with the spoils of the East, and he,
> like you, will be summoned with prayers.
> Then hard times will grow gentle as war is laid aside:
> white-haired Trust and Vesta, Remus with brother Quirinus
> will hand down justice; the grim gates of War will be locked
> with tight iron locks. Inside, wicked Rage,
> crouched on a savage heap of weapons, hands bound
> behind his back with a hundred brazen knots,
> will snarl horribly from gore-spattered mouth.
>
> *Aen.* 1.291–296

In this passage (discussed more fully in chapter 2 above), Jupiter makes clear that Aeneas' transfer of the Trojans to Italy will culminate in his deification and the reign of Augustus, which will bring the Golden Age of Saturn back to Italy. But even in that earthly paradise, "some trace of our ancestral deceit," as Vergil had written years earlier (*Buc.* 4.31), will remain. Rage (*Furor*) cannot be eliminated from the Roman soul or state; the best that can be hoped is that it can be restrained, as Neptune and the "man weighted with *pietas*" restrained theirs.

Helen Again

In Troy's final hours, before he begins his mission to Italy, Aeneas, another man weighted with duty and loyalty, wrestles with the complex dynamic of anger and *pietas*. Recall the scene—the passage in question is the notorious Helen episode (also discussed in chapter 1 above). Aeneas watches, helpless, while Achilles' son butchers Priam. He thinks of his own father, Anchises, and the rest of his family (*Aen.* 2.559–563). Prompted by that fundamental demand of *pietas*, he begins to climb down from the citadel to his own home. On the way, he sees Helen. She has taken refuge in the temple of Vesta, goddess of hearth and home—the best or perhaps most ironic place to seek sanctuary from the husband she deserted (2.572) and his Greek warriors. The sight of Helen enrages Aeneas. The fires consuming Troy seem to blaze up in his own mind (*exarsere ignes animo*, 2.575), and anger (*ira*) and a desire for vengeance rise up in him, just as thoughts of his family had arisen a few minutes before (*subit ira*, 2.575; compare *subiit*, 560, 562). He is also carried away by rage, *furor* (*furiata mente ferebar*, 2.588). But unlike the "man weighted with *pietas* and worth" (if my reading of the relation between the simile and Neptune is correct), Aeneas needs divine admonition—in the person of his mother, Venus—to check his anger and redirect him toward his family's mansion and onto the path of *pietas*. His anger, she reminds him, arises from pain (*dolor*, 2.594).

The Helen episode shows Aeneas, as he tells his story to Dido, reflecting on his own furious desire for retribution and reconstructing the hesitation that he felt about acting on it. It also links Aeneas to his antithesis, Juno. Should Helen get off scot-free and return to Sparta trailing a crowd of Trojan women as her slaves, now that Priam has been murdered, Troy burned, and the coast of Ilium bathed in blood? Even if there is no glory in killing a woman, killing Helen would at least remove an evil thing from the world, a kind of justice would have been done, and Aeneas would have exacted some vengeance for the loss of his home (*Aen.* 2.577–587). Venus interrupts that line of thought, and so we do not learn what decision Aeneas would have made in his anger. For him, anger has a distinct character. It issues from a desire for revenge and is accompanied by pain. It requires deliberation, as the angry person contemplates the best way to avenge a slight.

In constructing Aeneas' anger around revenge, pain, and deliberation, Vergil is working in a philosophical tradition that begins with Aristotle and continues through the Hellenistic philosophers Vergil studied. Aristotle defined anger as "a desire, accompanied by pain, for a perceived revenge, on account of a perceived slight on the part of people who are not fit to slight one or one's own" (*Rhetoric* 2.2.1378a31–33). For the Stoic Chrysippus, anger was "the desire to take vengeance against one who is believed to have committed a wrong contrary to one's deserts."[7] Vergil uses two words for "anger": *ira* and *furor* (along with a close relative, the plural *furiae*, and adjectives like *furiata* at *Aen.* 2.588).[8] Greek, like English, has a rich vocabulary for anger and its variations—irritation, bitterness, rage, fury, and so on—but Vergil seems to be building on a distinction that his Epicurean teacher Philodemus tried to draw between anger, *orgê*, and rage, *thymos*.[9] The distinction is not hard and fast, in Greek or in Latin; as Philodemus recognizes, *thymos* is, in its "more general linguistic usage," an "equivalent" of *orgê*.[10] But for Epicureans, he insists, there was a difference between *orgê*, natural anger from justified motives, and *thymos*, blind rage.[11] The sage will not fall victim to *thymos* but may feel *orgê*; Aeneas, who is neither sage nor philosopher, can feel both.

Aeneas tells Dido that his first thought on seeing Helen was to avenge his fatherland as it crashed down around him (*cadentem / ulcisci patriam*, *Aen.* 2.575–576), and Venus calls his attention to the fact that his anger (*ira*) stems from the pain (*dolor*) that he feels from the loss of his city (*dolor excitat iras*, 2.594). As he tries to justify killing a defenseless but wicked woman, Aeneas emphasizes the justice that will be done and the pleasure of vengeance. "I will be praised," he says, "for having blotted out a wicked thing and for exacting punishment from one who deserves it, and it will be pleasing to fill my mind with vengeance" (2.585–587).[12] As Aristotle says, "when human beings are angry, they feel pain, and when they avenge themselves, they feel pleasure" (*Nicomachean Ethics* 2.8.1117a5–15).

There is another character in the *Aeneid* for whom anger (*ira*) is a matter of revenge, pain, and deliberation. When Juno launches the action of the epic with her furious speech at the beginning of book 1, she focuses on what Aristotle might have called a "perceived slight" and on questions of status—that is, on the way in which other goddesses have been able to take vengeance on their human enemies while she, queen of the gods, wife and sister of Jupiter, can do nothing to keep the Trojans from Italy. Vergil has already set out the deep causes of her anger (*Aen.* 1.25–28). She has suffered at the hands of the Trojans, through her second-place finish in the Judgment of Paris, her husband Jupiter's lust for the Trojan prince Ganymede, and, even farther back in time, the descent of the "hated (Trojan) race" (*genus invisum*) from Dardanus, offspring of an alliance between Jupiter and the nymph Electra. Vergil makes it clear that Juno wants vengeance for all of those slights and that they are the causes of the cruel pain (*saevi dolores*, 1.25) that she feels. Neither the pain nor its causes have left her at the beginning of the second half of the *Aeneid*, when the sight of the "hated stock" (*stirpem invisam*, 7.293) on shore in Italy pierces her with sharp pain (*acri dolore*, 7.291) and provokes another furious speech (7.293–322). Once again she incites a minor divinity, this time the fury Allecto, to inflame Turnus and the Latins with lust for war against the Trojan invaders. Aeolus' winds reappear as the Italians' passions, and there is even another simile comparing political discord to a turbulent sea (7.585–590).[13] Rage, the *furor* that supplied weapons to the mob in the first simile of the poem, seems to begin its cycle anew.

Aeneas becomes angry when he contemplates Helen amid the collapsing embers of his homeland, but his justifiable anger (*ira*) is tinged with blind rage (*furor*). Venus asks him why he is raging (*quid furis*, *Aen.* 2.595) and tells him that Helen is not responsible for Troy's destruction (2.601–602). (Even if we expel the Helen episode altogether from the *Aeneid*, those lines with Venus indisputably belong in the text.) Aeneas' anger (*ira*) arises from a desire for revenge, prompted by the pain of a perceived wrong, and is accompanied by deliberation—by the need to think, to hesitate, before taking revenge. In these ways, his anger reflects that of Juno, his implacable foe, and his anger, like Juno's, is tinged with *furor*. He does not become angry again in the same way until the very end of the *Aeneid*.

In making this assertion, I exclude some episodes in which Aeneas is, by any reasonable definition, angry. Even those are hard to find between the Helen episode and the final three books of the *Aeneid*. It is hard to imagine physical combat without anger, and Aeneas joins in the collective rage of the surviving Trojans as *furor* and *ira* drive them on in battle (*Aen.* 2.316–317). As he prepares for the final combat in book 12, he uses *ira* to stir himself to action (*se suscitat ira*, 12.108), and *ira* carries him on during the succeeding melee (12.494, 499, 527). Philodemus might have called those incidents instances of *orgê*, natural anger from justified motives. From Troy to Italy, however, Aeneas is a man without anger, justified or not. In the face of Dido's *furor* (*reginam furentem*, 4.283), all he can manage is a speech from which he tries to expunge all passion (4.333–361). Weighted with *pietas* and his divine mission, he checks anger in himself and others. During the funeral games for Anchises in book 5, a boxing match, fought with the weighted gloves that the Romans called *caestus*, threatens to get out of hand and result in the death of one fighter. Aeneas does not allow the combatants' anger (*iras*, 5.461) to go any farther. Like the man in the initial simile of the poem, he soothes their raging spirits with words (*mulcens dictis*, 5.464).

Anger—not justified *orgê/ira*, but berserk rage, *thymos/furor*—returns when Aeneas rejoins his Trojans after his visit to Evander's city, bringing with him reinforcements led by the young prince Pallas. After Turnus kills Pallas, Aeneas launches a frenzied killing spree, an *aristeia* (or display of battle excellence) in which he seems to cast away all thoughts of *pietas* (as discussed in chapter 5). He rages through the enemy forces (*furit*, *Aen.* 10.545, 802), killing and killing like a torrent or dark whirlwind (*torrentis aquae vel turbinis atri / more furens*, 10.603–604). Ordinary anger, *ira*, returns to him only when *pietas* does, as young Lausus bravely—and pointlessly—tries to defend his wounded father, Mezentius.

> Aeneas endured the cloud of darts until
> it subsided, then spoke and menaced Lausus:
> "What are you doing? You're dead already. Your daring
> exceeds your power, your *pietas* deludes you."
> Lausus came on anyway, and *ira* mounted higher
> in the Trojan commander.
>
> *Aen.* 10.809–814

But *ira* is not or not quite *furor*. Deliberated anger, accompanied by pain and arising from perceived wrong, is not the raging red demon seen in an Achilles on the hunt for corpses. The same person can show now one and now the other form of anger (as Aeneas does in book 10), but the same person can also be inflamed by *ira* and *furor* at the same time, as Aeneas is when he makes his last decision in the *Aeneid*.

Killing Turnus

It is not easy for Aeneas to leave Troy, and in a sense, he never does.[14] In his first appearance in the *Aeneid* (1.92–101), he looks back to Troy and wishes he had died before its walls instead of in the storm that is overwhelming his exiled fleet. At every opportunity along the way, he seeks to replace the city that he has lost. His first stop is in Thrace, just north of Troy; there, as he tells Dido, he placed his first city walls and named the city Aeneadae, not realizing that the fates were against him (*Aen.* 3.17). At the very end of the poem, as he arranges a final, decisive duel with the Italian leader Turnus, he specifies that if he wins, his Trojans will build city walls for him, this time calling the city Lavinia (12.193–194). Between those two efforts comes a failed attempt to found a Pergamea in Crete (3.132–134), the mistaken venture in Carthage, and a visit to the sad miniature of Troy created by Helenus and Andromache. That experience shows him that his home must be renewed, not replicated (5.294–506). Replacing Troy and finding a home for his Trojans, not creating Rome, is always his goal.

One way to read the *Aeneid* is to discover in it a story about a man shaped by his heroic destiny, to trace his journey—from defeat in Troy, through exile, to victory in Italy—as a realization of that heroic self-discovery, a reworking of *pietas* to fit the demands of destiny in a changed world. The end of the *Aeneid* tugs at that easy story, and it begins to unravel. Aeneas' journey begins to look like a journey not of self-discovery but of self-abandonment. Aeneas gains personal agency at the cost of sacrificing the self that, grounded in community, made his *pietas* possible. The effect of that journey becomes clear when we examine his final choice in the *Aeneid*.

In the last book of the *Aeneid*, all the wars, exile, and struggle come down to two men. Turnus, the Rutulian prince who leads the Italian resistance to the invading Trojans, agrees to fight Aeneas in single combat. The victor will gain the hand of Lavinia, daughter of the Italian ruler Latinus, and, with her, a kingdom. As the champions parade to the sacrifice that will ratify their agreement, the Italians note, with foreboding, that Turnus seems no match for Aeneas. Then divine intervention evens the odds. The nymph Juturna, Turnus' immortal sister, stirs up the Italians, sends a misleading omen, and incites Tolumnius, an Italian seer, to hurl a spear into the Trojan ranks and break the truce. As Aeneas (once again called *pius*, at *Aen.* 12.311) begs his men to keep the truce and allow him to get at Turnus, an arrow flies from the Italian ranks and wounds him in the thigh. No one claims credit for that shot, and Vergil refuses to assign responsibility—it was a chance hit or a god (12.321). In the battle that follows, Juturna tries to keep her brother away from Aeneas, but Venus prompts her son to attack King Latinus' city, and the sight brings Turnus back to meet his opponent. At first, the combatants seem evenly matched: Turnus may be the less experienced warrior, but Aeneas is slowed by his wound (12.746–747). Each loses a weapon but regains it through divine intervention. They stand facing each other, Aeneas armed with his spear forged by Vulcan, Turnus relying on his father's sword, made by the same god (12.789–790).

As the two men stand there, panting and exhausted, Vergil shifts the scene to Olympus, where Jupiter and Juno cut a deal: Juno will cease her hostility toward the Trojans; in return, Jupiter will guarantee her that the hated Trojans will be assimilated into the Italian and Latin nation and that Trojan culture and language will be blotted from the face of the earth. The necessary condition of that arrangement is the death of Turnus. Jupiter sends a Dira, one of the demons who always stand ready to incite fear or panic at his command, to detach Juturna from her brother (*Aen.* 12.843–854). The demonic creature assumes the form of an owl, whose cry, the Romans believed, portended misfortune. The bird flutters in front of Turnus and beats his shield with its wings; Turnus knows that this means he is doomed. Juturna abandons her mortal brother, and he presses on to meet his death. Aeneas advances with his spear, and Turnus picks up a huge rock, a boundary marker, Vergil notes, such as twelve of today's men could barely lift. Vergil wants readers to think of *Iliad* 12.445–449, where Hector lifts a stone that two (not twelve) present-day men could not carry. The combat has become Homeric, with Aeneas as Achilles to Turnus' Hector.[15]

Readers can pause like gods in heaven, and it is worth taking a moment, as Turnus hefts his stone, to think about how that Homeric moment prompts a comparison not only between Aeneas and Achilles and between Turnus and Hector but also between the Aeneas of the end of the *Aeneid* and his Homeric counterpart.[16] In book 5 of the *Iliad*, the Greek champion Diomedes encounters Aeneas. Diomedes picks up a huge rock, "such as two men could not carry, as men are now" (*Iliad* 5.302–304) and throws it. It strikes Aeneas in the hip and disables him. Aeneas' mother, Aphrodite (Venus to the Romans) tries to save him, but as she is carrying him back to Troy, she herself is wounded by Diomedes. Then Diomedes goes in for the kill.

> Three times he leapt in homicidal frenzy,
> Three times Apollo flicked his lacquered shield,
> But when he charged a fourth, last time,
> He heard a voice that seemed to come
> From everywhere at once, and knew it was
> Apollo's voice, saying to him
> "Think it over, son of Tydeus, and get back.
> Don't set your sights on the gods. Gods are
> To humans what humans are to crawling bugs."
>
> *Iliad* 5.436–442, trans. Lombardo

Diomedes backs up a little; like Aeneas during the fall of Troy, he has encountered the Real in the form of the gods' anger. The Iliadic Aeneas, however, moves further from reality as he has his existence divided between the citadel of Troy and the battlefield.

> And Apollo took Aeneas from the swarm
> Up to his temple on sacred Pergamum.
> There Leto and arrowy Artemis healed him
> In the great sanctuary, and made him glorious.
> And silver-bowed Apollo made a phantom
> To look like Aeneas, armor and all,
> And over this wraith the Greeks and Trojans
> Battered each other with their rawhide shields
> Until the edges were tattered into leather fringe.
>
> *Iliad* 5.445–453, trans. Lombardo

Apollo makes arms and a man-like thing, and it may not be too far-fetched to suggest, as does James I. Porter (2004, 138), that Vergil had this passage in mind when he contemplated the first words of the *Aeneid* and its hero who is so hard to grasp.

As the *Aeneid* draws to a close, Vergil's evocation of Homer's rock-throwing heroes underlines the way in which the second half of the *Aeneid* repeats and reverses the Trojan War, making us wonder, for a moment, how Vergil's characters are doomed to repeat their archetypes.[17] Will Aeneas once again be wounded by a boulder? Instantly, Vergil resolves the doubt. This time around, Turnus is Hector. When he tries to throw the stone, his strength vanishes, and the boulder falls short of its target (*Aen.* 12.896–907). Turnus goes on like a man in a dream, like Hector at *Iliad* 22.199–201, trying to charge and fight but somehow unable to move. At the very end of this combat, though, Aeneas will become not only Achilles to Turnus' Hector but a projection of his greatest adversary in the poem. He will carry out the deal that Juno is making with Jupiter while he and Turnus go at each other.

Aeneas throws his spear; with a noise like a bolt from Roman siege artillery or like thunder, it passes through the air, drills into Turnus' shield, and wounds him in the thigh. Turnus is down. Aeneas has won. As Aeneas towers over him, with sword drawn, Turnus stretches out his hand and speaks.

"I earned this, and I am not begging off," he said.
"Enjoy your lot. But if any concern for an unhappy
parent can touch you—you had a father, Anchises,
like mine—I beg you, take pity on aged Daunus
and return me, or my lifeless body if you prefer,
to my people. You've won. The Italians have seen me
beaten and stretching out my hands to you.
Lavinia is yours. Don't carry hatred any farther."

Aen. 12.931–938

With his final words (*ulterius ne tende odiis*), Turnus unwittingly echoes Jupiter's command to Juno as they settled her anger earlier in the book: "I forbid you to make any further attempts" (*ulterius temptare veto*, 12.806).[18] Perhaps he also carries readers back to something that Aeneas himself said earlier in the poem, when he forbade the boxers at his father's funeral games to advance their anger any further (*procedere longius iras*, 5.461). Turnus' appeal to the memory of Anchises, the father whose death in Sicily, as Aeneas told Dido, marked a turning point in the long journey of exile (3.710–714), touches Aeneas' closest emotional attachment and the core of his *pietas*. Aeneas' moment has come. All eyes are on him, and with a single act of mercy, he can tie together divine reconciliation and human destiny and bring his exile, pain, and labors to a triumphant close. Perhaps *pietas* will restrain rage, as it did at the beginning of the *Aeneid*, and hope and history will rhyme at last.[19]

It nearly happens. Aeneas' gaze flickers, and he lowers his right hand. Turnus' speech has just begun to turn Aeneas away from his intention, and he hesitates. Vergil draws the moment out over nearly three lines (*Aen.* 12.938–941), which I translate here as literally as I can: "Aeneas stood, keen in his armor, rolling his eyes, and held back his right hand; and just at the moment when Turnus' speech began to bend him as he hesitated . . ."[20] Something catches Aeneas' eye. Across Turnus' shoulder stretches a familiar object, a sword belt. Turnus had taken it from the body of Pallas, the young son of Aeneas' ally King Evander of Pallanteum, the Arcadian Greek settlement on the future site of Rome. On it, a Greek artisan had engraved the story of the fifty daughters of Danaus, who had (all but one) murdered their husbands on their wedding night and, for that crime, been sentenced to eternal punishment in the underworld (10.495–500). The belt is an object freighted with meaning, both for Vergil's first readers and for Aeneas.[21] Aeneas had loved Pallas and, at the prince's burial, had wrapped the young man's body in a cloak, one of a pair made by Dido with her own hands (11.72–75). Aeneas makes a decision.

> Then, after his eyes took in these memorials and relics
> of cruel grief, he blazed up with rage and spoke,
> terrible in anger: "Will you, decked in my people's spoils,
> be snatched from me? Pallas, yes Pallas, sacrifices you
> with this wound and draws punishment from your wicked blood."
> As he says this, he plants the blade below the ribcage
> in boiling anger. Turnus' limbs relax in death's chill.
> Groaning, complaining, his soul escapes to the shades below.
>
> *Aen.* 12.945–952

I have read the *Aeneid* straight through many times. This ending never fails to stun me. I sit in silence, like the audience at a performance that they know has transformed their lives, before they break into applause. It is the end, and I am convinced that it is the end that Vergil planned, but it changes everything.

Not all readers of the *Aeneid* agree with me. For some, the ending is abrupt, unsatisfying, or incomplete; they want hope and history to rhyme. In the fifteenth century, Italian humanist Maffeo Vegio (1407–1458) wrote a thirteenth book to tie up the loose ends, and Robert Wells' 2001 poem "The Thirteenth Book" imagines Aeneas after the *Aeneid*.[22] For others, understanding the intent of the entire poem turns on correct interpretation of the final scene. Broadly speaking, interpretations fall into two groups. One sees Aeneas' action as the just fulfillment of all that he has done and of the poem's intent: Turnus stands in the way of the founder of Rome and of its foundation, so he must die. As Servius puts it, the *Aeneid* aims "to imitate Homer and to praise Augustus by way of his ancestors," and in killing Turnus and carrying the poem to its fitting conclusion, Aeneas confirms his status as ancestor of Rome and of Rome's second founder.[23] Another group sees the ending as subverting the poem's presentation of Aeneas as heroic forerunner of Augustus: in the end, Aeneas abandons his *pietas*, forgets the advice that Anchises in the underworld gave to him and future Romans to "subdue the proud in war and spare the conquered" (*Aen.* 6.853), and gives way to the rage (*furor*) that has, to this point and in the person of Juno, been blocking the inevitable path of history.[24] This dichotomy simplifies and almost caricatures complex nuances of interpretation. My own reading and perhaps my own temperament lead me to conclude that both positions are, in a way, true. The *Aeneid* is no exception to Walter Benjamin's assertion that every document of civilization is also a document of barbarism (2007, 255).

Aeneas chooses to kill Turnus, but before he does, he hesitates.[25] The entire *Aeneid* hangs on that instant when Aeneas' gaze turns aside and his right hand drops down. He deliberates, wonders what to do. As he did when leaving Troy, he makes his choice alone; no god shows him the way, no trusted adviser gives him counsel, no dream or vision confirms his choice. He does not ignore advice (as he ignored Hector's advice to flee Troy) or obey instructions (as he obeyed Jupiter's command to leave Carthage); there is no advice to ignore or command to obey. If *pietas* consists in part of attention to the divine and human context of advice and instruction and to the obligations that it encodes, what has happened to Aeneas' *pietas* at the end of the poem? What has happened to Aeneas?

The end of the *Aeneid* marks the final stage in the transformation of Aeneas into someone or something other than the "man marked out by *pietas*" whom Vergil introduced at the beginning of the poem (*insignem pietate virum*, *Aen.* 1.10). Some readers might be tempted to conclude that he has at last become himself, the unitary locus of will and action imagined by Kant and engrained in modern ideas about moral agency. Vergil suggests otherwise. Through a carefully crafted series of links to earlier episodes and persons in the *Aeneid*, he alienates Aeneas from his Trojan self and assimilates him to the forces that have opposed him: to his former Greek opponents, to rage (*furor*), and to Juno and the gods. For Vergil's Roman readers, Aeneas' departure from the realm of ordinary humanity would have been reinforced by their knowledge that after his death by drowning or in battle (versions varied, as with the death of Rome's other founder Romulus), Aeneas was worshipped as a god, Jupiter Indiges.[26]

Aeneas himself declares his alienation. As he prepares to stab Turnus, he attributes the action to Pallas, the young man Turnus had killed and whose plundered baldric Turnus now wears: "Pallas, yes Pallas, sacrifices you" (*Aen.* 12.948–949). The verb used here for "sacrifice," *immolare*, occurs in only two other places in the *Aeneid*, and in both occurrences, Aeneas is the subject while other human beings are the objects. At 10.517–520, Aeneas captures eight Italian youths to sacrifice to Pallas' ghost, and twenty lines later (10.537–542), Aeneas encounters a priest on the field of battle and sacrifices him. Perhaps Vergil is doing no more than suggesting that the killing of Turnus marks the third instance in that catalog of vengeance. Perhaps, as argued by John Esposito (2016), Aeneas' recovery of the stolen baldric from Turnus somehow restores the baldric to its proper owner, with Aeneas necessarily becoming or replacing

Pallas. Whether he avenges or restores, Aeneas chooses to do so by denying his agency and the *pietas* that drives it.

If the Aeneas who kills Turnus is different from the Aeneas who escaped from Troy and journeyed to Italy, who is this avenging Aeneas? The vestments of the priest sacrificed in book 10 provide a clue. As a priest of Apollo, Haemonides is recognizable by his gleaming white headband, *infula* (*Aen.* 10.537). The word occurs one other time in the *Aeneid*, in book 2, when Vergil turns from his narrative to address Panthus, a Trojan priest who had joined Aeneas' little band of fighters: "Your *pietas* did not protect you as you fell, Panthus, nor did Apollo's headband" (2.429–430). In killing a priest of Apollo, Aeneas is reenacting one of the events of the last night of Troy, but this time, he is taking on the role of the Greeks who killed Panthus, and he is refusing to recognize the claims of *pietas*. By the end of book 12, Aeneas' identification with the Greeks has become complete; he has become another Achilles, pursuing Turnus/Hector and killing him before the walls of the city that the Rutulian prince attempts to defend.[27] Aeneas has become one of the Greek killers who failed to respect the priest Panthus' *pietas*.

The final scene of the *Aeneid* is laced with pointers to Aeneas' new identity. The man marked out by *pietas* now becomes identified with the forces that have opposed his destined journey to Italy: not only Achilles and the Greeks, but also Juno and the raging anger that she has embodied from the first lines of the poem. Turnus' last words, *ulterius ne tende odiis*, recall Jupiter's words to Juno, *ulterius temptare veto*. After his momentary hesitation, Aeneas' response to the sight of Pallas' sword belt brings Juno back into the poem. The Danaids on Pallas' baldric are a reminder of savage grief (*saevi monimenta doloris, Aen.* 12.945) and a cause of Aeneas' anger. At the very beginning of the poem, Vergil introduced Juno with the same words; the prologue asks why the goddess was grieving (*dolens*, 1.9) and, a few lines later, describes the persistence of the causes of her anger and her cruel grievances (*causae irarum saevique dolores*, 1.25). Juno's enduring anger is a wound under her breast (*sub pectore vulnus*, 1.36). The image recurs at the beginning and end of book 4; Dido's unspoken love, which Juno helped to create, is "a silent wound under her breast" (*tacitum . . . sub pectore vulnus*, 4.67), transformed, at her death, from metaphor into a horribly literal sucking chest wound when she commits suicide with Aeneas' sword, as "the wound planted under her breast hisses" (*infixum stridit sub pectore vulnus*, 4.689). Aeneas' attribution of Turnus' wound to Pallas (*Pallas te hoc vulnere*, 12.948) may recall a different Pallas, the goddess Athena, in Juno's first great aria

(*Pallasne exurere classem*, 1.39). All these wounds culminate in Aeneas' final action as he plants a wound under Turnus' breast (*sub pectore*, 12.950). That action itself carries a reader back to the beginning of the poem, where it had a very different sense; the verb *condere*, which I have translated "plant," can mean "to bury" or "to found." Vergil introduces Aeneas as the man (*virum*) who must wander and suffer under Juno's anger until he founds (*conderet*) Rome (1.5), and Vergil ends his prologue by commenting, "So great a task it was to found [*condere*] the Roman race" (1.33). But in the end, Aeneas' founding has turned into a single act of killing, as he buries his blade in Turnus' chest (*ferrum adverso sub pectore condit*, 12.950).[28] Finally, Vergil uses the same words to describe Aeneas' final victim, Turnus, that he had used to describe Juno's first victim, Aeneas, twelve books earlier: the phrase *solvuntur frigore membra*, "his limbs relax in the chill [of death]," at 12.951 repeats 1.92, where they describe Aeneas cowering before the storm that Juno has sent to destroy his fleet. Foundation becomes burial, Juno's reconciliation becomes Aeneas' anger, the beginning of an empire turns into the end of a life, and victim and victimizer have changed places.

Cycles of Furor

The *Aeneid* ends by taking us full circle back to its beginning—to Juno's anger, savage grief, and the act of founding Rome. That returning, like the *Aeneid* itself, is embedded in another reiteration, the reenacting and reversal of the Homeric Trojan War as Aeneas becomes a second Achilles, an invader battling before a city's walls and killing, with help from the gods, a sympathetic defending champion.[29] In Michael Putnam's words, "we are made to dwell not on a golden future but on the fact that the past reiterates itself" (2001, 104). But the *Aeneid*'s final scene also operates within another cycle that had immediate relevance for Vergil's first readers: the seemingly endless round of civil war upon civil war that was all the generation of Vergil and Horace had ever known. As I suggested in chapter 2, the *Aeneid*'s golden future embraces two ideas: both the mythical Golden Age when Saturn ruled the earth and its Augustan counterpart envisioned by Jupiter at his first appearance in the *Aeneid* (1.283–296). When Vergil died in 19 BC, that second Golden Age could be only a hope, not a description. Horace, in his *Epodes*, and Vergil, in the *Bucolics* and again in Jupiter's speech at *Aeneid* 1.257–296, used the myth of a lost Golden Age to engage in a dialog about Rome's future and about the curse of civil war that seemed to loom over that city's past and present. The end of the *Aeneid* continues and extends that dialog by figuring Aeneas' final, solitary choice both as a reenactment of all that has gone before and as an enactment of what must happen again. His choice to kill Turnus answers Jupiter's unrolling of the secrets of fate and affirms Aeneas' condition as a man estranged from his life's meaning and from any possibility of knowing or understanding it.

When Aeneas left Troy, he also left the soil in which his characteristic excellence grew and flourished. *Pietas* had meaning for a subject, Aeneas, only in the presence of its objects: his home, his fellow citizens, and his family. Throughout the journeys and struggles of the *Aeneid*, Aeneas had to rediscover how to be *pius Aeneas* in the absence of that nourishing soil. *Pietas* became reconfigured as attention to the will of the gods and to the future that they dangled before him in a series of tantalizing hints—Hesperia, always receding in the west. *Pietas* became his personal, heroic virtue and no longer a quality grounded in the soil of Troy.

Without his Trojan *pietas*, though, Aeneas becomes, as we might say, a shadow of his former self. When Venus showed him the grim shapes of the great gods tearing Troy apart from its foundations, that glimpse of the reality behind his struggles made him seem unreal, directed by others like an actor on a stage (J. Porter 2004). In the underworld, Anchises showed him the future that could give meaning to his life, but he left through the gate of illusions and remembered nothing of what he had seen. At the end of the *Aeneid*, Vergil completes that pattern of unreality by showing the disappearance of Trojan Aeneas, the man marked out by *pietas*.[30]

The last hundred and fifty lines of the *Aeneid* contain two negotiations. In one, Turnus pleads for his life, and Aeneas answers; in the other, Jupiter lays down the necessary conditions of fate, as he had at the beginning of the poem, and Juno responds with her own conditions, to which Jupiter agrees. When Vergil has Turnus use Jupiter's language, "no farther," to appeal to Aeneas, he directs us to consider the relation between the two negotiations. Juno acknowledges Jupiter's lordship and recognizes, as she must, that Aeneas will win Lavinia and that their marriage will unite Trojans and Latins. Then the goddess makes a request.

> This one thing, because it is bound by no law of fate,
> I ask you for Latium and the glory of your Latins:
> when those two seal their people's peace with marriage

(so be it!), when they unite their laws and treaties,
do not require the native Latins to change their name,
become Trojans, be called people of Teucer,
change their language or wear different clothes.
Let there be Latium, Alban kings through the ages,
a Roman stock powered by Italian manliness:
Troy has fallen—let it die along with its name.

Aen. 12.819–828

Jupiter agrees. Turnus must die in order for Rome to come into being, and the Trojans will disappear by being assimilated into the Latin nation. Like their leader Aeneas, the Trojans will become someone else. By accepting the sense impression of Pallas' baldric and killing Turnus, Aeneas is fulfilling the pattern of fate and carrying out the will of Jupiter. He is, a Stoic might say, becoming part of the chain of auxiliary and proximate causes leading to Turnus' death and so to Rome's birth. But by killing Turnus in the way he does, by planting (*condere*) his sword in a blazing paroxysm of rage and anger (*furiis accensus et ira*, 12.946), Aeneas is becoming Juno and following her plan. When he plants his sword into Turnus' chest, Aeneas founds Rome, but in doing so, he also destroys Troy and himself.

Epilogue

The Hero Vanishes

Again and again, Aeneas fails. He fails to obey Hector's instructions to leave Troy and rushes into futile combat instead. He fails—or so it seems to many readers—to keep track of his wife during his family's escape from the burning city. He fails to interpret correctly the pictures in Juno's sanctuary at Carthage. He fails to express his emotions in his last encounters with Dido and yet fails to hide them entirely. He fails to protect the young warrior Pallas, who had been entrusted to him. Finally, in his last moment in the poem, with Turnus humbled before him, he fails to follow his father's advice to "spare the conquered, and subdue the proud" (*Aen.* 6.853). All these failures, I have suggested, stem from a crisis of identity and a larger failure to manage it, a doomed attempt to redefine his *pietas* and thus himself in the aftermath of the destruction of the home and society in which that *pietas* was grounded. The attempt is doomed because the meaning of Aeneas' life and struggle will be realized only centuries after his death, with the culmination of Roman history in Augustus.

Aeneas can identify himself by pointing to the quality by which he is distinguished: "I am *pius* Aeneas," he says as he introduces himself to his disguised mother (*Aen.* 1.378). After the fall of Troy, however, he struggles to say what that identity means, because he cannot know the future history that makes sense of his life. Halfway through his farewell to Dido, he sums up the crisis of identity that the Carthaginian queen poses. "Italy," he says—"this is my love, this is my country" (*hic amor, haec patria est*, 4.347). Like the agonized cry with which he ends the speech, "Italy—I seek it not of my own free will" (4.361), this summation recognizes the central movement of the *Aeneid*: Trojans will become Italians, and they will lose their identity in the process. Troy, the homeland that forms the ground of Aeneas' *pietas*, will be transformed into another *patria* in which he will still be a stranger and an exile by fate. The goal of his journey will always be receding into the distance. His fated *patria* will continue to be concealed from him, just as Vergil hides Rome, Roma, in its palindromic "secret name," Amor.[1] Aeneas knows that Italy must be his country and his love, but he cannot know that Trojans must become Italians, that his Amor will eventually become Roma, or that the price of that transformation will be his own identity, his *pietas*.

Pietas is central to the *Aeneid* and is not merely one of Aeneas' virtues or excellences in the conventional sense. It is not a disposition to act in certain ways that are aspects of a good human life. For Aeneas, *pietas* is an identity, bound up in his Trojanness. After the fall of Troy, that identity is liquid, something to be created, worked out, and negotiated in the absence of any moral framework within which it could exist. In the *Aeneid*, Aeneas seeks not what he ought to do but what he ought to be. He begins the *Aeneid* in a cosmos of literal liquidity in the chaos of the storm sent by Juno, and from that point on, he is in continual existential crisis. At the beginning of the second half of the poem, he is still trapped in a metaphorical billowing wave of worry (*magno curarum fluctuat aestu*, *Aen.* 8.19), and his thoughts are like light reflected from a mirror or a disturbed bowl of water (8.22–25). Italy, *Amor*, *Roma*, and the meaning of his existence are always fluid, somewhere else, or fleetingly present. "Finding a sense to life," Charles Taylor writes, "depends on framing meaningful expressions which are adequate" (1989, 18). Aeneas' silences, tears, and anger are markers of his failure to find a stable identity in his liquid existence. He begins the *Aeneid* as a damaged person, in an identity crisis that cannot be resolved, and ends it as a person without a personality. When he kills Turnus, he is not "doing the wrong thing." He simply ceases to be who he was, to be *pius Aeneas*.

When he buries his sword in Turnus' body, Aeneas founds Rome. At the end of the poem, "he plants/buries [*condit*] his sword below Turnus' breast" (*Aen.* 12.949). The verb there echoes the proclamation that caps the overture, "to plant/found the Roman race" (*Romanam condere gentem*, 1.33). At Rome, foundation requires death. The founding of Rome, like the founding of any of its colonies, began with three ritual acts: the taking of auspices; the killing of a pig, sheep, and bull in the sacrifice called *suovetaurilia*; and the marking out of a ritual boundary with a plow.[2] The legendary founding of Rome added another death to the necessary sacrifice, when Remus was killed—as some said, by his brother, Romulus. Aeneas, the founder before the founders, proclaims that his killing of Turnus is a sacrifice: "Pallas, yes Pallas, sacrifices you / with this wound and draws punishment from your wicked blood" (12.948–949).

Sacrifice, Terry Eagleton suggests, "is a critique of the ethic of self-sovereignty. It recognizes the self as an effect of the Other. One's identity is not one's own, but lies in the keeping of the gods" (2018, 12). Eagleton's insight illuminates Aeneas' final action in the *Aeneid*. In sacrificing Turnus, Aeneas also sacrifices himself. He ignores Turnus' evocation of Anchises' advice to "spare the conquered" and gives up the *pietas* with which he has been marked from the beginning of the *Aeneid*. In so doing, he gives up—sacrifices—any possibility of self-sovereignty or moral agency. With his final, founding sacrifice, he puts his identity away, into the keeping of the gods whom he will soon join.

Like all sacrifices—like the inaugural *suovetaurilia*, which had to be repeated every five years in the ceremony called *lustratio*—Aeneas' slaughter of Turnus will be reenacted in the civil wars of his descendants.[3] With the first word of his poem, Vergil turns the individual anger of the Iliadic Achilles into Rome's collective wars, *arma*, and especially the fratricidal civil wars of the poet's own lifetime. The man, *virum*, who accompanies those wars vanishes into collective identities that are tinged with fratricide. As he told Dido about the sacking of Troy, Aeneas merged his own will and actions with those of the resisting Trojans. Throughout the poem, his identity seems to draw on, foreshadow, and blend with others: Hercules, Romulus, or Augustus and even, in the end, Aeneas' rival Turnus. In the wars that conclude the poem, he relives and reenacts the Trojan War, but now he is a Paris to his enemies and an Achilles in his absences and anger.[4] Vergil brushes all these identities with the colors of civil war. Hercules' defeat of the monster Cacus, narrated in book 8, may evoke the culminating struggle of the Roman civil wars between Octavian and Antony, as well as that between Aeneas and Turnus (Morgan 2009). Romulus cannot be mentioned without conjuring up the shadowy image of his brother, Remus, and their fatal, fratricidal rivalry. The wars between Italians and Trojans that conclude the *Aeneid* are civil wars in all but name; Italians and Trojans share a common ancestry from Dardanus (*Aen.* 3.167–168) and are, Vergil declares, nations destined to live in peace forever (12.504).[5]

As Aeneas transfers Troy and its gods to Italy, he also enacts the future of the "Latin race, Alban elders, and walls of lofty Rome" (1.7) that will rise from his failures. If what he does will lead to Romulus, the elder Marcellus, and Augustus, it must also lead to Remus, Hannibal, Antony, and all the dead young sacrificed along the way to Rome: Marcellus the Younger, Lausus, Nisus, Camilla, and Turnus. Aeneas, as the progenitor and archetype of Rome, partakes in both sides of Rome's ancestral curse. He is victor, vanquished, and victim in the civil wars of his own soul. In the wake of his disappearance, the *Aeneid*'s central questions drift up from the depths of the text. Can we hold on to our identities when the society that created them is no more? Can a people cursed by its origins overcome them? What does an empire cost, and is it worth it?

Notes

Chapter 1

1. On the "lawyerly" (or, in Roman terms, rhetorical) aspects of Aeneas' speech, see Starr 2003. Feeney 1983 offers a reading of the entire passage that makes the best case possible for Aeneas.

2. Sentence boundaries are not always clear in Latin. Mynors' Oxford Classical Texts edition punctuates line 335 thus: *promeritam, nec me.*

3. Highet (1972, 29) describes it as "a brief but noble address."

4. Note *refert* at 1.208 and 4.333, *curis* at 1.208 and *curam* at 4.332, *premit* at 1.209 and *premebat* at 4.332, and *corde* at 1.209 and 4.332.

5. Line 361, *Italiam non sponte sequor*, is one of fifty-eight such incomplete hexameters in the *Aeneid.* Some scholars, such as Baldwin (Baldwin 1993), have argued that Vergil intended these incomplete lines to convey dramatic or other effects; my own belief is that the aesthetic canons of ancient poetry could not accommodate such an intention. See Miller 1909; Sparrow 1931; Pease 1935, 123–125; Highet 1974, 200–204; Moskalew 1982, 12–13.

6. Aeneas' great-grandfather Assaracus and Paris' great-grandfather Ilus were brothers, sons of Tros. So Aeneas and Paris are third cousins, as are Aeneas and Hector. For the genealogy, see *Iliad* 20.208–241.

7. Galinsky 1969, 3–46; see a synopsis at Casali 2014, 42–43. For reasons that I hope will become clear, *pietas* is untranslatable into English or, perhaps, from the mental and moral world of the first century into that of the twenty-first, and so I use the Latin term throughout this book.

8. Scafoglio 2013, 1–2 and n. 3; Sophocles, *Laocoön*, fr. 373 Radt. For the *Laocoön*, see Scafoglio 2006.

9. Lutatius Catulus, fr. 2 in Walter 2009, 5–6: *at uero Lutatius non modo Antenorem, sed etiam ipsum Aeneam proditorem patriae fuisse tradit*, "In fact, Lutatius transmits the story that not only Antenor, but also Aeneas himself was a traitor to his country."

10. Most of what scholars think they know about Vergil's life derives from a biography (here abbreviated as *VSD*) written by Aelius Donatus near the middle of the fourth century; most of that work derives, in turn, from a biography written by Suetonius at the end of the first century or beginning of the second. See Stok 2014. For a skeptical view on the reliability of that biographical tradition, see Horsfall 1995, 1–25.

11. Among the modern company are such disparate personalities as Samuel Johnson and Ezra Pound; see Farrell 2014, 442.

12. Gass 1970, 49; Sacks 2015.

13. Anderson, Moi, and Felski 2019; Zunshine 2006; Leverage et al. 2010; Vermeule 2010. For the *Aeneid*, see Scodel 2015.

14. For an overview of that ancient practice, with references to earlier literature, see Blom 2010, 1–17. For a comprehensive treatment, see Langlands 2018, especially 16–46.

15. For a similar analysis from a classicist's perspective, see Skinner 1983.

16. Wohl 2008, 89. On the general waning of Freud's influence, see Moyn 2016.

17. See, for an introduction to psychoanalytic criticism in general, Wright 1998; within classics, Oliensis 2009 and 2010; for Lacanian perspectives, Porter and Buchan 2004. Exemplary studies include duBois 1988, Janan 1994 and 2001, and Miller 2004.

18. For a sample, see Oliensis 2001 and 2009, 57–77; Reckford 1996; Mitchell-Boyask 1996; Gillis 1983. Quint (1993, 50–96) offers a subtle Freudian reading grounded in "repetition compulsion" and *Beyond the Pleasure Principle*.

19. On Achates' role in the poem, see Hexter 1997.

20. See Rogerson 2017, 137–138. Suppressed eroticism similarly tinges another intergenerational dialogue from the second half of the poem, when Amata, the mother of the princess for whom Aeneas and Turnus are rivals, begs Turnus not to fight Aeneas; see Ross 2007, 50–51.

21. For an introduction to Lacan's ideas, see Fink 1995. I note elsewhere (Pearcy 2005, 101), "Our human condition is made tragic by the fact that we must exist as grammatical beings in an ungrammatical world. A human who could construct no propositions about the world would be no human being at all, yet our innate power to construct propositions puts a veil of meanings between us and the world. We can only say things about the world. We will never be able to say the world itself."

22. Austin (1961) argues in favor of Vergilian authorship; Goold (1970) presents a thorough summary and concludes that the passage was written by a clever imitator of Vergil and should be excluded. Horsfall (2008, 553–591) offers a thorough discussion and opts for Goold's conclusion. Conte (2016, 76) calls it "a first, provisional, sketch, still awaiting the *labor limae*."

23. Line 462 (*sunt lacrimae rerum et mentem mortalia tangunt*), especially its first three words, are notoriously difficult. For an overview with sample translations, see Wharton 2008, 259–262. For further discussion, see chapter 5 in the present study.

24. Applying emphasis to Homer's Greek, as follows, makes the parallelism clear:

αἱ μὲν γὰρ κεράεσσι τετεύχαται, **αἱ δ'** ἐλέφαντι·
τῶν **οἳ μέν** κ' ἔλθωσι διὰ πριστοῦ ἐλέφαντος,
οἵ ῥ' ἐλεφαίρονται, ἔπε' ἀκράαντα φέροντες·
οἱ δὲ διὰ ξεστῶν κεράων ἔλθωσι θύραζε,
οἵ ῥ' ἔτυμα κραίνουσι, βροτῶν ὅτε κέν τις ἴδηται.

25. *Poetice apertus est sensus: vult autem intellegi falsa esse omnia quae dixit.*

26. For the journey as a dream, see Otis 1959, 173–179; Michels 1981. On Aeneas' corporeality contrasted with underworld spirits, compare *Aen.* 6.413–414, where Charon's skiff groans under the weight of Aeneas. On the time of night, see Horace, *Serm.* 1.10.33; Everett 1900. See also Norden 1957, 47–48, 348–349. Horsfall (2013, 2:612–618) has a thorough summary of approaches, with bibliography.

27. On Vergil's use of indirect discourse for aspects of character that he wishes to deemphasize, see Mackie 1988, 10–13.

28. That point is made with somewhat different emphasis in Most 2001, 162–164.

29. Hejduk (2009) sees this omission as part of Jupiter's general indifference to mortal suffering.

30. See further discussion in chapter 2 of this study.

31. Lacan noted that "Sade thus stopped at the point where desire and the law become bound up with each other" ("Kant with Sade," in Lacan 2006, 667).

32. Here I differ only slightly from Quint, who writes, "Aeneas is not allowed to transfer affective ties except to a collective Roman future; he is asked to give up the ties that constitute individual personality and will" (1993, 83). My reading suggests that "individual personality and will" mean something different in Aeneas' world than in ours and that rather than forming "affective ties to a collective Roman future," Aeneas remains largely ignorant of it. For a suggestion that Aeneas has affective ties to Italy, at least, see Fletcher 2014.

33. So argue Wilson (1979) and G. Williams (1983, 5–9).

34. See Wilson 1979, 369.

35. Jupiter predicts, "Indeed, harsh Juno, who now is wearying sea and lands and sky in fear, will change her mind for the better, and with me will cherish the Romans, lords of creation, the toga-clad race" (*Aen.* 1.279–282); Juno's change of heart occurs in dialogue with Jupiter, at 12.793–840.

36. For an analysis, see Michels 1997, 405–410.

37. Later, he will lose his trusted navigator, Palinurus (5.833–871), and finally, on the threshold of Italy, his old Trojan nursemaid, Caieta (7.1–4).

38. For a contrary view, see Hudson-Williams 1978; for a summary of the question, Seidman 2018.

39. See Gross 2003, 142–145.

40. Sophocles and Xenophon have been mentioned earlier in this chapter. See also, for example, [Cicero], *Ad Herennium* 4.46; *LIMC* 1:386–90.

41. Galinsky 1969, 3–10. On Aeneas before the *Aeneid*, see Gruen 1992, 6–51; Casali 2014. For an exemplary Aeneas in the Renaissance, see Schleiner 1975.

42. Fox is cited by, among others, Page (1894) and R. Williams (1972, ad loc.). See also W. B. Anderson 1930.

43. On the erotic elements in the relationship, see Putnam 1985.

44. I also venture to guess that most readers who encounter the *Aeneid* in Latin now are students between the ages of fifteen and twenty and that there are not more than a few thousand of them. In 2014, for example, only 6,542 students took the College Board's Advanced Placement Latin exam, which includes selections from the *Aeneid* (http://media.collegeboard.com/digitalServices/pdf/ap/apcentral/ap14-latin-scoring-score-dist.pdf).

45. So says the opening sentence of L. P. Hartley's novel *The Go-Between* (1953).

46. Foucault 1986; Gill 2006 and 1996. See also Riggsby 1998, 77–82.

47. C. Taylor 1989, 11–14. Taylor's important book came to my attention late in the making of the present study, and I regret not having been able to take full account of it herein.

48. See, for example, J. Porter 2017.

49. Dyson 2001, 50–53; Galinsky 1979 and 1969, 146–160.

50. See, for example, Bacon 1986.

Chapter 2

1. *Annales*, fr. 1 Vahlen: *Musae quae pedibus magnum pulsatis Olympum.*

2. Readable accounts from the past few years include Everitt 2003 and 2006, Goldsworthy 2014, and Alston 2015. For a full narrative, including political, social, and cultural history, see Crook, Lintott, and Rawson 1994; Bowman, Champlin, and Lintott 1996, 1–69. L. Taylor 1949 has been superseded in some details, but its framework is still sound; Scullard 1982 remains useful, and Syme 1939 is indispensable.

3. That comparison is made by Andrea Carandini (2013, 11), among others.

4. Q. Cicero, *Commentariolum Petitionis* 10. Levick 2015 gives a useful overview of Catiline.

5. Sallust, *Hist.* 1.44 Maurenbrecher = 1.36 McGushin (whose translation I use here).

6. Cicero, *In toga candida*, fr. 15: *Plenum animae et spiritus.*

7. Seneca, *De ira* 3.18.1–2; Hinard 1985, 377–380; Rawson 1987, 174–177.

8. Cicero, *In Defense of Roscius of Ameria* 89. The heads were displayed at the Lacus Servilius, close to the Basilica Julia (Richardson 1992, 232).

9. For a skeptical view of the idea that Catiline was Gratidianus' executioner, see Marshall 1985.

10. Sallust, *Catiline* 5.6: *Hunc post dominationem L. Sullae lubido maxuma invaserat rei publicae capiundae.* Caesar commented that by voluntarily laying down his dictator-

ship, Sulla had revealed that he didn't know his political ABCs (Suetonius, *Julius* 77). Caesar, as much as Pompey, may have been behind the remark that, according to Cicero (*Letters to Atticus* 9.10.2.), was on everyone's mind in 49 BC: "Sulla could do it—can't I?" (*Sulla potuit; ego non potero?*)

11. Sallust, *Catiline* 5.2: *Huic ab adulescentia bella intestina caedes rapinae discordia civilis grata fuere, ibique iuventutem suam exercuit.*

12. There had been no consuls in his family since the fifth century, although Gnaeus Sergius Fidenas Coxo had served as military tribune with consular power in 380 BC.

13. Sallust (*Catiline* 18.3) confusingly blends both possibilities: *post paulo Catilina pecuniarum repetundarum reus prohibitus erat consulatum petere, quod intra legitumos dies profiteri nequiverat,* "Somewhat later Catiline as defendant on a charge of extortion was kept from seeking the consulate, because he had been unable to declare his candidacy within the lawful number of days."

14. Suetonius, *Tiberius* 32: *Rescripsit boni pastoris esse tondere pecus, non deglubere.*

15. Sallust, *Catiline* 37.1. For the liquidity crisis, see Dyck 2008, 4–7; on the importance of funding in the civil wars, Westall 2017, 57–68.

16. Cicero, *In Defense of Murena* 51: *si quod esset in suas fortunas incendium excitatum, id se non aqua sed ruina restincturum.*

17. Appian (*Civil Wars* 2.2) reports that Catiline "collected much money from many women who hoped their husbands would be killed in the rising, and he formed a conspiracy with certain senators and knights."

18. Appian, *Civil Wars* 2.2: "He sent messengers throughout Italy to those of Sulla's soldiers who had squandered the profits of their former life and who longed for similar doings."

19. Appian *Civil Wars* 2.3: "He had the rods and axes borne before him like some proconsul."

20. Appian (*Civil Wars* 2.7) reports, "When Catiline had collected about 20,000 troops, of whom one-fourth part were armed, and was already moving toward Gaul in order to complete his preparations, Antonius, the other consul, caught up with him at the foot of the Alps."

21. Sallust, *Catiline* 59. A normal strength of six centuries, or 480 men, to a cohort plus a double-strength first cohort gives 4,320 men. Catiline may well have had fewer.

22. Sallust, *Catiline* 59.2–3: *Octo cohortis in fronte constituit, reliquarum signa in subsidio artius conlocat. Ab his omnis evocatos et centuriones, praeterea ex gregariis militibus optimum quemque [armatum] in primam aciem subducit*; "He posted eight cohorts on his front and placed the remaining formations in close order as a reserve; in addition, he took all the veterans and centurions, and also every best equipped man from the rank and file, and put them in his first line."

23. The image is Horace's (*Odes* 2.1.7–8).

24. Unlike the Second Triumvirate (the alliance of Octavian, Antony, and Lepidus), the First Triumvirate had no constitutional or legal basis. On *amicitia*, *dominatio*, and *factio*, see Brunt 1988, 351–381, 443–502.

25. I heard Ronald Syme offer that definition in a lecture many years ago. According to Tacitus, Pompey was less forthcoming, not better (*occultior, non melior, Hist.* 2.38.1). On *auctoritas*, see Galinsky 1996, 10–20; on Pompey's political character, Blom 2016, 113–145.

26. Suetonius, *Nero* 46; Pliny, *Natural History* 36.41. The complex stretched roughly from the modern Campo de' Fiori to Largo Argentina.

27. I have simplified a complex tactical picture; see Crook, Lintott, and Rawson 1994, 402–403.

28. Appian's report that ten thousand out of a total force of one hundred thousand survived (*Civil Wars* 2.18) is probably an exaggeration.

29. Gellius, *Attic Nights* 14.7.2–3.

30. Cicero, *Republic* 2.51: *Rector et gubernator civitatis*. See, further, Zarecki 2014.

31. Brunt 1988, 470–488; Robb 2010.

32. On *dignitas*, see Badel 2014.

33. Cicero's archenemy Publius Claudius Pulcher did so, changing his aristocratic name to Clodius along the way. (In modern times one thinks of the 2nd Viscount Stansgate, who morphed into Anthony Wedgwood Benn to keep his seat in the British Parliament and then into Tony Benn as he moved ever leftward.)

34. Morstein-Marx (2007) argues that fear of prosecution may not have been a major factor in Caesar's deliberations leading up to the civil war.

35. For the possibility that Caesar was preparing for civil war even before the crisis of December through January 49, see Westall 2017, 56–57.

36. The question of what to call the person who became the emperor Augustus is troublesome. Born Gaius Octavius Thurinus (Suetonius, *Augustus* 7.1), he became Gaius Julius Caesar after his great-uncle Julius Caesar almost but not quite adopted him by naming him as heir and granting him the right to his name. By degrees, he became Imperator Caesar Divi Filius, "Generalissimo Caesar son of the Deified One," and in 27 BC, the Senate conferred on him the honorary cognomen Augustus, "the Revered One." Most modern historians call him "Octavian" from 44 until 27 and "Augustus" thereafter, and so shall I. See Syme 1958.

37. See Cooley's edition of the *Res gestae* (2009). I use her translation here.

38. The exact provisions of this *Lex Titia* are obscure; see Alston 2015, 129 and n. 13.

39. On the triumviral proscriptions, see Hinard 1985, 227–318; Gowing 1992, 247–269; Goldsworthy 2014, 128–134. Still readable is R. Conway 1928, 1–13.

40. Osgood 2014. The inscription is *Inscriptiones Latinae Selectae* 8393; see also Valerius Maximus 6.7.2.

41. Appian's report (*Civil Wars* 4.5) that three hundred senators and two thousand *equites* were proscribed may be little more than a guess but is probably not unreasonable. Cassius Dio (47.3) says that 280 names were posted in the early days of the terror.

42. Reliable figures are hard to come by. In my estimate, I follow the conclusion of Brunt (1971, 493) that "the total number of veterans qualified for and seeking allotments

may not have exceeded 50,000," but I grant some validity to complaints that Octavian gave land to "the unworthy" (Appian, *Civil Wars* 5.16). Gabba (1956, 190), following Appian (*Civil Wars* 5.5), suggests a total of 170,000 veterans, which may be taken as an upper limit.

43. *VSD* 19–20. The tradition may be nothing more than an inference from lines in the *Bucolics*.

44. My account here of the Perusine War and events leading up to it follows the analysis in Alston 2015, 161–174.

45. Appian, *Civil Wars* 5.13. Note also *ut possessor* in *Bucolics* 9.3; the person who occupies Moeris' little farm seems to have no clear title to it.

46. Reasons for skepticism appear in Reid 1912.

47. Horace, *Odes* 2.7; *Satires* 1.6, 47–49; *Epistles* 2.2, 49–52; Nisbet and Hubbard 1978, 106–107.

48. For the literature of the civil wars, see Jal 1963; on Vergil, Perkell 2002.

49. Gatz 1967, 135. On later Augustan developments of the idea, see A. Zanker 2010.

50. Most but not all scholars still connect *Bucolics* 4 with the Treaty of Brundisium, negotiated between Octavian and Antony in the autumn of 40 BC. See Fraenkel 1957, 50–52; for a contrary view, Clausen 1994. The possibility of a connection between *Bucolics* 4 and Jewish literature is beginning to look likely: see Horsfall 2012; Bremmer 2013.

51. On *scelus* and *fraus* as ways of referring to the civil wars, see Clark 2004, 17–23. Vergil may be thinking of the Trojans' "ancestral fraud," when Laomedon, Priam's father, agreed to hire Apollo and Neptune to build the walls of Troy but then failed to pay them.

52. The *Phaenomena* also introduced the idea of Astraea (the maiden of *Buc.* 4.6). For an accessible translation of Aratus' poem, see Poochigian 2010; for an introduction to Cicero's translation, Gee 2001.

53. Lyne 1987. Lucretius (*On the Nature of Things* 3.68–73), writing at some point before the mid-fifties BC, had already associated civil war with fratricide and the breakdown of family ties. On fratricide and civil war, see Bannon 1997, 136–171.

54. On the date of Horace's *Epode* 16 and its relation to *Bucolics* 4, see Fraenkel 1957, 50–52, drawing on Snell 1938. For more recent discussion, which adds only a little, see Doblhofer 1992, 86–89; S. J. Harrison 1995, 11; Watson 2003, 487–488. Since the conditions of "publication" in the ancient world did not allow for a definitive publication date, it makes sense to speak of a dialogue between poems rather than of priority and influence.

55. Caesar, *Civil War* 3.59–61. Mankin (1995, 248) regards the Catilinarian episode as the least likely of several possibilities.

56. For war with Antony as war with his ally Cleopatra VII, see *Aen.* 8.675–713; Horace, *Odes* 1.37. On triumphs during the civil wars, see Havener 2014; Östenberg 2014; Lange 2016.

57. On Romans' feeling for the site of Rome, see Jenkyns 2014, 21–23.

58. Cicero, *Letters to Atticus* 7.11.3. For the rumor about Caesar's plans, see Suetonius, *Julius* 79.3. Another possible reflection of the anxiety appears in Horace, *Odes* 3.3 (23 BC); see Nisbet and Rudd 2004, 35–38.

59. On freedmen and magistracies, see Mouritsen 2011, 66–71, 248–278; on *adynata*, Rowe 1965, 387–396.

60. D. Porter 1995. Horace continued his engagement with *Bucolics* 4 in his *Odes*, published in 23 BC; see Clark 2004.

61. Bowman, Champlin, and Lintott 1996, 676–702.

62. For some of the complexities of spin in the conflict between Octavian and Antony, see P. Zanker 1988, 33–77; Gurval 1995, 137–178. The traditional view that triumphs in civil war always had to be reframed as victories over foreign enemies has been questioned; see Lange 2016.

63. Magie 1920 gives a concise account.

64. Cassius Dio 53.30. In *Epistles* 1.13, published in 20 BC, Horace asks a friend to deliver a book to Augustus only "if he is healthy." For early Augustan poets' concern for the physical safety and health of Augustus, see Lowrie 2016.

65. Stockton 1965; Goldsworthy 2014, 278–283.

66. Cassius Dio 53.33; Aldrete 2006, 131–132.

67. That milieu is emphasized by Schauer (2007, 1–25).

68. In his commentary on *Aeneid* 1, Austin (1971) gives arguments for and against identification of the "Trojan Caesar" as Julius or Augustus; for the possibility of deliberate ambiguity, see O'Hara 1990, 155–163.

69. For Romulus and Remus as avatars of civil war, see Bannon 1997, 158.

70. For the description "gates of War," see Plutarch, *Numa* 20. Augustus would announce the temple's closure a third time, but after Vergil's death.

71. See Ovid, *Fasti* 1.121–124 (for war locked in), 1.277–281 (for peace locked in); Statius, *Silvae* 4.1 (for Janus kept in).

72. See DeBrohun 2008. Note the hissing sounds in the Latin phrase *impius intus / saeva sedens super arma* and the roaring in *horridus ore cruento.*

73. Pliny, *Natural History* 35.27; Servius on *Aen.* 1.294.

74. For a detailed analysis of the grim aspects of Jupiter's speech, see Hejduk 2009, 283–292.

75. *Epode* 16.63 (*Piae . . . genti*), 66 (*piis*); both instances are translated "godly" in the quote in the preceding section of the present chapter. On *fides* as important to Vergil's generation, see Shearin 2015, 61–73; Konstan 1997, 122–142; Brunt 1988, 413–424.

76. *Buc.* 4.5: *Magnus ab integro saeclorum nascitur ordo*—. That line is the origin of the motto *Novus Ordo Seclorum* on the reverse of the Great Seal of the United States, found on every dollar bill.

77. Note *spoliis Orientis onustum* at *Aen.* 1.289.

78. Thucydides, *Hist.* 7.77. Pericles stated, "The Athens that I have celebrated is only what the heroism of these and their like have made her" (Thucydides, *Hist.* 2.42, trans. Crawley, from Strassler 1996).

79. *Moribus antiquis res stat Romana virisque* (quoted by Cicero in *De re publica* 5.1 = fr. 500 Vahlen).

Chapter 3

1. For a briefer but not conflicting account of Aeneas' points of decision, see Ross 2007, 12–18.

2. His mother, Venus, directs him in person at *Aen.* 1.335–401 and 2.589–620; the Penates, acting for Apollo, instruct him at 3.147–178; the god of the Tiber offers guidance at 8.36–70; and so on.

3. It makes little difference at this point whether we are fatalists or determinists; that is, whether we assume that all events unfold according to a cosmic plan or whether we hold that every event has a cause and, in turn, causes another event, so that the state of the world at any point must be what it is, given the way things were before it.

4. This so-called Idle Argument (discussed by Cicero at *On Fate* 28–29) is exhaustively analyzed by Bobzien 1998, 182–198.

5. For engagement with philosophical debates about fate in one of Vergil's models, Apollonius Rhodius, see Ojennus 2018.

6. For the difficulties involved, see Janko 2016.

7. The papyrus in question is designated *PHerc.Paris* 2; see Gigante 2004. For a concise account of Vergil's Epicurean affiliations, see D. Armstrong 2004, 1–3; for an introduction to Philodemus and the Herculaneum papyri, Gigante 1995.

8. On that passage in the context of Vergil's presentation of Aeneas as a model "good king," see Cairns 1989, 29–30.

9. *Letter to Menoeceus* 134 = Long and Sedley 20A.

10. Epicurus, *On Nature* 34.26–30 = Long and Sedley 20C.

11. Lucretius 2.216–224; Diogenes of Oenoanda 32.1.14–3.14 = Long and Sedley 20G. The connection between the atomic swerve and human free will is debated: see Englert 1987; Russell 2000.

12. Within the vast literature on Vergil and Stoicism, see Bowra 1933; Edwards 1960; G. Zanker 2017. For a skeptical view, see Galinsky 1988; for a sane overview, Braund 1997.

13. Chrysippus as cited in Plutarch, *On Stoic Self-Contradictions* (*De Stoicorum repugnantibus*) 1052c–d = Long and Sedley 46E, 1053b = Long and Sedley 46F.

14. As W. R. Johnson put it over forty years ago, "In his fear, in his vast Epicurean sensitivity to pain and suffering, Vergil nevertheless turned from the calm, austere garden back to the world where unreasoning power is a reality that must somehow be persuaded or suffered and where pain must be inflicted or endured. The garden was impossible because he could not teach himself not to hear the screams and riot outside" (1976, 152–153).

15. E. H. W. Conway (1921, 179) called the usage the "scenic plural."

16. Later in his tale to Dido, Aeneas describes himself and his band of exiles as "the second citadel of Troy" (*altera Troiae / Pergama, Aen.* 3.86–87).

17. At least since Servius' comment *hysteronproteron quidem est*, teachers have loved to point out that line 353, *moriamur et in media arma ruamus* ("Let us die and rush into battle"), is an example of the rhetorical figure hysteron proteron, putting first what logically or temporally belongs second—as in "put on your shoes and socks." Vergil's figure, which I have chosen not to keep in my translation, puts death, the thing uppermost in Aeneas' mind, first.

18. For the cinematic quality of Vergil's imagination, see Mench 1969.

19. Horsfall (2008, 553–567) argues that Vergil himself left a gap in the text, which the author of the Helen episode then filled.

20. Servius tries to offer explanation by citing a line from Catullus' friend Licinius Calvus and mentioning a statue of a bearded Venus in Cyprus. Macrobius (*Saturnalia* 3.8.1–2) confirms Servius' information and adds some details. Horsfall (2008, 452–453) gives arguments in support.

21. The verbs are *descendo* (632) and *expedior* (633). The latter, meaning "I am extricated, I extricate myself" (2.633), is passive or reflexive, but the former is active.

22. Note also *accingor* (671), *insertabam* and *ferebam* (672), *insternor* (722), *succedo* (723), *respexi* (741), *recondo* (748), *repeto* and *cingor* (749), *extuleram* and *repeto* (753), *sequor* (754), *refero* (757), *implevi* (769), *vocavi* (770), *obstipui* (774), *reviso* (795), *cessi* and *petivi* (804).

23. The date of the Trojan War and the coordination of Greek legendary and mythical history with the Roman past were of interest to Vergil's contemporaries, including Marcus Terentius Varro, Cornelius Nepos, and Livy. Eratosthenes, Timaeus, and other Greek historians give a range of dates in the thirteenth century BC; see Moatti 2015, 72–74.

24. For a summary, see Cantarella 2003.

25. For example, Otis (1964, 250) notes, "We are of course meant to sympathize with the grief of Aeneas . . . but we are also meant to see that Aeneas' attitude is far from a complete and sufficient *pietas*"; Grillo (2010, 43) writes, "I argue that the Aeneas who flees from Troy and loses Creusa is not a plain model of sensibility and virtue, as commentators have believed until recently. Virgil's language, intertextual references and narrative choices elicit open-ended and ambiguous interpretations and thus necessarily complicate the issue of Aeneas' *pietas*."

26. On Vergil's preference for the Greek form *Thybris* and on the problematic nature of that name, see Reed 2007, 5–6; Fletcher 2014, 70–73.

27. *Aen.* 3.495 = 2.780: *Maris aequor arandum*. Note also *Thybrim vicinaque Thybridis arva* at *Aen.* 3.500, *Lydius arva / inter opima virum leni fluit agmine Thybris* at 2.781–782.

28. Briggs (1979, 43) offers a concise summary:

> Orpheus and Aeneas both attempt their exits with their wives (*coniuge*—Geo. 4.504, *dulcis coniunx*—*Aen.* 2.777) behind them (*pone sequens*—487, *pone subit coni-*

> *unx*—125). As they near the end (*superas veniebat ad auras*—486, *Iamque propinquabam portis*—730), having escaped all danger (*Iamque . . . casus evaserat omnis*—485, *lamque . . . omnemque videbar evasisse viam*—730–731), each is distracted (Orpheus by a *dementia*, Aeneas by a *male numen amicum*), Orpheus and Creusa halt (*restitit*—490, *substitit*—139), the husbands look back (*respexit*—491, *respexi*—741) and are rebuked for their madness (*Quis tantus furor . . .*—495, . . . —776), losing their loves, never to be restored again (*neque . . . praeterea vidit*—500–502, nec *post ocuiis est reddita nostra*—740). After the loss, both men fill up the region around them with laments (Orpheus as a nightingale *maestis late loca questibus implet*—515, Aeneas says *implevi clamore vias, maestusque . . .*—769) and vainly clutch at their women (*prensantem nequiquam*—501, *ter conatus ibi collo dare bracchia circum*—792), who disappear like smoke or air (*ceu fumus in auras . . . tenuis*—499–500, *tenuisque recessit in auras . . . par levibus ventis*—791–794), saying, "iamque vale" (497, 798).

Note also that *Georgics* 4.475–477, where the ghosts greet Orpheus at the gates of the underworld, is repeated verbatim at *Aen.* 6.306–308, and a phrase from it describing the soul of unburied children, *pueri innuptaeque puellae*, echoes in *pueri circum innuptaeque puellae* (*Aen.* 2.238) as the Trojans drag the wooden horse into Troy at the beginning of the city's infernal last night.

29. Notably in Ennius' *Annales*; see Austin 1971, 286–289.

30. *Aen.* 1.466–493. The omens are the horses of Rhesus (469–473), the death of Troilus (474–478), and the loss of the Palladium (hinted at in 479–482); see Pandey 2017, 16.

31. *Aen.* 2.314, 735 (*amens*); 316 (*furor iraque*); 244, 355 (*furor*); 575 (in the Helen episode), 594 (*ira*).

32. *Aen.* 2.3: *Infandum, regina, iubes renovare dolorem.*

Chapter 4

1. *VSD* 24–25 and other ancient commentators on the *Bucolics* suggest that they were written between 42 and 39 BC. For a summary of the issue, see Coleman 1977, 14–21; Perutelli 1995, 28–31. Osgood (2006, 109) defends the commentators' date, but some scholars, such as Bowersock (1971) and Clausen (1972), have argued for a date closer to 35 BC.

2. For introductions to this complex genre, see Rosenmeyer 1969; Halperin 1983; Hubbard 1998.

3. My discussion here draws on the insights of Meban 2009. For a reading that downplays the importance of contemporary events for understanding *Bucolics* 9 and the related *Bucolics* 1, see Segal 1965.

4. I follow the division between speakers suggested by Coleman (1977, 268–269), which assigns 9.44–45 to Moeris instead of to Lycidas.

5. My account here is based on the description in Pliny, *Natural History* 2.93–94, which quotes Augustus' autobiography. Scott 1941 collects the abundant ancient evidence for the *sidus Iulium*. Gurval (1997, 41) tries to use the silence of some contemporary witnesses and contradictions in ancient accounts to argue that the comet "may be better understood as a construction of Augustan politics, an ideological myth," but Ramsey and Licht (1997) use Chinese astronomical records to demonstrate the comet's existence. Pandey (2013, 407) discusses interpretations of the *sidus* in the light of the "polysemous discourse of the [Augustan] age."

6. For *animum* with the sense "memory," note Servius' comment (ad loc.), *etiam memoriam*, and see Coleman 1977, 268.

7. Sulla, like Catiline, belonged to a branch of a patrician family that had fallen into relative decline; his paternal grandfather was praetor in 186 but seems never to have become consul.

8. Cicero, *Laws* 2.56; Valerius Maximus 9.2.1.

9. My account here of Caesar's reactions to Sulla follows Flower 2006, 104–109.

10. In a letter written to two of his close associates in early March of 49 BC, (Cicero, *Letters to Atticus* 9.7c), Caesar wrote,

> I shall willingly follow your advice, all the more willingly because I had of my own accord decided to show all possible clemency and to do my best to reconcile Pompey. Let us try whether by this means we can win back the good will of all and enjoy a lasting victory, seeing that others have not managed by cruelty to escape hatred or to make their victories endure, except only L. Sulla, whom I do not propose to imitate.

On Caesar's clemency and reactions to it, see Konstan 2005; for the rhetorical tradition about Sulla's cruelty and clemency, Dowling 2000.

11. Highet 1972, 19–20, 25–26. If the 1,516 lines of Aeneas' first-person flashback narrative in books 2 and 3 are counted as one speech and speech reported in it excluded, there are 290 speeches.

12. On Vergil's handling of Aeneas' silent deliberation, see Starr 2003, 36–41.

13. Compare Queen Arete's questions to Odysseus at *Odyssey* 7.237–239, Odysseus' encounter with the disguised Athena at *Od.* 14.217–235, and, especially, Odysseus' exchange with Nausicaa at *Od.* 6.149–210.

14. On Venus' augury and its importance in establishing a pattern of incomplete prophecy in the *Aeneid*, see O'Hara 1990, 9–13.

15. *Aen.* 6.700–702 = 2.792–794: *ter conatus ibi collo dare bracchia circum; / ter frustra comprensa manus effugit imago, / par levibus ventis volucrique simillima somno.*

16. On the episode and its links to Venus' augury in book 1, see O'Hara 1990, 31–35.

17. *Aen.* 2.729: *Pariter comitique onerique timentem.* Despite the efforts of commentators from antiquity on to make the singular *comiti*, "companion," include Creusa as well as young Ascanius, the line is unambiguous; see Horsfall 2008, 512.

18. Michels 1997, 412. Michels claims sixteen occasions on which Aeneas shows fear, nine of them in books 2 and 3.

19. Barchiesi (2015, 45) notes the similarity to Dido and reads Aeneas' relationship with Pallas, which is paternal as much as erotic, in the light of Homeric antecedents and the similar relationship between Mezentius and Lausus.

20. On Ascanius, see Rogerson 2017, especially 37–56 for his names. Some have even wondered how to pronounce the name Iulus; see Cowan 2009.

21. My discussion of memory in the *Aeneid* owes a great deal to Flower 2006, Most 2001, Quint 1982, and Seider 2013. My citations of them are intermittent, but their influence is ubiquitous.

22. Knauer 1964 is the fundamental detailed study of Vergil's use of Homer and can be useful even to those without German; Barchiesi 2015 complicates the matter in a good way.

23. *O socii* = ὦ φίλοι; *neque enim ante* = οὐ γάρ πώ; *ignari* = ἀδαήμονές; *sumus* = εἶμεν; *malorum* = κακῶν.

24. On Vergil's use of the so-called Alexandrian footnote, a term that seems to have been coined by Ross (1975), see Townshend 2015; Horsfall 2016, 111–134.

25. "The Choice of Hercules"—a parable in which the hero finds himself at a fork in the road, with one, harder path leading to virtue and another, easier one leading to vice (both personified as women)—goes back to the Sophist Prodicus (ca. 465–ca. 395) and is familiar from Xenophon, *Memorabilia* 2.1.21–34.

26. "Helmsman," the conventional translation of *gubernator*, misleads somewhat. In modern terms, Palinurus is a navigator or sailing master.

27. On inconsistencies in the *Aeneid*, see O'Hara 2007, 77–103; on sacrificial victims, Dyson 2001, especially 74–94 (on Palinurus).

28. Commentators sometimes create a difficulty by translating *cumque gubernaculo* at 6.859 as "with the rudder" and then wondering how Aeneas could have steered the ship if Palinurus had carried away the rudder (for example, Perkell 2004, 134–135). Ancient ships had steering oars to port and starboard. Aeneas presumably simply used the one remaining; that might be hard, in any kind of a breeze, if the remaining oar happened to be to windward, but it should be possible with a calm sea and favoring wind. The first two lines of book 6 may have originally ended book 5; according to Servius, they were moved to their present position by Varius and Tucca, the posthumous editors of the *Aeneid*.

29. In his comment on 5.832, Servius explains that *sua flamina* means "favorable, coming from astern."

30. For Palinurus as a doublet of Aeneas, see Nicoll 1988.

31. I construe *lenibat* and *ciebat* as conative imperfects; as Servius says, *ciere* is properly used of exciting someone else's emotions.

32. The echo of Catullus 66.39 (*invita, o regina, tuo de vertice cessi*) in Aeneas' *invitus, regina, tuo de litore cessi* is too close to be coincidence. For attempts to make it one, see Fordyce 1961, 334; R. Williams 1972, 488. Critics have found varied, plausible

answers by expanding Vergil's single line into a web of intertext and allusion to Catullus, Callimachus, and other authors and by probing the episode for what it can add to the characterization of Dido: see, among many others, Smith 1993; Johnston 1987; Tatum 1984; Skinner 1983.

33. Before he crosses into the world of the dead at *Aen.* 6.268, Aeneas gives two formal speeches, each just over twenty lines (6.56–77, 103–123). Afterward, only his greeting to Deiphobus at 6.500–508 comes close to the length of his anguished address to Dido.

34. At *Aen.* 2.107, Sinon "follows up [on the first part of his speech to the Trojans] trembling and speaks with feigning heart" (*prosequitur pavitans et ficto pectore fatur*); at 6.897–898, Anchises "follows his son with words" (*natum . . . prosequitur dictis*) as far as the Gates of Ivory; at 9.308–310, a band of the leading Trojans "follows with prayers" (*prosequitur votis*) as Nisus and Euralyus leave gates of the Trojan fort; at 11.107, when envoys from the Latins come to negotiate a cease-fire to bury the dead, Aeneas "follows with kindness and adds these remarks besides" (*prosequitur venia et verbis haec insuper addit*).

35. On Aeneas' experience on the last night of Troy as an anticipation of his underworld journey, see Hejduk 2013, 153–155, as well as discussion in chapter 3 of the present study.

36. The scheme is from Norden 1957, 152; Norden's rhetorical analyses are, as Nicholas Horsfall says (2013, 514), "of high quality."

37. For a summary of the literary and iconographic traditions around Hercules' and Theseus' descents into the underworld, see Verbanck-Piérard 2018.

38. See, especially, *Georgics* 4; *Aen.* 1.430–436. For introductions to the challenges of the apicultural sections of this poem, see Perkell 1978; Griffin 1979.

39. See Horsfall 2010; 2013, ad loc.

40. As Brooks Otis pointed out (1959, 167), the central concern of book 6 is with "Aeneas and the spiritual processes at work in his psyche."

41. Reed 2001 discusses Anchises' sensitivity to Aeneas' psychological state in book 6 and explores, from a slightly different angle than mine, Aeneas' hesitant and disillusioned underworld discoveries.

42. Horsfall (2013, 484–486) provides an introduction to what he describes as Vergil's "asystematic and impressionistic" eschatology.

43. On the "recovery of the standards," see Bowman and Lintott 1996, 90. In his *Centennial Hymn*, the *Carmen Saeculare*, commissioned by Augustus three years after Vergil's death, Horace trumpets the submission of the "Mede" to Roman axes. On the breastplate of the famous statue of Augustus from Prima Porta, the Parthians are shown surrendering the eagles.

44. Scholars have debated the construction sequence for the Mausoleum of Augustus; see Haselberger 2008, 160. For other resonances between the *Aeneid* and Augustus' reshaping of the civic landscape of Rome, see Kondratieff 2015; Pandey 2014.

45. On the importance of bonds between sons-in-law and fathers-in-law in Roman

society (and the importance of daughters in establishing those relationships), see Hallett 1984, 299–346.

46. For Cybele elsewhere in the *Aeneid*, see Wilhelm 1988.

47. Reed (2001, 163–164) argues that the repetition of *miserande puer* from *Aen.* 6.882 over the corpses of Lausus at 10.825 and Pallas at 11.42 suggests that Aeneas retains a subliminal memory of Anchises' teaching in the underworld. I elaborate on Reed's insight in chapter 5 of the present study.

48. Too many critics to name have noted how Vergil configures the wars in Italy in *Aen.* 7–12 as civil war. See, for example, Ahl 1976, 66–67; Lyne 1983; Cairns 1989, 85–108 (with focus on concord and discord as general themes); Pogorzelski 2009.

49. The name Cunctator was an improvement over his given cognomen, Verrucosus, "Warty."

50. These lines have attracted copious comment and dispute, and my translation slides over a few notorious difficulties, most notably *pacique imponere morem* in line 852. For a detailed discussion and analysis, see Horsfall 2011 and Horsfall's 2013 commentary.

51. See Horsfall 2011 and the bibliography at Horsfall 2013, 579.

52. Plutarch, *Life of Antony* 87; see also Freudenburg 2017, 118. For Julia, see Fantham 2006.

53. An example is the epitaph of Publius Cornelius Scipio (ca. 170 BC): "Death made sure that all your honor, fame, valor, glory and talent would be short-lived, but if you had been allowed a long life to enjoy them, you would easily have surpassed the deeds of your ancestors." The epitaph, *ILLRP* 311, is most easily found in volume 4 of the Loeb *Remains of Old Latin*, ed. E. H. Warmington (1940).

Chapter 5

1. On the whole episode, see Uden 2014.

2. On those two aspects of Aeneas' role, see Segal 1999. Putnam (1998) emphasizes Aeneas' role as interpreter of the murals and suggests that the Vergilian narrator "also posits Aeneas and his responses as a form of artisanship" (244).

3. For an account of previous views and another attempt to reconcile *amissis armis* and *versa . . . hasta*, see R. Williams 1960, 145–148.

4. Heslin 2015, 275. Heslin's analysis of the passage, if accepted, strengthens my argument that Aeneas operates from a position of necessary ignorance. His analysis depends, however, on a complex chain of iconographic and textual interpretations and on inference from a known building (the Temple of Apollo at Pompeii) to a vanished one (the Portico of Philippus at Rome) and then to Vergil's text. Heslin convinced me, but I am not a competent judge of the material evidence on which he rests early links in his chain of reasoning.

5. For a reading of Carthage and the Punic Wars as a tragic trope for Roman civil

war, see Giusti 2018. On Vergil's use of drama in general, see Galinsky 2003; Hardie 1997; Panoussi 2009. Roman readers knew very well that a gap of centuries separated the Trojan War from the foundation of Carthage and that a historical Aeneas and Dido could never have met (Hardie 2014, 52–55).

6. On Dido as Antigone, see Mac Góráin 2018, 137–141; as Medea, Giusti 2018, 115–127.

7. Harrison 1999, 69–72.

8. On the motif of ignorance and its relation to shepherds in the *Aeneid*, see Chew 2002.

9. Servius, ad loc.: *Quidam tamen 'lacrimas inanes' vel Aeneae, vel Didonis, vel Annae, vel omnium.*

10. For a summary of the question, see Seidman 2018; for a determinate view, Hudson-Williams 1978.

11. The definition is attributed to José Ortega y Gasset by Nancy Gardner Williams (widow of the novelist John Williams), in an interview in the *Paris Review*, February 20, 2019, https://www.theparisreview.org/blog/2019/02/20/mrs-stoner-speaks-an-interview-with-nancy-gardner-williams/

12. For an exhaustive catalog of the mentions of Hercules, see Zarker 1972.

13. For an exploration of the complex presentation of Romulus in the *Aeneid*, see Hejduk 2009, 285–288 with 318.

14. See, for example, Plutarch, *Life of Antony* 60.

15. On Vergil's use of Homer in book 10, see Barchiesi 2015, 1–52.

16. For the most effective presentation, see Putnam 1985.

17. Nielson 1983; Cleary 1982, 20–22.

18. In Vergil's lifetime, single combat between commanders was no mere relic of legendary times; on its appearance as a topic of political controversy, see Martino 2008.

19. Speculating about Aeneas' age is as useless as trying to guess his hair color, but if we allow for ten years of the Trojan War, seven years wandering the Mediterranean (*Aen.* 1.755–756), and most of a year in Carthage, we must imagine him as very near forty, on one side or the other. Lausus is still a *iuvenis* (10.816) and may not be much older than twenty.

20. On this episode, see Barchiesi 2015, 53–67.

21. The same might be said of *miserande puer*; see Reed 2001, 163–164.

22. Note, for example, *Aen.* 7.5, 133–140; 8.68–78; 10.2–3.

23. Here I follow the lead of Reed 2007, especially 182–186.

Chapter 6

1. See, for example, *Aen.* 2.362, 385.

2. The possible allusion was first noted, as far as I know, by Levitan (1993), followed by O'Hara (1996, 115–116) and many others.

3. *Quos ego—sed motos praestat componere fluctus.* Ever since Servius, teachers have pointed to this line as an example of the figure of speech called "aposiopesis."

4. *In Defense of Cluentius* 49, 138; note *quod saepe dictum est*, "a thing which has often been said." See Beck 2014, 73–74.

5. Cowan 2015, especially 105–107.

6. For an argument in favor of Augustus (and a nod to Popilius Laena), see Galinsky 1996, 21–23. In support of Cato the Younger, commentators refer to Plutarch, *Life of Cato the Younger* 44, but see the remarks in Pöschl 1962, 21–22. Morwood (1998) suggests the statesman Menenius Agrippa of the early fifth century BC.

7. The move from Aristotle's "slight" to Chrysippus' "injury," which Harris (2001, 61) takes as "a symptom of a certain shift from shame culture to guilt culture," need not concern us here; see also Konstan 2006, 66–67.

8. No meaningful distinction can be drawn between *furor* and *furiae*; see Thomas 1991.

9. In discussing this distinction, I draw on Indelli 2004.

10. Philodemus, *De ira* (*PHerc.* 182), cols. xliii.41–xliv.8.

11. Indelli (2004, 105) explains, "Even for the Epicureans, then, the difference was quite clear—underscored by Philodemus in col. xlv.33–37—between *orgē*, natural anger, springing from motives that are justified, moderate in its duration and its intensity, and *thymos* (which Philodemus seems also to call *kenē orgē*), blind and uncontrolled rage."

12. I approximate and truncate the meaning of line 587. As sometimes happens, the line has been irretrievably corrupted by generations of copying and recopying between Vergil's draft and our earliest manuscripts, and the obelus (†) before *famam* in Mynor's text, *ultricis †famam et cineres satiasse meorum*, is a funereal cross marking a dead text.

13. On the parallelism between books 1 and 7, see Cowan 2015, with bibliography at 97n2 and discussion of the two similes at 105–109.

14. For a framing of Aeneas' difficulty in terms of Freudian "repetition compulsion," see Quint 1993, 50–65.

15. For the Homeric motif, see also *Iliad* 20.285–287, where Aeneas hefts a stone described with the same formula, and *Iliad* 21.403–405, where Athena lifts a stone that men of old left to be a boundary.

16. On the whole passage, see Quint 1993, 70–74.

17. For further complexities in Vergil's use of Homeric descriptions of rock throwing, see the important discussion in Quint 1993, 68–72.

18. Those instances are Vergil's only uses of *ulterius*; note also the consonance of *tende/temptare*.

19. The sentiment here is drawn from Seamus Heaney's *The Cure at Troy*:

History says, don't hope
On this side of the grave.
But then, once in a lifetime
The longed-for tidal wave

Of justice can rise up,
And hope and history rhyme.

So hope for a great sea-change
On the far side of revenge.

20. *Stetit acer in armis / Aeneas volvens oculos dextramque repressit; / et iam iamque magis cunctantem flectere sermo / coeperat . . .*

21. The Danaids formed part of the sculptural ensemble surrounding the temple of Apollo dedicated by Octavian/Augustus in 28 BC, and Horace incorporates the story of Hypermnestra, the one Danaid who did not murder her husband, into *Odes* 3.11, published in 23 BC. Putnam (2001) suggests that the Danaids stand for revenge and, since their husbands were also their cousins, for the fratricidal conflicts of civil war.

22. Wells 2015; Maffeo Vegio's thirteenth book is conveniently available in Putnam 2004.

23. Servius, preface to commentary on *Aen.* 1; see also Kaster 2012. For a recent example of that "pro-Augustan" interpretation, see Stahl 2016. For overviews of the two schools from divergent perspectives, see Johnson 1976, 8–16; Galinsky 1996, 4–5; Hardie 1998, 94.

24. It has become conventional to refer to the second group as the "Harvard school" of interpretation, but that term probably has outlived its usefulness; see Hejduk 2017. For prominent examples, see Parry 1963; Johnson 1976 (especially 11, 156n10, for the original usage of the term "Harvard school" in this context); Thomas 2001.

25. On this and other hesitations in the *Aeneid*, see Putnam 1984 = 1995, 152–171.

26. Dyson 2001, 50–56; on the title Indiges, see Galinsky 1969, 149–150.

27. Among many discussions of the transformation of Aeneas into Achilles, see Callen King 1982.

28. Vergil may have been the first to extend the use of *condere* to burying a sword in an enemy's body; see, further, James 1995.

29. On repetition in the *Aeneid*, see W. S. Anderson 1957 and, especially, Quint 1993, 50–96.

30. Dyson (2001, 1–130) also argues that Aeneas' ultimate victory foreshadows his eventual death and disappearance.

Epilogue

1. Rome's secret name may go back to Ennius; see Stanley 1963.

2. The evidence for that ritual is collected in Eckstein 1979.

3. Cicero, *On Divination* 1.102; Eckstein 1979, 90–91. Note also Eagleton 2018, 12–13: "Like repression in the judgement of Freud, sacrifice is doomed to be a recurrent process rather than a punctual event. If its gestures of homage and reparation must be

endlessly repeated, it is among other things because the violence that sustains the social order cannot be fully dredged to consciousness."

4. See W. S. Anderson 1957, followed by, among others, Callen King 1982 and Quint 1993, 50–83.

5. The case for reading the wars in Italy as civil wars is concisely summarized in Camps 1969, 97–104.

Further Reading

For those who do not want or need to wander down all the bibliographic byways set out in the notes, I give here, with occasional comment, a list of two dozen books and articles that have shaped the way I read and teach the *Aeneid.*

Barchiesi, Alessandro. 2015. *Homeric Effects in Vergil's Narrative*. Princeton: Princeton University Press. Barchiesi complicates and enriches the idea that "Vergil imitated Homer."

Camps, W. A. 1969. *An Introduction to Virgil's "Aeneid."* Oxford: Oxford University Press. Camps' book and Ross 2007 are perhaps the best short introductions to the *Aeneid.* Together they will take a teacher or student a long way.

Dyson, Julia T. 2001. *King of the Wood: The Sacrificial Victor in Virgil's "Aeneid."* Norman: University of Oklahoma Press.

Galinsky, G. Karl. 1969. *Aeneas, Sicily, and Rome*. Princeton: Princeton University Press.

Galinsky, G. Karl. 1996. *Augustan Culture: An Interpretive Introduction*. Princeton: Princeton University Press. A comprehensive and thorough introduction to Augustan literary, visual, and political culture. He's in favor of it.

Goold, George P. 1970. "Servius and the Helen Episode." *Harvard Studies in Classical Philology* 74:101–168. After reading this example of classical philology at its best, it takes a will of iron to believe that the Helen episode belongs with the *Aeneid.*

Heinze, Richard. 1993. *Virgil's Epic Technique*. Berkeley: University of California Press. Heinze's *Virgils epische Technik* (3rd edition, 1915), of which this is a translation, and Pöschl 1962 revolutionized the reading of Vergil in the twentieth century and remain indispensable.

Hejduk, Julia. 2009. "Jupiter's *Aeneid: Fama* and *Imperium.*" *Classical Antiquity* 28:279–327.

Highet, Gilbert. 1972. *The Speeches in Vergil's "Aeneid."* Princeton: Princeton University Press.

Horsfall, Nicholas. 2016. *The Epic Distilled: Studies in the Composition of the "Aeneid."* Oxford: Oxford University Press. Horsfall, who died in 2020, may have been the most erudite, eccentric, and acute English-language commentator on the *Aeneid* since James Henry (1798–1896). While this reworking of an earlier essay in Italian does not substitute for Horsfall's voluminous commentaries on books 2, 3, 6, 7, and 11, it makes a good introduction to his approach.

Johnson, W. R. 1976. *Darkness Visible: A Study of Vergil's "Aeneid."* Berkeley: University of California Press. Johnson delineates an *Aeneid* suitable for the era of Vietnam and Watergate and perhaps for our own. With Lyne 1987 and O'Hara 1990, this book casts shadows onto the comparatively sunny *Aeneid* of Otis 1964 and other studies.

Lyne, R. O. A. M. 1987. *Further Voices in Vergil's "Aeneid."* Oxford: Clarendon.

Most, Glenn W. 2001. "Memory and Forgetting in the *Aeneid*." *Vergilius* 47:148–170.

O'Hara, James J. 1990. *Death and the Optimistic Prophecy in Vergil's "Aeneid."* Princeton: Princeton University Press.

Oliensis, Ellen. 2009. *Freud's Rome: Psychoanalysis and Latin Poetry*. Cambridge: Cambridge University Press.

Otis, Brooks. 1964. *Virgil: A Study in Civilized Poetry*. Oxford: Oxford University Press.

Pöschl, Viktor. 1962. *The Art of Vergil: Image and Symbol in the "Aeneid."* Ann Arbor: University of Michigan Press.

Putnam, M. C. J. 1995. *Virgil's "Aeneid": Interpretation and Influence*. Chapel Hill: University of North Carolina Press. Putnam gets closer to the way words in Latin whisper to each other than any other critic I know.

Quint, David. 1993: *Epic and Empire: Politics and Generic Form from Virgil to Milton*. Princeton: Princeton University Press.

Ross, David O. 2007. *Virgil's "Aeneid": A Reader's Guide*. Malden, MA: Blackwell.

Syme, Ronald. 1939. *The Roman Revolution*. Oxford: Clarendon.

Taylor, Lily Ross. 1949. *Party Politics in the Age of Caesar*. Berkeley: University of California Press. Taylor perhaps exaggerates the *populares/optimates* distinction, but this study and Syme 1939 still provide a sound introduction to the events that shaped the *Aeneid*.

Thomas, Richard. 2001. *Virgil and the Augustan Reception*. Cambridge: Cambridge University Press.

Zanker, Paul. 1988. *The Power of Images in the Age of Augustus*. Ann Arbor: University of Michigan Press.

Works Cited

Ancient Sources

In text and notes, I cite ancient sources by standard pagination (e.g., Stephanus for Plato, Bekker for Aristotle) or by title, book number, and section or line numbers. These references should transfer to any reliable edition. References to the *Aeneid* and other works of Vergil are to the Oxford Classical Texts edition by Roger Mynors, *P. Vergili Maronis Opera* (Oxford: Clarendon, 1969). The ancient commentator Servius is cited from Georg Christian Thilo and Hermann Hagen, *Servii Gramatici qui feruntur in Vergilii carmina comentarii*, 3 vols. (Leipzig: Teubner, 1881). For other ancient sources, I have used the Oxford Classical Texts series whenever possible or the Loeb Classical Library. For Sallust, Suetonius, and Valerius Maximus, respectively, I have used Bibliotheca Teubneriana editions by A. Kurfess (1976), M. Ihm (1967), and C. Kempf (1888). Commentaries and translations, listed below, are cited by surname of commentator or translator.

ILLRP	*Inscriptiones Latinae Liberae Rei Publicae*. Edited by Attilio Degrassi. 2 vols. Florence: La Nuova Italia, 1957–1963.
LIMC	*Lexicon Iconographicum Mythologiae Classicae*. Edited by the Fondation pour le Lexicon iconographicum mythologiae classicae. 8 vols. Zurich: Artemis Verlag, 1981.
Long and Sedley	*The Hellenistic Philosophers*. Edited by A. A. Long and D. N. Sedley. 2 vols. Cambridge: Cambridge University Press, 1987.
VSD	*Vita Suetonii vulgo Donatiana*. Edited by C. Hardie. Oxford Classical Texts. Oxford, 1954. 2nd edition, 1966. This ancient biography that

the grammarian Donatus (fourth century AD) prefaced to his commentary on Vergil's works is generally believed to reflect a biography written by Suetonius much closer to Vergil's lifetime. For further information, see Stok 2014.

Modern Scholarship

Ahl, Frederick M. 1976. *Lucan: An Introduction*. Ithaca, NY: Cornell University Press.

Aldrete, Gregory S. 2006. *Floods of the Tiber in Ancient Rome*. Baltimore: Johns Hopkins University Press.

Alexander, William H. 1954. "*Aeneid*, I, 462: A New Approach." *American Journal of Philology* 75:395–400.

Alston, Richard. 2015. *Rome's Revolution: Death of the Republic and Birth of the Empire*. Oxford: Oxford University Press.

Anderson, Amanda, T. Moi, and R. Felski. 2019. *Character: Three Inquiries in Literary Study*. Chicago: University of Chicago Press.

Anderson, W. B. 1930. "*Sum Pius Aeneas*." *Classical Review* 44:3–4.

Anderson, W. S. 1957. "Vergil's Second *Iliad*." *Transactions and Proceedings of the American Philological Association* 88:17–30.

Armstrong, David, ed. 2004. *Vergil, Philodemus, and the Augustans*. Austin: University of Texas Press.

Armstrong, Richard H. 2005. *A Compulsion for Antiquity: Freud and the Ancient World*. Ithaca, NY: Cornell University Press.

Austin, R. G. 1961. "Virgil, *Aeneid* 2.567–88." *Classical Quarterly* 11:185–198.

Austin, R. G. 1971. *P. Vergili Maronis Aeneidos Liber Primus*. Oxford: Oxford University Press.

Bacon, Helen H. 1986. "The *Aeneid* as a Drama of Election." *Transactions of the American Philological Association* 116:305–334.

Badel, Christophe. 2014. "La dignitas à Rome: Entre prestige et honneur (fin de la République)." In *Le prestige: Autour des forms de las différenciation sociale*, edited by F. Hurlett, I. Rivoal, and I. Sidéra, 107–118. Paris: Editions de Boccard. http://www.jstor.org/stable/j.ctt175x2zj

Baldwin, Barry. 1993. "Half-Lines in Virgil: Old and New Ideas." *Symbolae Osloenses* 68:144–151.

Bannon, Cynthia. 1997. *The Brothers of Romulus: Fraternal Pietas in Roman Law, Literature, and Society*. Princeton: Princeton University Press.

Barchiesi, Alessandro. 1999. "Representations of Suffering and Interpretation in the *Aeneid*." In Hardie 1999, 324–344. Originally published as "Rappresentazioni del dolore e interpretazione nell'*Eneide*." *Antike und Abenland* 40 (1994): 109–124.

Barchiesi, Alessandro. 2015. *Homeric Effects in Vergil's Narrative*. Princeton: Princeton University Press.

Barchiesi, Alessandro, and Walter Scheidel, eds. 2010. *The Oxford Handbook of Roman Studies*. Oxford: Oxford University Press.

Beck, Deborah. 2014. "The First Simile of the *Aeneid*." *Vergilius* 60:67–83.

Benjamin, Walter. 2007. *Illuminations*. Edited by Hannah Arendt. New York: Schocken Books. First published 1968.

Blom, Henriette van der. 2010. *Cicero's Role Models: The Political Strategy of a Newcomer*. Oxford: Oxford University Press.

Blom, Henriette van der. 2016. *Oratory and Political Career in the Late Roman Republic*. Cambridge: Cambridge University Press.

Bobzien, Susanne. 1998. *Determinism and Freedom in Stoic Philosophy*. Oxford: Clarendon.

Bowersock, Glen W. 1971. "A Date in the Eighth *Eclogue*." *Harvard Studies in Classical Philology* 75:73–80.

Bowman, Alan K., Edward Champlin, and Andrew Lintott, eds. 1996. *The Cambridge Ancient History*. Vol. 10, *The Augustan Empire, 43 B.C.–A.D. 69*. 2nd edition. Cambridge: Cambridge University Press.

Bowra, Maurice. 1933. "Aeneas and the Stoic Ideal." *Greece and Rome* 3:8–21.

Braund, S. M. 1997. "Virgil and the Cosmos: Religious and Philosophical Ideas." In Martindale 1997, 204–221.

Bremmer, Jan M. 2013. "Virgil and Jewish Literature." *Vergilius* 59:157–164.

Briggs, Ward W. 1979. "Eurydice, Venus, and Creusa: A Note on Structure." *Vergilius* 25:43–45.

Broadie, Sarah, and Christopher Rowe, eds. 2002. *Aristotle, "Nichomachean Ethics": Translation, Introduction, and Commentary*. Oxford: Oxford University Press, 2002.

Brooks, Peter. 1987. "The Idea of a Psychoanalytic Literary Criticism." *Critical Inquiry* 13:334–338.

Brunt, P. A. 1971. *Italian Manpower, 225 B.C.–A.D. 14*. Oxford: Oxford University Press.

Brunt, P. A. 1988. *The Fall of the Roman Republic and Related Essays*. Oxford: Clarendon.

Cairns, Francis. 1989. *Virgil's Augustan Epic*. Cambridge: Cambridge University Press.

Callen King, Katherine. 1982. "Foil and Fusion: Homer's Achilles in Vergil's *Aeneid*." *Materiali e discussioni per l'analisi dei testi classici* 9:31–57.

Camps, W. A. 1969. *An Introduction to Virgil's "Aeneid."* Oxford: Oxford University Press.

Cantarella, Eva. 2003. "Fathers and Sons in Rome." *Classical World* 96:281–298.

Carandini, Andrea. 2013. *La Roma di Augusto in 100 monumenti*." Rome: Università di Roma "La Sapienza."

Carrithers, Michael, Steven Collins, and Steven Lukes, eds. 1985. *The Category of the Person: Anthropology, Philosophy, History*. Cambridge: Cambridge University Press.

Casali, Sergio. 2014. "The Development of the Aeneas Legend." In Farrell and Putnam 2014, 37–51.

Chatman, Seymour. 1978. *Story and Discourse: Narrative Structure in Fiction and Film*. Ithaca, NY: Cornell University Press.

Chew, Kathryn. 2002. "*Inscius Pastor*: Ignorance and Aeneas' Identity in the *Aeneid*." *Latomus* 61:616–627.

Clark, Raymond J. 2004. "Horace on Vergil's Sea-Crossing in *Ode* I.3." *Vergilius* 50:4–34.

Clausen, Wendell V. 1972. "On the Date of the First *Eclogue*." *Harvard Studies in Classical Philology* 76:201–205.

Clausen, Wendell V. 1994. *A Commentary on Virgil, "Eclogues."* Oxford: Oxford University Press.

Cleary, Vincent J. 1982. "To the Victor Belong the *Spolia*: A Study in Vergilian Imagery." *Vergilius* 28:15–29.

Coleman, Robert. 1977. *Vergil, "Eclogues."* Cambridge: Cambridge University Press.

Conte, Gian Biagio. 2016. *Critical Notes on Virgil: Editing the Teubner Text of the "Georgics" and the "Aeneid."* Berlin: De Gruyter.

Conway, E. H. W. 1921. "The Singular *Nos* in Vergil." *Classical Quarterly* 15:177–182.

Conway, Robert Seymour. 1928. *Harvard Lectures on the Vergilian Age*. Cambridge, MA: Harvard University Press.

Cooley, Alison, ed. 2009. *Res Gestae Divi Augusti: Text, Translation, and Commentary*. Cambridge: Cambridge University Press.

Cowan, Robert. 2009. "Scanning *Iulus*: Prosody, Position, and Politics in the *Aeneid*." *Vergilius* 55:3–12.

Cowan, Robert. 2015. "On the Weak King according to Vergil: Aeolus, Latinus, and Political Allegoresis in the *Aeneid*." *Vergilius* 61:97–124.

Crawford, Jane W., ed. 1994. *M. Tullius Cicero, the Fragmentary Speeches: An Edition with Commentary*. 2nd edition. Atlanta: Scholars Press, 1994.

Crook, J. A., Andrew Lintott, and Elizabeth Rawson, eds. 1994. *The Cambridge Ancient History*. Vol. 9, *The Last Age of the Roman Republic, 146–43 B.C.* 2nd edition. Cambridge: Cambridge University Press.

Crostini, B., G. Iversen, and B. M. Jensen, eds. 2016. *Ars Edendi Lecture Series*. Vol. 4. Stockholm: Stockholm University Press.

DeBrohun, Jeri Blair. 2008. "The Gates of War (and Peace): Roman Literary Perspectives." In *War and Peace in the Ancient World*, edited by Kurt A. Raaflaub, 256–278. London: John Wiley and Sons.

de Sélincourt, Aubrey. *Livy, "The Early History of Rome."* London: Penguin Books, 1960.

Doblhofer, Ernst. 1992. *Horaz in der Forschung nach 1957*. Darmstadt: Wissenschaftliche Buchgesellschaft.

Dowling, Melissa Barden. 2000. "The Clemency of Sulla." *Historia* 49:303–340.

duBois, Page. 1988. *Sowing the Body: Psychoanalysis and Ancient Representations of Women*. Chicago: University of Chicago Press.

Dyck, Andrew. 2008. *Cicero, "Catilinarians."* Cambridge: Cambridge University Press.

Dyson, Julia T. 2001. *King of the Wood: The Sacrificial Victor in Virgil's "Aeneid."* Norman: University of Oklahoma Press.

Eagleton, Terry. 2018. *Ritual Sacrifice*. New Haven: Yale University Press.

Eckstein, A. 1979. "The Foundation Day of Roman *Coloniae*." *California Studies in Classical Antiquity* 12:85–97.

Edwards, Mark. 1960. "The Expression of Stoic Ideas in the *Aeneid*." *Phoenix* 14:151–165.

Eliot, Thomas Stearns. 1945. *What Is a Classic?* London: Faber and Faber.

Englert, Walter. 1987. *Epicurus on the Swerve and Voluntary Action*. Atlanta: Scholars Press.

Esposito, John. 2016. "Who Kills Turnus? 'Pallas' and What Aeneas Sees, Says, and Does in *Aeneid* 12.939–52." *Classical Journal* 111:463–481.

Everett, William. 1900. "Upon Virgil, *Aeneid* VI, Vss. 893–898." *Classical Review* 14:154–155.

Everitt, Anthony. 2003. *Cicero: The Life and Times of Rome's Greatest Politician*. New York: Random House.

Everitt, Anthony. 2006. *Augustus: The Life of Rome's First Emperor*. New York: Random House.

Fantham, Elaine. 2006: *Julia Augusti, the Emperor's Daughter*. London: Routledge.

Farrell, Joseph. 2014. "Vergil's Detractors." In Farrell and Putnam 2014, 435–448.

Farrell, Joseph, and Michael Putnam, eds. 2014. *A Companion to Vergil's "Aeneid" and Its Tradition*. Chicester: John Wiley and Sons. First published 2010.

Feeney, Denis. 1983. "The Taciturnity of Aeneas." *Classical Quarterly* 33:204–219.

Fink, Bruce. 1995. *The Lacanian Subject: Between Language and Jouissance*. Princeton: Princeton University Press.

Fletcher, K. F. B. 2014. *Finding Italy: Travel, Colonization, and Nation in Vergil's "Aeneid."* Ann Arbor: University of Michigan Press.

Flower, Harriet. 2006. *The Art of Forgetting: Disgrace and Oblivion in Roman Political Culture*. Chapel Hill: University of North Carolina Press.

Foley, Helena, ed. 1981. *Reflections of Women in Antiquity*. New York: Gordon and Breach Science Publishers.

Fontaine, Michael. 2015. "Aeneas in Palestine." *Eidolon*. https://www.academia.edu/12126645/Aeneas_in_Palestine

Fordyce, C. J. 1961. *Catullus: A Commentary*. Oxford: Clarendon.

Foucault, Michel. 1986. *The Care of the Self*. New York: Pantheon Books.

Fraenkel, Eduard. 1957. *Horace*. Oxford: Clarendon.

Frede, Dorothea. 2003. "Stoic Determinism." In Inwood 2003, 179–205.

Freudenburg, Kirk. 2017. "Seeing Marcellus in *Aeneid* 6." *Journal of Roman Studies* 107:116–139.

Gabba, Emilio. 1956. *Appiano e la Storia delle Guerre Civile*. Florence: La Nuova Italia.

Galinsky, G. Karl. 1969. *Aeneas, Sicily, and Rome*. Princeton: Princeton University Press.

Galinsky, G. Karl. 1979. "The 'Tomb of Aeneas' at Lavinium." *Vergilius* 20:2–11.

Galinsky, G. Karl. 1988. "The Anger of Aeneas." *American Journal of Philology* 109:321–348.

Galinsky, G. Karl. 1996. *Augustan Culture: An Interpretive Introduction.* Princeton: Princeton University Press.

Galinsky, G. Karl. 2003. "Greek and Roman Drama and the *Aeneid*." In *Myth, History and Culture in Republican Rome: Studies in Honour of T. P. Wiseman*, edited by David Brand and Christopher Gill, 275–294. Exeter: University of Exeter Press.

Galinsky, G. Karl, ed. 2014. Memoria Romana*: Memory in Rome and Rome in Memory*. Supplements to the Memoirs of the American Academy in Rome 10. Ann Arbor: University of Michigan Press.

Gass, William H. 1970. *Fiction and the Figures of Life*. New York: Alfred A. Knopf.

Gatz, Bodo. 1967. *Weltalter, goldene Zeit, und sinnverwandte Vorstellungen*. Hildesheim: Olms.

Gee, Emma. 2001. "Cicero's Astronomy." *Classical Quarterly* 51:520–536.

Gigante, Marcello. 1995. *Philodemus in Italy: The Books from Herculaneum*. Translated by Dirk Obbink. Ann Arbor: University of Michigan Press.

Gigante, Marcello. 2004. "Vergil in the Shadow of Vesuvius." In D. Armstrong 2004, 85–99.

Gill, Christopher. 1996. *Personality in Greek Epic, Tragedy, and Philosophy: The Self in Dialogue*. Oxford: Oxford University Press.

Gill, Christopher, 2006. *The Structured Self in Hellenistic and Roman Thought*. Oxford: Oxford University Press.

Gilligan, Carol. 1989. "Mapping the Moral Domain: New Images of Self in Relationship." *CrossCurrents* 39:50–63.

Gillis, Dan. 1983. *Eros and Death in the "Aeneid."* Rome: "L'Erma" di Bretschneider.

Giusti, Elena. 2018. *Carthage in Vergil's "Aeneid": Staging the Enemy under Augustus*. Cambridge: Cambridge University Press.

Goldsworthy, Adrian. 2014. *Augustus: First Emperor of Rome*. New Haven: Yale University Press.

Goold, George P. 1970. "Servius and the Helen Episode." *Harvard Studies in Classical Philology* 74:101–168.

Gowing, Alain. 1992. *The Triumviral Narratives of Appian and Cassius Dio*. Ann Arbor: University of Michigan Press.

Graves, Robert. 1962. "The Virgil Cult." *Virginia Quarterly Review* 38:13–35. Reprinted as "The Anti-Poet," in *Oxford Addresses on Poetry*, 29–53.

Green, Peter, trans. 2018. *Homer, The "Odyssey."* Oakland: University of California Press.

Griffin, Jasper. 1979. "The Fourth *Georgic*, Virgil, and Rome." *Greece and Rome* 26:61–80.

Griffith, Mark. 1985. "What Does Aeneas Look Like?" *Classical Philology* 80:309–319.

Grillo, Luca. 2010. "Leaving Troy and Creusa: Reflections on Aeneas' Flight." *Classical Journal* 106:43–68.

Gross, Nicholas. 2003. "Mantles Woven with Gold: Pallas' Shroud and the End of the *Aeneid*." *Classical Journal* 99:135–156.

Gruen, Erich. 1992. *Culture and National Identity in Republican Rome*. Ithaca, NY: Cornell University Press.

Gurval, Robert Alan. 1995. *Actium and Augustus: The Politics and Emotions of Civil War*. Ann Arbor: University of Michigan Press.

Gurval, Robert Allen. 1997. "Caesar's Comet: The Politics and Poetics of an Augustan Myth." *Memoirs of the American Academy in Rome* 42:39–71.

Hallett, Judith P. 1984. *Fathers and Daughters in Roman Society: Women and the Elite Family*. Princeton: Princeton University Press.

Halperin, David M. 1983. *Before Pastoral: Theocritus and the Ancient Tradition of Bucolic Poetry*. New Haven: Yale University Press.

Hancock, Ange-Marie. 2016. *Intersectionality: An Intellectual History*. New York: Oxford University Press.

Hardie, P. 1997. "Virgil and Tragedy." In Martindale 1997, 312–326.

Hardie, P. 1998. *Virgil*. Oxford: Oxford University Press.

Hardie, P., ed. 1999. *Virgil: Critical Assessments of Classical Authors*. 4 vols. London: Routledge.

Hardie, P. 2014. *The Last Trojan Hero: A Cultural History of Virgil's "Aeneid."* London: I. B. Tauris.

Harris, William V. 2001. *Restraining Rage: The Ideology of Anger Control in Classical Antiquity*. Cambridge, MA: Harvard University Press.

Harrison, E. L. 1999. "Why Did Venus Wear Boots? Some Reflections on *Aeneid* 1.314f." In Hardie 1999, 59–75. First published in *Proceedings of the Virgil Society* 12 (1972–1973): 10–25.

Harrison, S. J., ed. 1995. *Homage to Horace: A Bimillennary Celebration*. Oxford: Oxford University Press.

Haselberger, Lothar, ed. 2008. *Mapping Augustan Rome*. Journal of Roman Archaeology Supplementary Series 59. Portsmouth, RI: Journal of Roman Archaeology.

Havener, Wolfgang. 2014. "A Ritual against the Rule? The Representation of Civil War Victory in the Late Republican Triumph." In Lange and Vervaet 2014, 165–180.

Heinze, Richard. 1915. *Virgils epische Technik*. 3rd edition. Leipzig: Teubner.

Heinze, Richard. 1993. *Virgil's Epic Technique*. Berkeley: University of California Press.

Hejduk, Julia. 2009. "Jupiter's *Aeneid*: *Fama* and *Imperium*." *Classical Antiquity* 28:279–327.

Hejduk, Julia. 2013. "The Bough and the Lock: Fighting Fate in the *Aeneid*." *Illinois Classical Studies* 38:149–157.

Hejduk, Julia. 2017. "Introduction: Reading Civil War." *Classical World* 111:1–5.

Heslin, Peter. 2015. *The Museum of Augustus: The Temple of Apollo in Pompeii, the Portico of Philippus in Rome, and Latin Poetry*. Los Angeles: J. Paul Getty Museum.

Hexter, Ralph. 1997. *The Faith of Achates: Finding Aeneas' Other*. Morrison Library Inaugural Address Series 8. Berkeley: University of California Doe Library. https://escholarship.org/uc/item/8vb3r3p4

Highet, Gilbert. 1972. *The Speeches in Vergil's "Aeneid."* Princeton: Princeton University Press.

Highet, Gilbert. 1974. "Speech and Narrative in the *Aeneid.*" *Harvard Studies in Classical Philology* 78:189–229.

Hinard, François. 1985. *Les proscriptions de la Rome républicaine*. Rome: École Française de Rome.

Horsfall, Nicholas. 1995. *A Companion to the Study of Vergil*. Leiden: Brill.

Horsfall, Nicholas. 2008. *Virgil, "Aeneid" 2: A Commentary*. Leiden: Brill.

Horsfall, Nicholas. 2010. "Bees in Elysium." *Vergilius* 56:39–45.

Horsfall, Nicholas. 2011. "*Excudent alii.*" *Vergilius* 57:63–73.

Horsfall, Nicholas. 2012. "Virgil and the Jews." *Vergilius* 58:67–80.

Horsfall, Nicholas. 2013. *Virgil, "Aeneid" 6: A Commentary*. 2 vols. Berlin: De Gruyter.

Horsfall, Nicholas. 2016. *The Epic Distilled: Studies in the Composition of the "Aeneid."* Oxford: Oxford University Press.

Hubbard, Thomas K. 1998. *The Pipes of Pan: Intertextuality and Literary Filiation in the Pastoral Tradition from Theocritus to Milton*. Ann Arbor: University of Michigan Press.

Hudson-Williams, A. 1978. "*Lacrimae Illae Inanes.*" *Greece and Rome* 25:16–23.

Indelli, Giovanni. 2004. "The Vocabulary of Anger in Philodemus' *De ira* and Vergil's *Aeneid.*" In D. Armstrong 2004, 103–110.

Inwood, Brad, ed. 2003. *The Cambridge Companion to the Stoics*. Cambridge: Cambridge University Press.

Itkin, Alan. 2017. *Underworlds of Memory: W. G. Sebald's Journeys through the Past*. Evanston, IL: Northwestern University Press.

Jal, Paul. 1963. *La guerre civile à Rome, etude littéraire et morale*. Paris: Presses Universitaires de France.

James, Sharon. 1995. "Establishing Rome with the Sword: *Condere* in the *Aeneid.*" *American Journal of Philology* 116:623–637.

Janan, Micaela. 1994. "*When the Lamp Is Shattered*": *Desire and Narrative in Catullus*. Carbondale: Southern Illinois University Press.

Janan, Micaela. 2001. *The Politics of Desire: Propertius IV*. Berkeley: University of California Press.

Janko, Richard. 2016. "How to Read and Reconstruct a Herculaneum Papyrus." In Crostini, Iversen, and Jensen 2016, 117–161. http://dx.doi.org/10.16993/baj.f

Jenkyns, Richard. 2014. "The Memory of Rome in Rome." In Galinsky 2014, 15–26.

Johnson, W. R. 1976. *Darkness Visible: A Study of Vergil's "Aeneid."* Berkeley: University of California Press.

Johnston, Patricia. 1987. "Dido, Berenice, and Arsinoe: *Aeneid* 6.460." *American Journal of Philology* 108:649–654.

Kaster, Robert. 2012. "Honor Culture, Praise, and Servius' *Aeneid.*" In *Reception and the Classics: An Interdisciplinary Approach to the Classical Tradition*, edited by William

Brockliss, Pramit Chaudhuri, Ayelet Halmson Lushkov, and Katherine Wasdin, 45–56. Cambridge: Cambridge University Press.

Kirk, G. S. 1990. *The "Iliad": A Commentary*. Vol. 1, *Books 5–8*. Cambridge: Cambridge University Press.

Knauer, G. N. 1964. *Die Aeneis und Homer*. Göttingen: Vandenhoeck und Ruprecht.

Kondratieff, E. 2015. "Future City in the Heroic Past: Rome, Romans, and Roman Landscapes in *Aeneid* 6–8." In *Urban Dreams and Reality in Antiquity*, edited by A. Kemezis, 165–228. Leiden: Brill.

Konstan, David. 1997. *Friendship in the Classical World*. Cambridge: Cambridge University Press.

Konstan, David. 2005. "Clemency as a Virtue." *Classical Philology* 100:337–346.

Konstan, David. 2006. *The Emotions of the Ancient Greeks: Studies in Aristotle and Classical Literature*. Toronto: University of Toronto Press.

Körte, A. 1892. "Augusteer bei Philodem." *Rheinisches Museum für Philologie* 45:172–177.

Lacan, Jacques. 1978. *The Seminar of Jacques Lacan*. Book 11, *The Four Fundamental Concepts of Psychoanalysis*. Translated by Alan Sheridan. New York: W. W. Norton. First published 1973.

Lacan, Jacques. 2006. *Écrits: The First Complete Edition in English*. Translated by Bruce Fink, in collaboration with Héloise Fink and Russell Grigg. New York: W. W. Norton.

Lange, Carsten Hjort. 2016. *Triumphs in the Age of Civil War: The Late Republic and the Adaptability of Triumphal Tradition*. London: Bloomsbury Academic.

Lange, Carsten Hjort, and Frederik Juliaan Vervaet, eds. 2014. *The Roman Republican Triumph: Beyond the Spectacle*. Rome: Edizioni Quasar.

Langlands, Rebecca. 2018. *Exemplary Ethics in Ancient Rome*. Cambridge: Cambridge University Press.

Lattimore, Richmond. 1947. *The Odes of Pindar*. Chicago: University of Chicago Press, 1947.

Leach, Eleanor Windsor. 1988. *The Rhetoric of Space: Literary and Artistic Representations of Landscape in Republican and Augustan Rome*. Princeton: Princeton University Press.

Leverage, Paula, Howard Mancing, Richard Schweikhert, and Jennifer Marston William. 2010. *Theory of Mind and Literature*. West Lafayette, IN: Purdue University Press.

Levick, Barbara 2015. *Catiline*. London: Bloomsbury Academic.

Levitan, William. 1993. "Give Up the Beginning?" Juno's Mindful Wrath (*Aeneid* 1.37)." *Liverpool Classical Monthly* 18:14.

Lombardo, Stanley, trans. 1997. *Homer, The "Iliad."* Indianapolis: Hackett, 1997.

Lowrie, Michèle. 2016. "Le salut, la sécurité et le corps du chef: Transformations dans la sphere publique à l'époque d'Horace." In *La poésie lyrique dans la cité antique: Les*

"Odes" d'Horace au miroir de la lyrique grecque archaïque, edited by Bénédicte Delignon, Nadine Le Meur, and Olivier Thévenaz, 71–86. Lyon: Université Jean Moulin Lyon 3.

Lyne, R. O. A. M. 1983. "Vergil and the Politics of War." *Classical Quarterly* 33:188–203.

Lyne, R. O. A. M. 1987. *Further Voices in Vergil's "Aeneid."* Oxford: Clarendon.

Mac Góráin, Fiachra. 2018. "Vergil's Sophoclean Thebans." *Vergilius* 64:131–156.

Mackay, L. A. 1963. "Hero and Theme in the *Aeneid.*" *Transactions and Proceedings of the American Philological Association* 94:157–166.

Mackie, C. J. 1988. *The Characterisation of Aeneas.* Edinburgh: Scottish Academic.

Magie, David. 1920. "Augustus' War in Spain (26–25 B.C.)." *Classical Quarterly* 15:323–339.

Mankin, David, ed. 1995. *Horace, "Epodes."* Cambridge: Cambridge University Press.

Marshall, Bruce. 1985. "Catilina and the Execution of M. Marius Gratidianus." *Classical Quarterly* 35:124–133.

Martindale, Charles, ed. 1997. *The Cambridge Companion to Virgil.* Cambridge: Cambridge University Press.

Martino, John. 2008. "Single Combat and the *Aeneid.*" *Arethusa* 41:411–444.

McGushin, Patrick, ed. and trans. 1992. *Sallust, The "Histories."* 2 vols. Oxford: Clarendon, 1992.

Meban, David. 2009. "Virgil's *Eclogues* and Social Memory." *American Journal of Philology* 130:99–130.

Mench, Fred. 1969. "Film Sense in the *Aeneid.*" *Arion* 8:380–397. Reprinted in *Classical Myth and Culture in the Cinema*, edited by Martin Winkler (Oxford: Oxford University Press, 2001), 220–236.

Michels, Agnes K. L. 1981. "The *Insomnium* of Aeneas." *Classical Quarterly* 31:140–146.

Michels, Agnes K. L 1997. "The Many Faces of Aeneas." *Classical Journal* 92:399–416.

Miller, Frank Justus. 1909. "Evidences of Incompleteness in the *Aeneid* of Vergil." *Classical Journal* 4:341–355.

Miller, Paul Allen. 2004. *Subjecting Verses: Latin Love Elegy and the Emergence of the Real.* Princeton: Princeton University Press.

Mitchell-Boyask, Robin. 1996. "*Sine fine*: Vergil's Masterplot." *American Journal of Philology* 117:289–307.

Moatti, Claudia. 2015. *The Birth of Critical Thinking in Republican Rome.* Cambridge: Cambridge University Press.

Morstein-Marx, Robert. 2007. "Caesar's Alleged Fear of Prosecution and His *Ratio Absentis* in the Approach to the Civil War." *Historia* 56:159–178.

Morwood, James. 1998. "Virgil's Pious Man and Menenius Agrippa: A Note on *Aeneid* 1.148–53." *Greece and Rome* 45:195–198.

Moskalew, Walter. 1982. *Formular Language and Poetic Design in the "Aeneid."* Leiden: Brill.

Most, Glenn W. 2001. "Memory and Forgetting in the *Aeneid.*" *Vergilius* 47:148–170.

Mouritsen, Henrik. 2011. *The Freedman in the Roman World*. Cambridge: Cambridge University Press.

Moyn, Samuel. 2016. "Freud's Discontents." *Nation*, November 2, 2016. https://www.thenation.com/article/freuds-discontents/

Nicoll, W. S. M. 1988. "The Sacrifice of Palinurus." *Classical Quarterly* 38:459–472.

Nielson, Kristina. 1983. "The *Tropaion* in the *Aeneid*." *Vergilius* 29:27–33.

Nisbet, R. G. M., and Margaret Hubbard. 1978. *A Commentary on Horace, "Odes," Book II*. Oxford: Clarendon.

Nisbet, R. G. M., and Niall Rudd. 2004. *A Commentary on Horace, "Odes," Book III*. Oxford: Oxford University Press.

Norden, Eduard. 1957. *P. Vergilius Maro Aeneis Buch VI*. Stuttgart: Teubner.

Nussbaum, Martha. 2001. *The Fragility of Goodness*. 2nd edition. Cambridge: Cambridge University Press. 1st edition 1986.

O'Hara, James J. 1990. *Death and the Optimistic Prophecy in Vergil's "Aeneid."* Princeton: Princeton University Press.

O'Hara, James J. 1996. *True Names: Vergil and the Alexandrian Tradition of Etymological Wordplay*. Ann Arbor: University of Michigan Press.

O'Hara, James J. 2007. *Inconsistency in Roman Epic: Studies in Catullus, Lucretius, Vergil, Ovid and Lucan*. Cambridge: Cambridge University Press.

Ojennus, Paul. 2018. "Apollonius of Rhodes, Hellenistic Philosophy, and Fate." *American Journal of Philology* 139:215–248.

Oliensis, Ellen. 2001. "Freud's *Aeneid*." *Vergilius* 47:39–63.

Oliensis, Ellen. 2009. *Freud's Rome: Psychoanalysis and Latin Poetry*. Cambridge: Cambridge University Press.

Oliensis, Ellen. 2010. "Psychoanalysis and the Roman Imaginary." In Barchiesi and Scheidel 2010, 295–308.

Osgood, Josiah. 2006. *Caesar's Legacy: Civil War and the Emergence of the Roman Empire*. Cambridge: Cambridge University Press.

Osgood, Josiah. 2014. *Turia: A Roman Woman's Civil War*. Oxford: Oxford University Press.

Östenberg, Ida. 2014. "Triumph and Spectacle: Victory Celebrations in the Late Republican Civil Wars." In Lange and Vervaet 2014, 181–196.

Otis, Brooks. 1959. "Three Problems of *Aeneid* 6." *Transactions and Proceedings of the American Philological Association* 90:165–179.

Otis, Brooks. 1964. *Virgil: A Study in Civilized Poetry*. Oxford: Oxford University Press.

Page, T. E. 1894. *The "Aeneid" of Virgil, Edited with Introduction and Notes*. 2 vols. London: Macmillan. Frequently reprinted.

Pandey, Nandini. 2013. "Caesar's Comet, the Julian Star, and the Invention of Augustus." *Transactions of the American Philological Association* 143:405–449.

Pandey, Nandini. 2014. "Reading Rome from the Farther Shore: *Aeneid* 6 in the Augustan Urban Landscape." *Vergilius* 60:85–116.

Pandey, Nandini. 2017. "Sowing the Seeds of War: The *Aeneid*'s Prehistory of Interpretive Contestation and Appropriation." *Classical World* 111: 7–25.

Panoussi, Vassiliki. 2009. *Greek Tragedy and Vergil's "Aeneid": Ritual, Empire, and Intertext*. Cambridge: Cambridge University Press.

Parry, Adam. 1963. "The Two Voices of Virgil's *Aeneid*." *Arion* 2:66–80.

Pearcy, Lee T. 2005. *The Grammar of Our Civility: Classical Education in America*. Waco: Baylor University Press.

Pease, A. S. 1935. *P. Vergili Maronis Aeneidos Liber Quartus*. Cambridge, MA: Harvard University Press.

Perkell, Christine. 1978. "A Reading of Vergil's Fourth Georgic." *Phoenix* 32:211–221.

Perkell, Christine. 1981. "On Creusa, Dido, and the Quality of Victory in Virgil's *Aeneid*." In Foley 1981, 355–377.

Perkell, Christine. 2002. "The Golden Age and Its Contradictions in the Poetry of Vergil." *Vergilius* 48:3–39.

Perkell, Christine. 2004. "Irony in the Underworlds of Dante and Virgil: Readings of Francesca and Palinurus." *Materiali e discussioni per l'analisi dei testi classici* 52:127–142.

Perutelli, A. 1995. "Bucolics." In Horsfall 1995, 27–62.

Pogorzelski, Randall. 2009. "The 'Reassurance of Fratricide' in the *Aeneid*." *American Journal of Philology* 130:261–289.

Poochigian, Aaron. 2010. *Aratus, "Phaenomena."* Baltimore: Johns Hopkins University Press.

Porter, David. 1995. "*Quo, Quo Scelesti Ruitis*: The Downward Momentum of Horace's *Epodes*." *Illinois Classical Studies* 20:107–130.

Porter, James I. 2004. "Vergil's Voids." In Porter and Buchan 2004, 127–156.

Porter, James I. 2017. "Time for Foucault? Reflections on the Roman Self from Seneca to Augustine." *Foucault Studies* 22:113–133.

Porter, James I., and Mark Buchan, eds. 2004. "Before Subjectivity? Lacan and the Classics." Special issue, *Helios* 31, nos. 1–2.

Pöschl, Viktor. 1962. *The Art of Vergil: Image and Symbol in the "Aeneid."* Ann Arbor: University of Michigan Press.

Putnam, M. C. J. 1984. "The Hesitation of Aeneas." In *Atti dei Convegno Mondiale Scientifico di Studi su Virgilio*, edited by Marco Beck, 233–252. Milan: Mondadori.

Putnam, M. C. J. 1985. "Possessiveness, Sexuality and Heroism in the *Aeneid*." *Vergilius* 31:1–21.

Putnam, M. C. J. 1987. "Daedalus, Virgil and the End of Art." *American Journal of Philology* 108:173–198.

Putnam, M. C. J. 1995. *Virgil's "Aeneid": Interpretation and Influence*. Chapel Hill: University of North Carolina Press.

Putnam, M. C. J. 1998. "Dido's Murals and Virgilian Ekphrasis." *Harvard Studies in Classical Philology* 98:243–275.

Putnam, M. C. J. 2001. "Vergil's *Aeneid*: The Final Lines." In *Poets and Critics Read Vergil*, edited by Sarah Spence, 86–104. New Haven: Yale University Press.

Putnam, M. C. J. 2015. *Maffeo Vegio, Short Epics*. Cambridge, MA: Harvard University Press.

Quint, David. 1982. "Painful Memories: *Aeneid* 3 and the Problem of the Past." *Classical Journal* 78:30–38.

Quint, David. 1993. *Epic and Empire: Politics and Generic Form from Virgil to Milton*. Princeton: Princeton University Press.

Radt, Stefan, ed. *Tragicorum Graecorum Fragmenta*. Vol. 4, *Sophocles*. Göttingen: Vandenhoeck und Ruprecht, 1977.

Ramsey, J. T., and A. L. Licht. 1997. *The Comet of 44 B.C. and Caesar's Funeral Games*. Atlanta: Scholars Press.

Raven, D. S. 1975. "A Note on Vergil *Aen.* IV 9–14." *Acta Classica* 18:147–148.

Rawson, Elizabeth. 1987. "Sallust on the Eighties." *Classical Quarterly* 37:163–180.

Reckford, Kenneth. 1996. "Recognizing Venus (I): Aeneas Meets His Mother." *Arion* 3:1–42.

Redfield, James. 1975. *Nature and Culture in the "Iliad": The Tragedy of Hector*. Chicago: University of Chicago Press.

Reed, J. D. 2001. "Anchises Reading Aeneas Reading Marcellus." *Syllecta Classica* 12:146–168.

Reed, J. D. 2007. *Virgil's Gaze: Nation and Poetry in the "Aeneid."* Princeton: Princeton University Press.

Reid, J. S. 1912. "Human Sacrifices at Rome and Other Notes on Roman Religion." *Journal of Roman Studies* 2:34–52.

Richardson, L. 1992. *A New Topographical Dictionary of Ancient Rome*. Baltimore: Johns Hopkins University Press.

Riggsby, Andrew M. 1998. "Self and Community in the Younger Pliny." *Arethusa* 31:75–98. Reprinted in *The "Epistles" of Pliny*, edited by Roy Gibson and Christopher Whitton (Oxford: Oxford University Press, 2016), 225–245.

Rimmon-Kenan, Shlomith. 2002. *Narrative Fiction: Contemporary Poetics*. 2nd edition. London: Routledge.

Robb, M. A. 2010. *Beyond* Populares *and* Optimates*: Political Language in the Late Republic*. Historia Einzelschriften 213. Stuttgart: Franz Steiner Verlag.

Rogerson, Anne. 2017. *Virgil's Ascanius: Imagining the Future in the "Aeneid."* Cambridge: Cambridge University Press.

Rosenmeyer, Thomas G. 1969. *The Green Cabinet: Theocritus and the European Pastoral Lyric*. Berkeley: University of California Press.

Ross, David O. 1975. *Backgrounds to Augustan Poetry: Gallus, Elegy, and Rome*. Cambridge: Cambridge University Press.

Ross, David O. 2007. *Virgil's "Aeneid": A Reader's Guide*. Malden, MA: Blackwell.

Rowe, Galen O. 1965. "The Adynaton as a Stylistic Device." *American Journal of Philology* 86:387–396.

Russell, Daniel C. 2000. "Epicurus and Lucretius on Saving Agency." *Phoenix* 54:226–243.

Sacks, Sam. 2015. "The Rise of the Nameless Narrator." *New Yorker*, March 3. http://www.newyorker.com/books/page-turner/the-rise-of-the-nameless-narrator

Scafoglio, Giampiero. 2006. "Le Laocoon de Sophocle." *Revue des Études Grecques* 119:406–420.

Scafoglio, Giampiero. 2013. "The Betrayal of Aeneas." *Greek, Roman, and Byzantine Studies* 53:1–14.

Schauer, Markus. 2007. *Aeneas dux in Vergils Aeneis*. Munich: C. H. Beck.

Schein, Seth L. 1984. *The Mortal Hero: An Introduction to Homer's "Iliad."* Berkeley: University of California Press.

Schleiner, Winfried. 1975. "Aeneas' Flight from Troy." *Comparative Literature* 27:97–112.

Scodel, Ruth. 2015. "*Sunt Lacrimae Rerum*." *Classical Journal* 111:219–230.

Scott, Kenneth. 1941. "The *Sidus Iulium* and the Apotheosis of Caesar." *Classical Philology* 36:257–272.

Scullard, Howard Hayes. 1982. *From the Gracchi to Nero: A History of Rome from 133 B.C. to A.D. 68*. 5th edition. New York: Methuen.

Segal, Charles. 1965. "*Tamen Cantabitis, Arcades*—Exile and Arcadia in *Eclogues One and Nine*." *Arion* 4:237–266. Reprinted in *Poetry and Myth in Ancient Pastoral: Essays on Theocritus and Vergil* (Princeton: Princeton University Press, 1981), 271–300..

Segal, Charles. 1999. "Art and the Hero: Participation, Detachment, and Narrative Point of View in the *Aeneid*.":, In Hardie 1999, 42–58. First published in *Arethusa* 14 (1981): 67–85.

Seider, Aaron M. 2013. *Memory in Vergil's "Aeneid": Creating the Past*. Cambridge: Cambridge University Press.

Seidman, Jessica. 2018. "Dido's (?) Tears: A Brief History of a Sorrowful Ambiguity." In Quasi Labor Intus: *Ambiguity in Latin Literature. Papers in Honor of Reginald Thomas Foster, OCD*, edited by M. Fontaine, C. J. McNamara, and W. M. Short, 123–142. Middletown, DE: Amazon Kindle Direct.

Seo, Mira. 2013. *Exemplary Traits: Reading Characterization in Roman Poetry*. Oxford: Oxford University Press.

Shearin, W. H. 2015. *The Language of Atoms: Performativity and Politics in Lucretius' "De rerum natura."* Oxford: Oxford University Press.

Shields, John C. 2001. *The American Aeneas: Classical Origins of the American Self*. Knoxville: University of Tennessee Press.

Skinner, Marilyn. 1983. "The Last Encounter of Dido and Aeneas: *Aen.* 6.450–476." *Vergilius* 29:12–18.

Skulsky, Susan. 1985. "*Invitus, Regina*: Aeneas and the Love of Rome." *American Journal of Philology* 106:447–455.

Smith, R. A. 1993. "A Lock and a Promise: Myth and Allusion in Aeneas' Farewell to Dido in *Aeneid* 6." *Phoenix* 47:305–312.

Snell, Bruno. 1938. "Die 16. Epode von Horaz und Virgils 4. Ekloge." *Hermes* 13:231–242.

Sparrow, John. 1931. *Half-Lines and Repetitions in Vergil*. London: Oxford University Press.

Stahl, Hans-Peter. 2016. *Poetry Underpinning Power: Virgil's "Aeneid," the Epic for Emperor Augustus: A Recovery Study*. Swansea: Classical Press of Wales.

Stanley, Keith. 1963. "Rome, Ἔρως, and the *Versus Romae*." *Greek, Roman, and Byzantine Studies* 4:237–249.

Starr, Kenneth J. 2003. "Aeneas the Rhetorician: *Aeneid* IV, 279–295." *Latomus* 62:36–46.

Stewart, Douglas J. 1971. "*Sunt Lacrimae Rerum*." *Classical Journal* 67:116–122.

Stockton, David. 1965. "Primus and Murena." *Historia* 14:18–40.

Stok, Fabio. 2014. "The Life of Virgil before Donatus." In Farrell and Putnam 2014, 107–120.

Strachey, James, ed. 1966. *The Standard Edition of the Complete Psychological Works of Sigmund Freud*. In collaboration with Anna Freud, assisted by Alix Strachey and Alan Tyson. Vol. 1, *Pre-Psycho-Analytic Publications and Unpublished Drafts*. London: Hogarth.

Strassler, Robert B. 1996. *The Landmark Thucydides: A Comprehensive Guide to "The Peloponnesian War."* New York: Free Press, 1996.

Syme, Ronald. 1939. *The Roman Revolution*. Oxford: Clarendon.

Syme, Ronald. 1958. "Imperator Caesar: A Study in Nomenclature." *Historia* 7:172–188.

Tatum, James. 1984. "Allusion and Interpretation in *Aeneid* 6.440–76." *American Journal of Philology* 105:434–452.

Taylor, Charles. 1989. *Sources of the Self: The Making of Modern Identity*. Cambridge, MA: Harvard University Press.

Taylor, Lily Ross. 1949. *Party Politics in the Age of Caesar*. Berkeley: University of California Press.

Thomas, Richard. 1991. "*Furor* and *Furiae* in Virgil." *American Journal of Philology* 112:261.

Thomas, Richard. 2001. *Virgil and the Augustan Reception*. Cambridge: Cambridge University Press.

Townshend, James R. 2015. "Stop Me If You've Heard This: Faux Alexandrian Footnotes in Vergil." *Vergilius* 61:77–96.

Treggiari, Susan. 2019. *Servilia and Her Family*. Oxford: Oxford University Press.

Trilling, Lionel. 1951. "Freud and Literature." In *The Liberal Imagination: Essays on Literature and Society*, 34–57. London: Martin Secker and Warburg.

Uden, James. 2014. "The Smile of Aeneas." *Transactions of the American Philological Association* 144:71–96.

Vahlen, Iohannes, ed. 1903. *Ennianae Poesis Reliquiae*. 2nd edition. Leipzig: Teubner, 1903.

Varner, Eric R. 2004. *Mutilation and Transformation:* Damnatio Memoriae *and Roman Imperial Portraiture*. Leiden: Brill.

Verbanck-Piérard, Annie. 2018. "Round Trip to Hades: Herakles' Advice and Directions." In *Round Trip to Hades in the Eastern Mediterranean Tradition*, ed. Gunnel Ekroth and Ingela Nilsson, 163–193. Leiden: Brill.

Vermeule, Blakey. 2010. *Why Do We Care about Literary Characters?* Baltimore: Johns Hopkins University Press.

Walter, Uwe. 2009. "Die *Communes Historiae* des Lutatius: Einleitung, Fragmente, Übersetzung, Kommentar." *Göttinger Forum für Altertumswissenschaft* 12:1–15.

Watson, L. C. 2003. *A Commentary on Horace's "Epodes."* Oxford: Oxford University Press.

Wells, Robert. 2015. "The Thirteenth Book." *TLS*, August 23.

Westall, Richard. 2017. *Caesar's "Civil War": Historical Reality and Fabrication*. Leiden: Brill.

Wharton, David. 2008. "*Sunt Lacrimae Rerum*: An Exploration in Meaning." *Classical Journal* 103:259–279.

Wilhelm, Robert M. 1988. "Cybele, the Great Mother of the Augustan Order." *Vergilius* 34:77–101.

Williams, Gordon. 1983. *Technique and Ideas in the "Aeneid."* New Haven: Yale University Press.

Williams, R. D. 1960. "The Pictures on Dido's Temple (*Aeneid* I.450–93)." *Classical Quarterly* 10:145–151.

Williams, R. D. 1972. *The "Aeneid" of Virgil*. 2 vols. London: Macmillan.

Wilson, C. H. 1979. "Jupiter and the Fates in the *Aeneid*." *Classical Quarterly* 29:361–371.

Wohl, Victoria. 2008. "Review Essay: The Romance of Tragedy and Psychoanalysis." *Helios* 35:89–110.

Wright, Elizabeth. 1998. *Psychoanalytic Criticism: A Reappraisal*. 2nd ed. New York: Routledge.

Zanker, Andreas. 2010. "Late Horatian Lyric and the Virgilian Golden Age." *American Journal of Philology* 131:495–516.

Zanker, Graham. 2017. "*Paremus Ovantes*: Stoicism and Human Responsibility in *Aeneid* 4." *Classical Quarterly* 66, no. 2: 580–597.

Zanker, Paul. 1988. *The Power of Images in the Age of Augustus*. Ann Arbor: University of Michigan Press.

Zarecki, Jonathan. 2014. *Cicero's Ideal Statesman in Theory and Practice*. London: Bloomsbury Academic.

Zarker, John W. 1972. "The Hercules Theme in the 'Aeneid.'" *Vergilius* 18:34–48.

Zunshine, Lisa. 2006. *Why We Read Fiction: Theory of Mind and the Novel*. Columbus: Ohio State University Press.

Index of Passages Cited

Index of Names and Subjects